332.63244
C549p

D1302594

PRIVATE MORTGAGE INVESTING

How to Earn 12% or More on Your Savings, Investments, IRA Accounts, and Personal Equity

A Complete Resource Guide with 100s of Hints, Tips, and Secrets from Experts Who Do It Every Day

By
Teri B. Clark

Co-Author
Matthew Stewart Tabacchi

OCT   2007

SHERWOOD FOREST LIBRARY
7117 W. 7 MILE RD.
DETROIT, MI 48221

PRIVATE MORTGAGE INVESTING: How to Earn 12% or More on Your Savings, Investments, IRA Accounts, and Personal Equity: A Complete Resource Guide with 100s of Hints, Tips, and Secrets from Experts Who Do It Every Day

Copyright © 2006 by Atlantic Publishing Group, Inc.
1210 SW 23rd Place • Ocala, Florida 34474 • 800-814-1132 • 352-622-5836–Fax
Web site: www.atlantic-pub.com • E-mail: sales@atlantic-pub.com
SAN Number: 268-1250

No part of this publication may be reproduced, stored in a retrieval system, or transmitted in any form or by any means, electronic, mechanical, photocopying, recording, scanning, or otherwise, except as permitted under Section 107 or 108 of the 1976 United States Copyright Act, without the prior written permission of the Publisher. Requests to the Publisher for permission should be sent to Atlantic Publishing Group, Inc., 1210 SW 23rd Place, Ocala, Florida 34474.

ISBN-13: 978-0-910627-62-7 • ISBN-10: 0-910627-62-2

Library of Congress Cataloging-in-Publication Data

Clark, Teri B.
  Private mortgage investing : how to earn 12% or more on your savings, investments, IRA accounts, and personal equity : a complete resource guide with 100s of hints, tips & secrets from experts who do it every day / Teri B. Clark, Matthew Stewart Tabacchi.
    p. cm.
  Includes index.
  ISBN-13: 978-0-910627-62-7 (alk. paper)
  ISBN-10: 0-910627-62-2 (alk. paper)
  1. Mortgage loans--United States. 2. Real estate investment--United States. 3. Real property--United States--Finance. 4. Investments--United States. I. Tabacchi, Matthew Stewart. II. Title.

HG2040.5.U5C585 2006
332.63'2440973--dc22
                                2006012582

LIMIT OF LIABILITY/DISCLAIMER OF WARRANTY: The publisher and the author make no representations or warranties with respect to the accuracy or completeness of the contents of this work and specifically disclaim all warranties, including without limitation warranties of fitness for a particular purpose. No warranty may be created or extended by sales or promotional materials. The advice and strategies contained herein may not be suitable for every situation. This work is sold with the understanding that the publisher is not engaged in rendering legal, accounting, or other professional services. If professional assistance is required, the services of a competent professional should be sought. Neither the publisher nor the author shall be liable for damages arising herefrom. The fact that an organization or Web site is referred to in this work as a citation and/or a potential source of further information does not mean that the author or the publisher endorses the information the organization or Web site may provide or recommendations it may make. Further, readers should be aware that Internet Web sites listed in this work may have changed or disappeared between when this work was written and when it is read.

ART DIRECTION & INTERIOR DESIGN: Meg Buchner • megadesn@mchsi.com
FRONT COVER DESIGN: Jackie Miller
BOOK PRODUCTION DESIGN: Lisa Peterson, Michael Meister • info@6sense.net
EDITOR: Jackie Ness • jackie_ness@charter.net
EDITOR: C. L. Hogan • wordwerks@msn.com • Cell: 812-219-1340

Printed in the United States

TESTIMONIALS

"Overall the book offered a great foundation into many different concepts of real estate investing that are not as commonly found or covered by most other books. Private mortgages, 1031 exchange concepts (tax deferred investing) etc. I think this book would be a great handbook and reference point for many new to experienced investors. It presented concepts that most real estate orientated investors forget are out there. It was easy to read and worded in language that even the newbie investor can understand."

AJ Beach
Managing partner in DRB Properties LLC

"This book is written for the investor who wants the best return for their hard earned money or for the mortgager who wants a fast and private closing. Not only can you learn how to invest your money, but also the do's and don'ts of private mortgage investing! As a licensed mortgage broker I enjoyed reading and learning from this book."

Jennifer Arch
Licensed Mortgage Broker

"It is refreshing to see knowledgeable material that talks about something other than the get rich quick real estate strategies. I believe that this book is right for today's market offering the beginning investor as well as the advanced investor in depth insight to the lending side of real estate investing. I highly recommend this book to any individual and/or small business that wants to own real estate without the element of property management. Last but not least, I do feel that the book is well written and organized to communicate to readers of varying levels of intelligence."

Craig Emmanuel, Founder
Commercial Realty Advisors & Investment Group, Inc.
www.craigemmanuel.com

"A must read for Investors. If you want a good return on investing in private mortgages, or if you need private money to buy other investments, then you need to read this book."

Kevin A. Dunlap
Trident Investments
Real Estate Investor

SAY HELLO TO PRIVATE MORTGAGE INVESTING!

C*ongratulations on having the foresight* to buy this book. Not only will you learn how to earn double-digit interest on your hard-earned money, you'll also learn how to invest it virtually risk-free.

ARE YOU ...

New to investing?

Chapter 1 compares investment alternatives and guides you in your first foray into the world of private mortgage investing.

Interested in diversifying?

In the pages that follow, you'll find dozens of reasons to include private mortgages in your portfolio.

An experienced real estate pro?

Read on to discover how to enjoy safe, lucrative

investing in the area you know and love without tying up your money for decades.

Tired of trusting stockbrokers and fund managers with your money?

This book shows you how to "be the bank" and take control of your own investing destiny.

TABLE OF CONTENTS

CHAPTER 2: Private Mortgages –Why You Want To Be Involved

CHAPTER 3: Why Borrowers Seek Private Mortgages

CHAPTER 4: Five Investment Parameters

CHAPTER 5: The World Of Mortgages, Interest Rates, and Fees

CHAPTER 6: Ways to invest

CHAPTER 7: Getting The Most from Your IRA

CHAPTER 8: Selling Mortgages and Notes

CHAPTER 9: Finding Potential Borrowers

CHAPTER 10: Verifying Property Information

CHAPTER 11: Insurance to Keep Your Investment Safe

CHAPTER 12: More Safety Measures for the Private Lender

CHAPTER 13: Real Estate Attorneys Are Worth the Price

CHAPTER 14: Bookkeeping and Taxes

CONCLUSION

APPENDIX

APPENDIX 1: Forms

APPENDIX 2: Loan Package from Broker

APPENDIX 3: Glossary

APPENDIX 4: Calculations

APPENDIX 5: Self-Directed IRA Trustees

APPENDIX 6: State Usury Laws

APPENDIX 7: Mortgage Procedures by State

APPENDIX 8: Resources

Index

About the Author

PRIVATE MORTGAGE INVESTING

In my 30 years in the financial services industry, I've learned that there are as many different investing styles as there are investors. Many invest defensively, reacting to events and circumstances, fearing the future, and never becoming fully engaged in the process. Then there are those who take the future by the horns, planning ahead, seeing the possibilities, anticipating the challenges, adapting to change, seizing the opportunities. This is what I call creative self-direction. It's what drives my business, and I believe it's integral to a productive, fulfilling life as well. I know you agree or, chances are, you wouldn't be reading this book.

In the chapters that follow, you'll find out all about private mortgage investing and how it could help you get a firm grip on your financial future. Not only will you learn how to potentially earn double-digit interest on your money, you'll also learn how to invest it and minimize the risk. If you're new to investing, you'll learn about different investment alternatives and how to get your feet wet in private mortgage investing. If you've been investing for some time and are interested in diversifying, you'll find myriad reasons to include private mortgages as a part of your portfolio. If you're an experienced real estate pro, you'll discover how to enjoy relatively safe, lucrative investing in the area you know and love without tying up your money for decades. And, if you're just tired of trusting stockbrokers and fund managers with your hard-earned money, you'll get a crash course in how to "be the bank" and take control of your own investing destiny.

This book takes the mystery out of private mortgage investing. Its pages are filled with practical information, Web sites, product recommendations, and case studies of people just like you who began investing in private mortgages and never looked back. You'll find out exactly what you need to do and when to do it to increase your earnings and decrease your worries. For example, you'll learn:

- What sets private mortgage investing apart from other types of investments.

- Exactly what private mortgages are and how to configure them to help you meet your personal investing objectives.

- The reasons that so many good borrowers want to use private lenders instead of banks.

- Five criteria that you must consider before you make a mortgage loan.

- Proven ways to protect yourself against loss.

- All about making interest, fees, points, and the magic of compounding work overtime for you.

- The pros and cons of going it alone or partnering with other investors.

- Why you should consider making private mortgage loans from your self-directed IRA.

- How to make quick cash through buying and selling mortgages and notes.

In buying this book, you've just taken a bold step toward creative self-direction. Whether you're a brand-new investor just learning the ropes or a seasoned veteran with a diversified portfolio and years of experience under your belt, this book will change your life and your attitude toward investing. All the information you need to get started in private mortgage investing is here; all you have to do is get out there and use it. Turn the page, and get ready to say good-bye to traditional investment vehicles. Now you're in the driver's seat!

James R. Wagner
President and Chief Executive Officer
Trust Administration Services Corporation
(800) 455-9472, ext. 222

Direct Fax: (760) 602-1300
E-mail: jwagner@trustlynk.com
Web Site: **www.trustlynk.com**

James Wagner has more than 30 years of experience as a business owner in the areas of securities, trust administration, retirement planning, and employee benefits. He has been actively involved in the self-directed retirement plan industry since 1977.

CHAPTER 1

PRIVATE MORTGAGES BEAT TRADITIONAL INVESTMENTS HANDS DOWN

R*eal estate is an often overlooked* investment option. In fact, most investors are unaware that an investment vehicle exists beyond the more traditional opportunities of stocks, bonds, CDs, and the like. For you, that is going to change. Here you will learn about a real estate investment opportunity that gives you the ability to earn double-digit interest rates, while other investors around you are hoping to cross the 5 percent line. Not only that, but these investments are backed by real property.

Private mortgages have stable returns and fit well within a portfolio of stocks, bonds, and real estate. Adding these to a portfolio will make the returns of the total portfolio more consistent. Let's take a look at some typical returns for other investment vehicles before focusing on private mortgage investing. In this way, you will be able to see for yourself why you should include private mortgages in your portfolio.

INVESTING BASICS

When you make an investment, you are assigning funds to a particular asset to be held for a period of time. Your expectation is that these dedicated funds will increase in value over the years and that, at some point, often retirement, you will have the ability to live off those investments.

The purpose of investing is to improve your future welfare. As an investor, you believe that by forgoing consumption today and investing the savings, you can do better in the future. This future may include college tuition for your children, a retirement home in the mountains, or simply a comfortable retirement. Regardless of why you invest, you should seek to manage your wealth effectively so that you can get the most from it.

BASIC PARAMETERS FOR CHOOSING YOUR INVESTMENT VEHICLE

How Much to Get Started?

There are some basic points to consider when you choose your investment vehicle. For instance, how much money do you have to invest? Some products allow you to get started with as little as $100, while others require much, much more.

Although you can't start investing in private mortgages with $100, you can get started with much less than is required by many traditional vehicles. And later, you will learn how to use money in your IRA to help you.

Depending upon the state where you do business, there may or may not be a requirement for a private mortgage investor to have or maintain a given net worth. However, to be an "accredited investor" under federal law, you must have a net worth of $1 million or an income of $200,000 annually. Every time an investor gives money to a broker to lend out, that investor must also submit a letter certifying that he or she has fulfilled any net worth or minimum annual income requirements that may exist.

Accessibility and Investment Period

Another thing to consider is accessibility or liquidity. Some investments allow you to withdraw money throughout the investment process, while others make you wait until full maturity. Always consider how tying up your funds in long-term investments will affect you.

For many investment opportunities, the longer you are willing to hold the investment, the higher the interest rate. This means that if you want accessibility, you often have to give up increased growth.

This is not true of private mortgage investments. When

you invest in mortgages, you are typically investing your money for a period of 6 months to 2 years. Despite the short term of your investment, you will earn an interest rate of well over 10 percent.

Growing Capital Versus Earning Income

Next you need to consider what you want your money to do for you while it is invested. Are you hoping to live off the income, or do you want to build your capital?

When you choose to invest in mortgages, you can do either. For instance, if you have loaned out $60,000 at 12 percent, your interest payments will be $600 a month. You can determine if that money will go toward your living expenses or if you would rather put it into another investment. You have total control.

What Interest Rate Would Make You Happy?

Most investment opportunities are influenced heavily by outside factors. They are controlled by money market rates or are fixed for the entire length of the investment. Or they are determined by the bank.

Private mortgage interest rates are determined, in large part, by you. There are certainly guidelines to follow, but in the end, you determine the rate, and the mortgagee will pay it or go elsewhere.

The typical interest rate for a direct private mortgage ranges from 10 to 16 percent. This range is dependent upon many factors, including the length of the loan, the purpose for the loan, your exit strategy, and so on.

The interest rate can be either fixed or floating. If you choose a floating rate, it is often set so that there is a floor, allowing you to raise your rates if the prime rate goes up and protecting you from loss if the prime goes down.

Once again, you are in control.

A LOOK AT TRADITIONAL INVESTMENT OPTIONS

When it comes to investing, you have many options. Let's look at the pros and cons of the most common ones.

Savings Account

Pros: Savings accounts can be used as collateral and are insured by the FDIC for up to $100,000. Money is easily accessible, and interest is paid monthly. You can start this account with any amount of money.

Cons: Interest rates are low, often less than 0.5 percent today. Interest is subject to federal and state income taxes.

Money Market Account

Pros: Interest on money market accounts is slightly higher than that of savings accounts, currently about 1.5 percent. Money is easily accessible and liquid.

Cons: There are penalties for not maintaining the

minimum balance. Interest rates are still quite low and subject to change. Interest income is subject to federal and state income taxes.

Money Market Fund

Pros: There are no penalties for withdrawal, making the account very accessible. Interest is figured daily instead of monthly.

Cons: There is no FDIC guarantee on your money. Interest rates vary according to the market. Interest income is subject to state and federal income taxes. You need to have a minimum deposit to get started.

Certificate of Deposit

Pros: You can determine if you wish to grow your capital investment or take the interest as quarterly payments. Your investment is federally insured.

Cons: CDs require that you keep your money invested for a specific period of time. You are penalized for early withdrawal, and your interest earnings are subject to federal and state income taxes.

U.S. Savings Bond, Series EE

Pros: Your investment is guaranteed. There are no fees associated with buying these bonds. They are very liquid, and there are no penalties for redeeming them before maturity. Interest earnings are exempt from state income taxes and, if used for tuition, are also exempt from federal taxes.

Cons: This is a very long-term investment, and interest is reduced if redeemed early. If you hold a bond longer than 18 years, it stops paying interest.

Municipal Bond

Pros: This investment is fairly safe. You can check on the safety by looking at Moody's and Standard & Poor's. Municipal bonds are also exempt from federal income tax. Expect a return on this investment of 7 to 8 percent.

Cons: Because the interest rate is fixed, you may earn more or less than is paid by other investments.

Federal Agency Bond

Pros: This is a very low-risk investment with returns of about 7 percent. You can pick bonds with maturities from 1 to 40 years.

Cons: You typically need at least $5,000 to get started. The interest earned is subject to state and federal income taxes.

U.S. Treasury Bill, Note, Bond

Pros: These investment vehicles are guaranteed by the government and are considered risk-free. You immediately get a check for the difference between the bond amount and the auction price. The interest is exempt from state taxes.

Cons: The initial investment requirement may be large. The earned interest is subject to federal income taxes. On bills, you must send your money without knowing the exact price until the auction ends. On notes and bonds, you won't know the price until after competitive bidding at auction.

Corporate Bond

Pros: Corporate bonds are a fairly safe investment, as rated by Moody's and Standard & Poor's, and typically return 6 to 8 percent.

Cons: These bonds take a long time to mature. Some bonds can be redeemed by the company before the maturity date. As interest rates go up, bond yields go down. All interest earnings are subject to federal and state income taxes.

Mutual Fund

Pros: A small outlay can get you into mutual fund investing. The fees associated with trading in the stock market are smaller when you use a fund than when you trade independently. There are 9,000 fund portfolios to choose from, allowing you to find one that meets your needs.

Cons: There are no guarantees of your principal. Earned interest is subject to federal and state income taxes. If interest rates are low, the trading and management fees can exceed your return.

Corporate Stock

Pros: You can start investing in corporate stocks with

very little money. These stocks are liquid, because there is no maturity date or time period that they must be held.

Cons: Corporate stocks can be quite risky, and without a financial advisor, determining which ones will make a lot of money is very difficult. Commissions are charged by the broker when you buy stocks. Dividends, if paid, are subject to federal and state income taxes. Stock prices may fall, and you may lose money. Additionally, you will lose your principal if your company goes bankrupt.

If you mix these different investment vehicles, you will get a portfolio that earns about 3.2 percent. If you have $500,000 invested, that gives you about $1,300 a month as a return.

For most people, living on $1,300 a month will not cut it. Additionally, most people do not have $500,000 invested.

Private Mortgage Investing

And that brings us to private mortgage investing. That same $500,000 invested in mortgages would yield between 10 and 16 percent, and depending upon the loan, it could even go as high as 25 percent. Let's use 12 percent for this example. That gives you $5,000 a month to live on. Much, much better! And if you only have half that amount to invest, you are still earning double what you would be earning with a traditional portfolio.

Not many investments can dependably generate such strong returns, and few other investments have an asset like real estate as a "backstop" providing real protection.

Pros: Privately held mortgages provide a high return on investment (ROI). Real estate can be traded or exchanged for like-kind property on a tax-free basis.

Cons: This is not a terribly liquid investment. It requires that you stick with the mortgage for the time specified. To get started, you have to make a relatively large initial investment—typically no less than $5,000.

One of the advantages is that private mortgage investing brings in a high return on investment. What does high mean? Let's look at an example of an initial investment held over 5 years, 10 years, and 20 years:

5 YEARS (COMPOUNDED)			
Amount	7%	15%	Net Increase
$10,000	$14,176	$21,071	$6,895
$25,000	$35,440	$52,679	$17,239
$50,000	$70,881	$105,359	$34,478
$100,000	$141,762	$210,718	$68,596

10 YEARS (COMPOUNDED)			
Amount	7%	15%	Net Increase
$10,000	$20,096	$44,402	$24,036
$25,000	$50,241	$111,005	$60,764
$50,000	$100,483	$222,010	$121,527
$100,000	$200,966	$444,021	$243,055

20 YEARS (COMPOUNDED)			
Amount	**7%**	**15%**	**Net Increase**
$10,000	$40,387	$197,155	$156,768
$25,000	$100,968	$492,887	$391,919
$50,000	$201,937	$985,774	$783,837
$100,000	$403,837	$1,971,549	$1,567,712

As you can see, if you have $10,000 to invest for 20 years, the difference between investing that money at an annual rate of 7 percent versus an annual rate of 15 percent is $156,768.

Now, let's find out what private mortgage investing is all about.

CHAPTER 2

PRIVATE MORTGAGES – WHY YOU WANT TO BE INVOLVED

Welcome to the world of high-yield mortgage investing. Never again will you want to accept the paltry returns available from banks and other lending institutions. Once you understand private mortgages, you will realize that high investment returns do not necessarily mean high risk. If you know what you are doing and use common sense, you will find that mortgage investments can be safer than government bonds.

WHAT IS A PRIVATE MORTGAGE NOTE?

A private mortgage is similar to a bank mortgage, except that it is provided through an individual rather than a financial institution or a government agency such as Fannie Mae or Freddie Mac. Additionally, these loans are determined not by the borrower's credit score, but by the value of the property.

These loans are very safe, because they are backed by actual collateral—the real estate property. And to further ensure the safety of your principal, these loans are only for 65 to 70 percent of the appraised value of the property. (For construction loans or lots, the typical loan is 55 percent of the appraised value.) If someone can't pay, you can sell the property and easily recoup your principal.

If the loan goes into default, you, as the investor, can start foreclosure proceedings. This means that you can get the house for 65 to 70 percent of its value. Then you can sell the property for a substantial gain or use it for rental income.

When you invest in a private mortgage, you can set your own interest rate depending upon the situation. In most cases, first liens yield about 12 to 14 percent, while second liens yield from 16 to 18 percent. Generally, you will be able to get 6 points over the current prime rate.

PRIVATE MORTGAGE INVESTING VERSUS RENTAL INCOME

Let's imagine that you buy a house and rent it to tenants for $1,000 a month. If the house cost $100,000, you're getting a return on investment (ROI) of 12 percent. This sounds great, but it's not the whole picture.

In real life, if you buy a rental house, where will most of your rental income go? You will be spending a good portion of the $1,000 a month. It will go not only to the bank in the form of a mortgage payment, but it will also go into the maintenance of the property.

Every time a toilet leaks or a hot water heater fails, part of your interest is eaten up. Yes, you are building equity, but at a very slow rate. In the meantime, you are dealing with tenants.

It seems that banks have it pretty good. They just collect the mortgage every month. They are not in charge of toilets and tenants. Even if a property goes into foreclosure, banks have attorneys to take care of it. They make money while you do the work.

How would you like to be the bank? This is what private mortgage investing is all about. You get the monthly payments, and the real estate investor deals with everything else.

YOU ARE THE BANK

Let's look at a simplified loan transaction:

1. A potential buyer finds a piece of property.

2. The buyer heads to the local bank to take out a loan. If he or she qualifies, the loan is approved.

3. After approval, the ownership of that property is transferred to him or her.

4. The previous owner gets paid from money out of the loan.

5. The new homeowner begins making mortgage payments to the bank.

In a private mortgage transaction, the property is sold, not with money from a bank, but with money from an individual — you. You become the bank, and you make money from the transaction.

The mortgage note that you hold is fully collateralized by income-producing real estate. These loans are usually for the duration of one year and provide a monthly income of interest-only payments. At the end of the year, you receive the full amount of your initial principal.

MORTGAGE VERSUS DEED OF TRUST

When someone borrows money, the lending institution or individual usually requires that the borrower sign a promissory note, thereby agreeing to pay the lender back according to specific conditions. This note can be a mortgage or a deed of trust, which is completely dependent upon the laws of the state in which the transaction takes place.

In title-theory states, a mortgage is used. The title is held by the lender and is transferred to the borrower upon payment in full.

In lien-theory states, a mortgage is also used. The difference is that the title is held by the borrower, but a lien is charged against the property. The lien is removed when the property is paid off.

In California, a deed of trust or trust deed is used to tie the mortgage note to the property and create a lien. The note is not recorded — just the deed of trust.

Then there are the deed-of-trust states. A deed of trust is similar to a mortgage, but instead of just a borrower and a lender, there are a borrower, a lender, and a trustee. The title is put in the name of the trustee and given to the borrower when the loan is paid in full.

RECORDING THE LOAN

All mortgages or deeds of trust should be recorded with the county clerk of the county in which the real property is located. If you are recording a deed or a mortgage, you must take the proper steps to ensure that the documents meet all the legal requirements for recording. Believe it or not, more than 30 percent of all deeds received by county clerks are rejected and have to be returned for correction.

Although this is part of the title company's job, here are some of the things you need to understand about recording a deed of trust or mortgage:

- Every deed must contain the names and addresses of the purchaser and the seller. Post office boxes are not acceptable.

- The deed must contain a complete description

of the property, including the state, county, township, and village in which the property is located.

- The document must be signed and properly acknowledged by a notary public (notarized).

- If a deed incorporates exhibits, such exhibits must be included with the deed at the time of recording.

A perfected deed or mortgage is one for which the creditor has secured the proper documentation necessary to make it valid. A mortgage is perfected by recording a deed of trust or mortgage with the county recorder. Your deed is considered complete when it has been signed, sealed, and delivered.

Recording the deed is not required by law for the transfer from the seller to the buyer to take place. However, some people underestimate the importance of recording deeds of trust, a sure way for private lenders to lose their money.

To protect yourself from future claims on the title, you should record the deed. This should be done simultaneously with the closing or as soon after the close of escrow as possible.

To record a deed yourself, you need only to take the deed to the appropriate recording office in your area. The recorder will then index and transcribe the deed in the public records, and it will be available for anyone

to see.

"Constructive notice" is said to have been given once the deed is recorded. Unrecorded deeds, while valid between the grantor and grantee, don't give constructive notice to the world.

For example, suppose you lend $100,000 on a piece of property. The deed is notarized and ready to be recorded. However, you forget to do so, and it simply sits on your desk.

Several months later, another lender comes along and lends money to the very same borrower for the very same piece of property. This lender, too, gets a deed in recordable form and heads straight to the clerk's office.

Now, the borrower skips out on both of you, and you both go in to foreclose on the property. Here is the problem. The first lender—you—never recorded the deed. So who owns the lot?

The answer is the second lender, who had no knowledge of the previous sale of the property, but won the race to the courthouse.

This extreme example shows why it is so critical to promptly record every property deed or any document affecting real estate titles.

The deed becomes part of the property's chain of title. If anyone were to look up your property, your name would show up as the official owner.

The document must be acknowledged by an

authorized person, such as a judge or notary public. Documents that are not witnessed by a notary public are usually not recordable. The acknowledgment will verify the identity of the person signing the document, but will not make any statement or guarantee as to the validity of the document itself.

In some states, whenever a deed is recorded, the buyer must also file a Preliminary Change in Ownership Report. These reports are used by the assessor to determine which properties are exempt from property tax.

In most states, a transfer tax must be paid when a deed is recorded. Depending on your area, the amount of the tax will vary, but generally is based on a rate per $1,000. For example, it may be $1.10 per $1,000 of the value or the consideration or price paid for the property. Transfer taxes are typically paid by the borrower.

Now let's take a look at getting started. You have the option of creating the note yourself or using a hard-money lender, also known as a mortgage broker.

CREATING THE NOTE YOURSELF

If you decide that you want to create the note yourself, you will need to find a borrower. What do you look for in a borrower?

Professional real estate investors are usually a safer bet than individual homeowners. Why? They can show a proven track record, and they have experience. Typically, they are using the property to generate income and can pay you out of the rent monies, or they are planning to sell quickly after making improvements. Individuals, on the other hand, typically live in the house and have to come up with the money for payments. That is a much riskier investment.

Then you have to determine the factors you will use when lending money, in addition to doing your due diligence— finding out what you can about the property. You also want to determine if a particular borrower is going to work well with you.

The legal aspects of the loan process will also be up to you as well. You have to draw up a note and deed of trust. Your best bet would be to find a good real estate attorney to draw up these forms for you. Keep in mind that these documents should favor you, the lender, and not the borrower. Therefore, do not use the borrower's attorney or let the attorney change the note in any way. If you do, you are risking your principal.

The best place to lend money is in nonjudicial states. These are states that do not require a judicial proceeding to foreclose on a property.

Here is a list of nonjudicial states:

- Alabama
- Alaska
- Missouri
- Nevada

- Arkansas
- California
- Colorado
- District of Columbia
- Georgia
- Hawaii
- Idaho
- Massachusetts
- Michigan
- Minnesota
- Mississippi
- New Hampshire
- North Carolina
- Oregon
- Rhode Island
- South Dakota
- Tennessee
- Texas
- Virginia
- Washington
- West Virginia
- Wyoming

What does this mean to you? You can begin foreclosure on a property as soon as one payment is missed. This keeps you from losing too much interest income or allowing the property to deteriorate.

USING A MORTGAGE BROKER

Why would you consider using a private mortgage broker instead of doing it yourself? Because a mortgage broker can save you time — and time is money. Additionally, mortgage brokers often have a number of investments available that would not be available to you as an individual.

Instead of your having to find a borrower, the broker determines the parameters of the loan and handles all the legal work.

The problem with this approach to originating the loan is that most mortgage brokers are borrower-friendly instead of investor-friendly. In other words, they create deals that favor the borrower. If you decide to use a mortgage broker, you should find one who considers the investors to be clients as well as borrowers. If you do this, you won't have to worry as much about the state of the property or the borrower.

At this point, you're probably thinking that using a broker will certainly eat into your interest earnings. Amazingly, this is not true! Mortgage brokers do not earn their money from you, but from the borrower. The borrower pays fees to the broker to initiate the loan and find an investor.

A good broker will make sure that the client pays on your loan for 12 months, because it is beneficial to the borrower, to the investor, and to the broker. If the borrower pays perfectly for 12 months, the broker can show a good mortgage history for 12 months and help the borrower straighten out his or her credit. Then the broker can help the borrower find a loan with less interest. Who wouldn't want that? The broker benefits by getting to do another loan. The investor benefits because his or her money will be invested out again, and he or she will get a new point (1 percent to initiate the loan).

An established broker can help you with all of this.

LOAN SERVICING COMPANIES

For some, the idea of dealing with the monthly hassle of payment collection seems like too much trouble. If you want to try private investing but want to be as "hands-off" as possible, a loan servicing company may be just what you need.

A broker sets up the loan and, from that day forward, the broker doesn't have to do anything in connection with that loan. The borrower sends the check directly to the investor. If you choose, you can have a loan servicing company step in between.

Loan servicing companies typically offer the following types of services:

- Setting up, maintaining, and safeguarding the loan files.

- Sending out welcome letters to new borrowers.

- Sending out coupon books or monthly billing statements to each borrower.

- Collecting monthly principal and interest payments, along with taxes, insurance, and other escrow or impound payments, if applicable.

- Analyzing each loan account annually to ensure that an appropriate amount is collected for all escrow payments.

- Performing due diligence reviews of all loan files to ensure that all required documents are contained in each.

- Enforcing collection procedures, as required, to manage, mitigate, and minimize delinquencies.

- Posting payments to each borrower's account, ensuring that the correct amounts are applied to principal, interest, late charges, escrows, and so forth, as appropriate.

- Preparing and mailing reminder notices, late notices, and delinquency notices.

- Producing monthly delinquency reports that group loans by the age of the delinquency (30 days, 60 days, 90 days, and so on).

- Preparing, filing, and mailing the annual IRS 1098 reports and providing borrowers with copies of their respective reports.

- Performing other billing and collection services, as required.

Not all loan servicing companies perform all of these tasks, but this will give you a good idea of the types of services you can expect. The typical cost is 1 percent of your portfolio.

A good loan servicing company will send you a report and a check every month. It is similar to working with a bank and receiving bank statements, or giving your money to Merrill Lynch, which takes care of your investments and sends you a monthly statement, and you don't have to worry in between.

Many loan servicing companies just service loans, while some service and collect. If you only have a servicing company and not a collection company, it will be up to you to take care of delinquent payments through a real estate attorney.

Let's look at an example: Let's say Jack has $50,000 to invest. His broker arranges for Jack to make a loan to John. Every month, John sends a payment to Jack. Jack doesn't want to deal with the hassle of collecting the payments and keeping the records. So the loan servicing company steps in between John, the borrower, and Jack, the lender.

NOTE: If your broker is licensed, then he or she cannot service your loans. It is illegal to do both. It is not illegal, however, if your broker is also a lender.

In this case, John would start sending a check to the loan servicing company, payable to the servicing company. The servicing company would keep up with the loan and, in turn, charge Jack a fee.

Mortgage Broker Case Study – Allstate Mortgage Loans and Investments, Inc.

809 NE 25th Ave.
Ocala, FL 34470
Phone: 352-351-0200
Fax: 352-351-4557
E-mail: **info@allstateocala.com**
Web site: **www.allstateocala.com**

I spent some time talking with Matt Tabacchi about his real estate brokerage firm, and here are his answers to a few questions:

What exactly does a mortgage broker do?

As a mortgage broker, people come to me looking for money. I turn around and find them the money through people looking to invest. I connect the match together. These investors can be private individuals who lend money, as well as banks and other institutions. When someone comes in for a loan, we try to run them through the bank. If a bank can't do it, then we turn around and try to do a private mortgage. I guess you could call me the go-between.

Why do private investors use a mortgage broker?

Private investors use brokers because we have the loans to give them, and we have the license to do it. As a private investor, you might be able to find a loan or two on your own, but as a mortgage broker, I can find several. And you don't have all the work involved. You can loan out one or two mortgages without a license, and you don't have all the work involved. But if you want to do lots, you may be considered a lender, and may need to get a license. How much can you do without a license? The law is very gray. My advice is to always use a broker.

How safe do you think private mortgage investing is? Have you ever had problems?

Out of 2,000 private mortgages I have brokered, we have never had an issue. I know of brokers who have issues, but they are not following safe practices. They are too busy chasing the money and making unwise investments.

Do you worry about clients not paying on time?

No, I never worry. In fact, you make more money when they don't pay you on time. That is what late fees are for. When you do a loan for somebody, the interest keeps coming, and after ten days, you get a late fee, and that is true for each ten days late. We enter these at such a low LTV, and it is such a harsh penalty for these guys that they want to pay on time.

Do you have any recommendations for someone just starting in private mortgage investing?

I recommend driving by every piece of property that you lend money out on. Just by driving by, you can know if the property is a $100,000 house or a $200,000 house. You can get a feel for what is going on. You can see the neighborhood. Once you have a good trust with your broker, then you don't have to do it with every piece of property, but I would still do spot-checks.

Find a team that consists of a good broker, a good accountant, and a good appraiser. It is also a good idea to have a real estate attorney.

Start small, and see how you feel about it.

Doing what I do is a pretty complicated thing, because every deal is so different. There are basic guidelines, but there is a lot of gut feeling involved.

Do you have any good stories about real people who have begun private mortgage investing?

My mother and father owned a little rental store in Pittsburgh, Pennsylvania, and wanted to move to Florida to be with the grandkids and us. They are in their late 50s and have been self-employed their whole life. They are just simple, hard-working, blue-collar people with a bit of property.

About five years ago, I started helping them with investing their money—they began with $50,000. That is what they had in the bank. They started making $500 a month in interest. They were able, because of making the type of interest that they make every month, to sell all of their property and retire and move to Florida and live off the interest. Their money is getting ready to double.

They now have three of their best friends from Pennsylvania involved, and they have all moved to their little retirement community in Florida. Not only that, but they enjoyed it so much that both have become part-time brokers with me!

Mortgage Broker Case Study – January Financial

7700 Irvine Center Drive, Suite 800
Irvine, CA 92618
Phone: 949-305-6355
Fax: 949-753-2891
E-mail: **carey@januaryfinancial.com**
Web site: **www.januaryfinancial.com**

January Financial was formed in 2005 to serve the needs of its valued clients in the residential and commercial lending areas. It operates on a "referral-only" basis, meaning the majority of its business comes from referrals from clients, business partners, friends, and family members. January Financial guarantees that you will have an outstanding experience each and every time you do business there, from beginning to end.

I spoke with Carey Pott of January Financial and asked the following questions:

Do people use private mortgages as their sole source of income? Is it beneficial?

In my experience, people very rarely use private mortgages as a sole source of income. Generally, the investors who supply capital for private mortgages are financially savvy individuals and have fully diversified their investment capital.

I'd say the only time I've seen individuals using private mortgages as their only source of income is when they've acquired a large amount of property over their lives, are nearing retirement age, and are utilizing private mortgages as a way to trade equity for income. These people generally are lending money for properties they're selling, not to anyone who walks in off the street.

What is the best story you have ever heard while helping someone with a private mortgage?

The best story I've heard is a borrower I worked with who was able to save her house from foreclosure, replace a broken-down car, and fly back to Columbia to visit her sick grandmother. This woman had horrible credit scores and was unable to qualify for a conventional mortgage but had lots of equity in her home. I was able to pair her up with a group of investors who supplied funds for private mortgages, among other things. This group was able to replace the existing mortgage and give our borrower enough cash out to accomplish her goals when every bank was saying no.

How many people use their private mortgages wisely? What ways are there to prevent people from misusing them?

I can't recall a single instance when one of my borrowers used their private mortgage unwisely. Generally, the private mortgages are set up in such a way so as to ensure the borrower can make the payments in the short term, while making it sufficiently uncomfortable that they have an incentive to refinance themselves out of the private mortgage as soon as they are able. This benefits both the borrower and the investor. The borrower has a short-term solution to their problem and is able to get their financial lives [sic] back on track, and the investors get their capital back to invest in another venture, most likely another private mortgage.

In my opinion, the best way to prevent private mortgages from being used unwisely is to structure them correctly right from the beginning—a payment that is bearable, but not comfortable, and no prepayment penalty. As stated previously, this ensures that the borrower has incentive to refinance after fixing their problem and returns the investment capital to the investor.

Do you think that private mortgages are a good source of investment and income? Why?

Yes, I do, if structured correctly. As long as the loan-to-value ratio is kept sufficiently low (generally under 65 percent, rarely more than 70 percent), the investor's capital is protected. Even if the borrower ceases to make their payments, the investor is all but guaranteed to get their money back.

Additionally, private mortgages can provide much higher rates than are generally available in the security or money markets with very little additional risk. Couple this with the fact that if private mortgage lending is done ethically, it allows investors to solve problems for people who [sic] the conventional banks can't help, and I feel that it's a win-win.

From your perspective, investing in mortgages is quite beneficial. You get a high rate of interest with very little risk. What is in it for the borrower?

Let's look at the next chapter to find out.

CHAPTER 3

WHY BORROWERS SEEK PRIVATE MORTGAGES

It would seem that private mortgage investing is good for the investor but not for the borrower. With high interest rates and points, why would a borrower go to a private investor rather than a bank? To follow are the ten biggest reasons.

1. When Time Is An Issue

Traditional loans typically take six weeks or more to be approved. Sometimes, however, the borrower needs to get the deal closed sooner. For instance, a borrower may be waiting for a conventional loan, but the closing date on the property is coming faster than the approval. In this case, the borrower may get a "bridge loan" with a private lender. He or she then can close on the deal and wait for the bank to provide a permanent loan without worrying about deadlines.

Another situation in which time might be a factor is if a borrower purchases vacant property with the intent of turning it into something else. Banks would prefer to loan the money after the property has been converted and is fully rented out, not before.

Why does it take so long for conventional loans to be approved? For one thing, due diligence must be completed on both the borrower and the property. This means looking at the borrower's credit history, tax returns, and financial statements. Banks also need to know about all other property owned by a borrower. All of this takes time.

2. When Privacy Is An Issue

There are times when a borrower may not wish to have all of his or her financial information in the hands of a banking institution. For instance, if the borrower is going through a divorce or business separation, that information could be used against him or her. Perhaps the borrower has not yet filed income taxes for the year or does not have all the financial information needed by a traditional lender.

Any of these situations would keep the borrower from getting a conventional loan. However, if the property is producing income and the borrower has a good track record, none of these things should keep you from loaning money as a private lender.

3. When Ease Is An Issue

Private mortgages are easy to do. There is simply less paperwork involved. A borrower doesn't have to find all of the past years' paperwork, bank statements, tax forms, and so forth. Not only that, but the costs are actually less, because he or she doesn't have to get all of the expensive appraisals that the bank would require.

4. When The Amount Is An Issue

It is quite possible that a borrower will be able to get more money from a private lender than he or she is able to get from an institutional mortgage lender. Institutions lend money based on a percentage of either the cost of the property or the appraised value — whichever is lower. This means that if someone finds a good deal and gets a piece of property at a steal, the bank is going to lend him or her money based on that price rather than the true value.

The private lender, however, always bases the loan on the appraised value of the property. In this way, the borrower does not get penalized for finding a good deal.

5. When Credit Is An Issue

Sometimes the credit of the borrower is the issue for traditional loans. Perhaps the borrower's credit score or debt-to-income ratio is too low. He or she may not meet all the qualifications for a traditional bank to make the loan.

Since private mortgage lenders are mainly concerned with the appraised value of the property, credit issues often do not arise. The biggest factors are whether the property is currently producing or can produce enough income to pay the note and whether the value of the property will more than cover the note. If these two conditions are met, then the borrower's credit is not an issue.

6. When Foreclosure Is An Issue

If someone is delinquent with his or her payments and at risk of foreclosure, sometimes a private mortgage investor can help. Let's look at this scenario: If the homeowner has a $200,000 home and owes just $70,000, you may decide to give that homeowner a second chance and lend him or her $80,000. In this way, the borrower can pay off the bank and start making payments to you. Keep in mind that the loan-to-value (LTV) ratio is just 40 percent, so even if the borrower goes into foreclosure again, you will be able to get your money back out of the deal.

7. When Self-Employment Is An Issue

If you are or ever have been self-employed, you know that getting a loan is often much tougher. You have to show more financial statements. You have to prove you are even more financially sound than your corporate-employed counterpart.

Oftentimes, self-employed people simply do not have the financial depth to prove their creditworthiness to a bank. That is why self-employed people often seek private mortgages. This is especially true if they have been self-employed for less than five years and if their initial years of self-employment show small or even negative earnings.

None of this will matter to you as a private mortgage investor. You only need to be concerned with the property and not the financial records of the borrower.

8. When A Short-Term Loan Is An Issue

Trying to get a short-term loan from a bank is not always easy. For these loans, a borrower is often required to have a larger down payment and much better financial standing. Therefore, if a real estate investor is looking for a 2- to 3-year loan, he or she is often better off looking to a private lender.

One such short-term loan is a construction loan. Matt Tabacchi tells of one client who was given a private mortgage construction loan, and once the home was built, this borrower easily qualified for a regular loan. The private mortgage investor bridged the gap.

9. When A Commercial Property Is An Issue

The criteria for borrowing on a commercial property at a traditional lending institution are strict. As a borrower, you can't have any gut instincts about a property—you have to have cold, hard facts. You also have to have quite a bit of money backing you. Once again, in this situation, many investors look to private mortgages.

10. When The Property Itself Is An Issue

Some properties just don't qualify. Banks have criteria, and they make no exceptions.

Let's look at an example of an old, historic house that is partially renovated. The house is owned free and clear and is worth $200,000. The owner needs $75,000 to finish it. Most banks will not touch this property, but a private mortgage investor can and will.

Another type of property that often doesn't qualify is a mobile home. For instance, let's look at the case of a double-wide mobile home on 10 acres of land that is worth $250,000. The owner wants to borrow $50,000 — a 20 percent LTV. Most banks just say no.

BUT IS IT SAFE?

Your money is guaranteed. For every $100,000 that you invest, you will make between $1,000 and $1,200 in interest. This is a fact. If you take somebody who has invested $500,000, he or she is going to make close to $6,000 per month. The only way you can lose money in private mortgage investing is by fraud.

What do I mean by fraud? Let's suppose that I want you to lend out $50,000 on a home that I say is worth $100,000, but in reality, the home is only worth $30,000. In this case, you can and will lose money.

I can tell you how to loan money in private mortgages so that it never happens.

The first thing you must do is your own research. Let's look at a non-real estate example. If you go to Merrill Lynch and say that you want to buy stock, and you follow the broker's recommendation to buy XYZ stock, you just trusted him or her. XYZ stock may drop by half tomorrow, and you won't know this is coming, because you didn't spend the time to research it.

The same applies to private mortgage investing. Your research consists of the following:

- An appraisal

- A title search

- A proper LTV ratio (see Chapter 4)

If someone tells you that the property is worth $100,000 and the appraisal comes back with the same numbers, then you can feel pretty good about knowing the true value of the house. Here are some other ways to find the value of the house. In Florida, you can go to **www.floridapropertyappraisers.com**, put in the parcel number, and find out what that property is worth. This is what you will find:

41551-000-00

```
                               MARION COUNTY
41551-000-00 Alt Key:1031109   ** Property Information **   Map It!  As of  10/07/05
-----------------------------------------------------------------------------------
XXXXX XXXXX X X XXXXXX       TAXES/ASSESSMENTS:        $1,622.30    M.S.T.U.
XXXXX XX XXXXXXX XXX         LOCATION:                 MAP: 218 D2    PC: 01
XXXXXXXXX XX                 013369 SE HWY 484         IMAGES Mill Grp 9001
                            344205827 SEE LETTER IN HX FILE          .60 Acres
-----------------------------------------------------------------------------------
```

```
                    **      Current Values        **

Property Values: Land Just Val        7,498
               : Buildings           80,268
               : Miscellaneous       14,551
               : Total Just         102,317
               : Total Assessd        86,704   Amendment 10 Impact      -15,613
               : Exemptions          -25,000   Ex Codes: 01
               : Total Taxable        61,704
-----------------------------------------------------------------------------------
```

```
                    **  History of Assessed Values  **

Year      Land    Building  Misc Impr    Just    Assessed  Exemption  Taxable
2005 1   7,498     80,268    14,774    102,540    84,179    25,000    59,179 TN
2004 1   6,504     73,546    12,395     92,545    81,728    25,000    56,728 TN
2003 1   6,079     70,813    12,565     89,457    79,027    25,000    54,027 TN
-----------------------------------------------------------------------------------
```

```
                    **  Property Transfer History   **

(Official Records Transfer)                  Qualified/     Vacant/
Book Page Date  Instrument      Code         Unqualified    Improved Price
3827/1968   09/04 07 WARRANTY    7 PORTIONUND INT U            I       100
3383/0283   03/03 05 QUIT CL     0             U               I       100
3383/0280   03/03 07 WARRANTY    0             U               I       100
2127/0441   04/95 07 WARRANTY    2 V-SALES VERIFI Q QUALIFIED  I     88500
2093/1229   09/94 71 DTH CER     0             U               I       100
2095/1961   12/91 74 PROBATE     0             U               I       100
```

```
                    **  Property Description       **

01  -  SEC 12 TWP 17 RGE 22
02  -  BEG AT PT ON W BDY OF E 1/2 OF NW 1/4 N 00-02-52 W
03  -  634.5 FT FROM SW COR OF E 1/2 OF NW 1/4 TH
04  -  N 00-02-52 W 210 FT TO SELY ROW OF SR 484 BEING ON
05  -  A CURVE AND BEGINNING 30 FT FORM THE RADIAL TO THE
06  -  CENTERLINE OF SAID ROD, TH NELY AL ROW LINE CURVE
07  -  A CHORD BEARING OF N 48-58-40 E 150 FT TH S 42-19-53 E
08  -  RADIAL TO ROW LINE CURVE 143.79 FT TH S 00-02-52 E
09  -  201.98 FT TH S 89-57-08 W 210 FT TO POB LESS ANY PART OF
10  -  PROPERTY THAT LIES WITHIN FOLLOWING DESCRIPTION:
11  -  FROM SW COR OF NW 1/4 OF SEC 12 RUN N 89-42-17 E 1340.54 FT
12  -  TH N 00-16-03 E 708.19 FT FOR POB TH N 00-16-03 E 138.55 FT
13  -  TO POINT ON EXZISTING ROW LINE OF CTY RD 484 S ROW LINE
14  -  BEING A NONTANGENT CURVE CONCAVE NW'LY RAD OF 3849.55 FT TH
15  -  FROM TANGENT BEARING OF N 50-13-02 E RUN NE'LY 148.69 FT
16  -  ALONG ARC OF CURVE & EXISTING ROW LINE CHORD BEARING OF
17  -  N 49-06-38 E THRU CENTRAL ANGLE OF 02-12-47 TO POINT ON
18  -  E'LY BDRY OF PARCEL OF LAND BEING DESC IN OR BK 2127/PG 441
19  -  TH S 41-47-06 E 147.12 FT TH S 00-25-32 W 21.84 FT ALONG
20  -  E'LY BDRY TO POINT ON AFORESAID LINE BEING PARALLEL WITH
21  -  & 100 FT SE'LY OF CTY RD 484 TH S 63-40-48 W 235.31 FT
22  -  ALONG SAID PARALLEL LINE TO POB
```

```
**   Land Data                      **
```

LN	Use	Front	Depth	Zone	C	Notes	Units	Type	Rate	Dph	Loc	Shp	Phy	Just Val
01	0100			A1		IRREGULAR	.60	AC	4500.00	100	100	215	110	6,386
02	9990			A1		CR484	150.00	UT	7.41	100	100	100	100	1,112
Neighborhood	9400 17/22 & 17/23 W of Hwy 441						Total Land		–		Class			6,386
Mkt: 10 70							Total Land		–		Just			7,498

```
**   Building Characteristics   **
```

Building 01 of 02

FGR01=U29R23D29L23.U3
RES02=L50U26R20U20R30D46.
FOP03=D1R1D3L21U4R20.U26
FOP04=R23U6L23D6.U20
EPA05=R21U18L10U20L25U3L20D10L10D31R44.

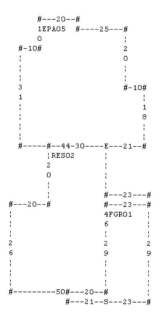

```
Improvement Type 1F SFR      - 01 FAMILY RESID
Effective Age      3 10-14 YRS                        Obsolesence: Functional  0%
Condition          6 GOOD                Year Built   1965               Locational  0%
Quality Grade      500                   Architecture    0 STANDARD SFR
Inspected on 09/02/03 by 174-XXXXX XXXXXXXX                       Base Perimeter    192
```

(Section)			Nbr	Year	Attic	/- Basement Data -/		Ground
Type	ID	/- Exterior Walls -/	Stories	Bilt	Finish	% Area	% Finish	Flr Area
FGR	01	29 VINYL SIDING	1.00	1965	N	0	0	667 SF
RES	02	29 VINYL SIDING	1.00	1965	N	0	0	1,900 SF
FOP	03	01 NO EXTERIOR	1.00	1965	N	0	0	83 SF
FOP	04	01 NO EXTERIOR	1.00	1980	N	0	0	138 SF
EPA	05	01 NO EXTERIOR	1.00	1985	N	0	0	2,260 SF

```
Roof Type   10 GABLE            Floor Finish 24 CARPET          Bedrooms 3 Kitchen     Y
Roof Cover  08 FBRGLASS SHNGL Wall  Finish 16 DRYWALL-PAINT   4FixBath 0 Dishwasher Y
Heat Type1  22 DUCTED FHA      Heat Source1 10 ELECTRIC        3FixBath 2 Disposal   Y
     Type2  00                     Source2 00                  2FixBath 0 Compactor  N
Foundation   7 BLK PERIMETER  Fireplaces    1                 Xfixture 2 Intercom   N
A/C          Y                                                            Vacuum     N
```

```
**   Building Characteristics   **
```

Building 02 of 02

APT01=L30U16R30D16.
PT002=R13U16L13D16.

```
#--------------------30--------------------#--------13-------#
| APT01                                     | PT002          |
|                                           |                |
|                                           |                |
|                                           |                |
|                                           |                |
|                                           |                |
| 1                                         | 1              | 1
| 6                                         | 6              | 6
|                                           |                |
|                                           |                |
|                                           |                |
|                                           |                |
|                                           |                |
#--------------------30--------------------E--------13-------#
```

```
Improvement Type 1F SFR     - 01 FAMILY RESID
Effective Age     3 10-14 YRS                    Obsolesence: Functional  0%
Condition         5 AVERAGE           Year Built  1980           Locational  0%
Quality Grade   200                   Architecture    0 STANDARD SFR
Inspected on 09/02/03 by 174-XXXXX XXXXXXXX                Base Perimeter    92
```

```
(Section)              Nbr   Year Attic /- Basement Data -/    Ground
Type  ID  /- Exterior Walls -/ Stories Bilt Finish % Area  % Finish   Flr Area
APT   01  20 MH ALUM SIDING   1.00   1980  N        0        0        480 SF
PTO   02  01 NO EXTERIOR      1.00   1980  N        0        0        208 SF
```

```
Roof Type  02 FLAT WOOD STR  Floor Finish 24 CARPET      Bedrooms 1 Kitchen   Y
Roof Cover 17 KOOL SEAL/MTL  Wall  Finish 16 DRYWALL-PAINT 4FixBath 0 Dishwasher N
Heat Type1 22 DUCTED FHA     Heat Source1 06 GAS         3FixBath 1 Disposal   N
     Type2 00                     Source2 00             2FixBath 0 Compactor  N
Foundation  7 BLK PERIMETER  Fireplaces   0             Xfixture 2 Intercom   N
A/C         N                                                      Vacuum     N
```

** Miscellaneous Improvements **

Type		Number Units/Type	Life	EYB	Grade	Length	Width	Just Value
256	WELL 1-5 BTH	1.00 UT	99	2003	2			1,200
190	SEPTIC 1-5 BTH	1.00 UT	99	1965	2			730
190	SEPTIC 1-5 BTH	1.00 UT	99	1980	1			460
226	RES SWIM POOL	648.00 SF	20	1984	5	36.0	18.0	5,876
099	DECK	444.00 SF	50	1984	1			711
UDS	SCRN PORCH-UNF	380.00 SF	40	1980	1	20.0	19.0	1,197
UDU	UTILITY-UNFINS	120.00 SF	40	1980	1	12.0	10.0	441
159	PAV CONCRETE	2582.00 SF	20	1980	3			1,756
UDC	CARPORT-UNFIN	420.00 SF	40	1993	2	20.0	21.0	1,942
114	FENCE BOARD	128.00 LF	10	1993	4			238
				Total Just Value as of 10/20/03				14,551

** Appraiser Notes **

01 - COULD NOT DO A COMPLETE REVIEW

** Planning and Building **
County Permit search

	Permit Number	Permit Amount	Date Issued	Date Complete	Construction Description	
01	M041073	2,315	04/03	04/03	WELL PUMP ELECTRIC	-
02	M120194	450	12/03	06/04	ABANDON WELL	-

** Cost/Market Summary **

			Bldg Nbr	Reproduction Cost New	Amount of Depreciation	R.C.N. Less Depreciation
Buildings R.C.N.	100,203	03/28/01	01	85,251	16,197	69,054
Total Depreciatio	-19,935		02	14,952	3,738	11,214
Bldg - Just Value	80,268					
Misc - Just Value	14,551	10/20/03				
Land - Just Value	7,498	05/18/05				
Total Just Value	102,317					

Other states have similar Web sites. You can go to **www.searchsystems.net** to find appraisals in many different states.

You can also find the parcel ID number on the title search and ask a local appraiser what he or she believes the property is worth. Or you can give a local Realtor the parcel ID number and ask what the property is worth, since Realtors know their areas.

When you conduct the title search, be sure that it has the same parcel ID number as the property you are lending on. If an unscrupulous party changed the ID number, you could be signing on something else! Also, double-check with the title company that you will have a first mortgage.

Finally, keep your LTV ratio at no more than 65 percent of the property's value. All of these things will help you check for fraud. As long as no fraud is involved, your money truly is safe.

Now we've seen some of the main reasons why a borrower would want to take out a private mortgage. It is a win-win deal for all concerned. Even though it is a win-win, there are times when loaning money is not a good idea. The parameters described in Chapter 4 will help you determine when loaning your money is right for you.

FIVE INVESTMENT PARAMETERS

LOAN-TO-VALUE RATIO

When private lenders consider whether to offer a
loan, they consider many different variables. The most
important — the one that the deal really hinges on — is the
loan-to-value ratio (LTV). This is a simple calculation of
the value of a property versus the loan amount.

$$\frac{\text{Loan Amount}}{\text{Property Value}}$$

For instance, if you loan $63,000 on a $100,000 piece of
property, then the LTV is 63 percent.

Let's look at one without such even numbers. If you loan
out $56,000 on a $96,500 piece of property, the LTV would
be $56,000 divided by $96,500 or 58 percent.

For private mortgage lenders, the LTV is typically:

- Up to 55 percent on undeveloped or raw property.

- Up to 65 percent for commercial properties, such as shopping centers and office complexes.

- Up to 70 percent on residential properties, such as houses, duplexes, and apartment complexes.

Of course, these are merely guidelines, and the LTV is only one parameter used to determine whether you should make the loan. Depending upon the other criteria, you may only want to go 55 percent on a commercial property or even on a residential property. As you become more experienced with real estate investors and property, you will be able to make these decisions instinctively.

What makes you decide to lower an LTV ratio? Someone like Matt Tabacchi drives by the piece of property and determines how much he wants to lend. There are basic guidelines, but there is also a lot of gut feeling involved. What is your sense of the person? How do you feel about the property?

> "If someone has a piece of property that is well maintained, it is a very good-looking piece of property, and the person needs 67 percent, then I may do it. On the other hand, if the property is run down, in bad shape, and in a poor location, then I might only loan 40 to 50 percent. A lot of it is gut feeling. The more you do it, the better your gut feelings about these things."

You can literally stay at 65 percent and not go wrong, even if the property is not as good. You can get 65 percent out of a piece of property regardless of its shape.

The other real concern is to be sure that you are loaning 65 percent of the real value of the property and not some inflated value. We are in an inflated market. If somebody paid $100,000 for a piece of property six months ago and is now asking for $150,000 because the house is worth $300,000, that should raise a red flag. The probability that it appreciated that much in six months is pretty small.

Any time someone has owned a house for less than a year, you want to find out what they paid for it, and then you also want to see why it appreciated so much. Was it totally remodeled? Was it inherited or bought cheaply from a relative? Or is the house just not worth that much money? There may be legitimate reasons why it appreciated so quickly, but you need to check it out. A Realtor and an appraiser will give you the true value of a house.

NOTE: Find yourself a real estate appraiser or a real estate agent who you can trust in the area in which you are going to lend. Ask your real estate professional what he or she thinks is the value of a house. This person should be "working for you" and for the seller of the property. In return, the real estate professional can bill for his or her services, which is charged back to the borrower.

TYPE OF PROPERTY

This parameter is dependent upon your comfort level. Let's look quickly at the different types of properties and the ability to dispose of them quickly in case of a default.

Single-family dwellings – These often take up to a year to sell. Unless you can get them rented while you are attempting to sell them, you stand to lose money. Not only will you not be getting a monthly interest check, but you will not be able to use the capital toward other investments.

Single-use buildings – Some buildings can only be used for one thing. For instance, a building built specifically for an oil-changing company can only be used by other oil-changing businesses. Trying to sell one quickly is not going to be very easy, and finding a renter will also be difficult.

Multi-tenant, multiuse buildings – Office buildings usually sell quickly, especially if you are selling below market value to simply get your initial capital back. Additionally, an office building can produce income while you attempt to sell, thus helping you to retain the monthly payments you had counted on in the original deal.

CASH FLOW OR INCOME POTENTIAL OF THE PROPERTY

This is an area that requires a bit more intuition. If you believe that the borrower will be able to come up with the interest payments, then you may be a bit more broad-minded with this parameter.

To be on the safe side, you, as the lender, would like to see the property producing income, and you would want this income to pay for the note as well as all the expenses. This gives the mortgage a larger degree of safety.

A private lender can look at the borrower's overall cash flow from other properties. Lending money, however, when there is no apparent cash flow is quite risky.

YOUR EXIT STRATEGY

Private loans are short-term loans. Therefore, it is essential that you know how the borrower plans to repay the loan at the end of the term. Once you know the plan, you have to decide if the plan is a good one. If the exit strategy is too risky, you may determine that you don't want to be a part of the deal or you may decide that the deal needs higher interest rates or a lower LTV or both.

There are many ways that a borrower can "exit" the private mortgage that you hold:

1. **Selling the property before the note is due.** This is a good strategy for a single-family dwelling as long as the note is at least a year in length. It is also quite likely to happen if the building is an office complex or other easily sold real estate.

2. **Financing through a traditional lender.** This is a good exit strategy as long as the borrower has good enough credit to get a traditional loan, and the property is such that a bank will want to loan the money.

3. **Obtaining a blanket mortgage on all properties owned.** Once again, this will be dependent upon the borrower's credit and the properties involved.

4. **Borrowing equity from another property is another strategy.** This is a good exit strategy as long as the equity in the other property is sufficient to cover the mortgage and as long as you feel comfortable that the borrower will use that equity toward your loan and not for something else.

5. **Finding a partner for investment purposes.** Once again, this is dependent upon the property and the likelihood of someone wanting that property as an equity investor.

6. **Self-amortizing the exit.** A self-amortization exit involves full repayment of the loan from the property cash flow. This is uncommon, because most property cannot produce enough income to repay the loan in full during the short duration of the loan.

These are not the only strategies, but they are the most common. There is no one right exit strategy. It depends upon the borrower and the property. You, as the lender, must decide if a particular strategy is feasible.

BORROWER'S EXPERIENCE

Finally, you want to look at the borrower's experience. This parameter is more than numbers — it is also ability. Has the borrower done this type of thing before?

If you are dealing with a borrower who has a long list of successful real estate ventures, you will feel that it is a pretty safe bet to loan him or her the money.

On the other hand, new real estate investors taking on huge renovation projects may not be such a good idea. What kind of experience do they have? Have they worked in real estate at all? Do they know construction? Have they ever acted in the capacity of landlord? Each of these questions will help you determine your comfort level.

The borrower's abilities are inversely proportional to the interest rate. If you feel safe, then you can provide the maximum loan amount at the minimum interest rate. If you don't feel safe but are still going to go with the loan, then you can provide a smaller loan with a much higher interest rate.

Experienced borrowers have practical, hands-on knowledge concerning the project. You can feel confident that they know how to renovate a building and how to sell it quickly. You can feel confident that they understand their exit strategy. You can feel confident that they will be purchasing property that will make them money.

Once you look at these parameters as a whole, you can determine the interest rate as well as the LTV. High marks in all the categories lead to high LTVs. Doubt about any of the parameters will lead to higher interest rates and lower LTVs.

The only way you would consider making a loan to a borrower if the parameters looked poor is if you would like to own the property yourself. That is, in case of foreclosure, would you be happy to get that property? If the answer is yes, then it might be worth the risk.

CREDIT SCORES AND WHAT THEY MEAN

Despite the fact that the credit of the borrower is not really a factor, as part of the "experience" category, you may find yourself looking at his or her credit rating. This section will help you figure out how the rating is determined and what the number really means, especially to you as a private mortgage investor.

A credit score is simply a number calculated based on the borrower's credit history. The borrower gets points based on information in his or her credit report. These points are compared to those of other similar consumers and help the lending agency identify the risk of loaning money to this particular person or entity.

Based on the number, the lending agency predicts how likely the borrower is to repay money. The higher the score, which can range from 300 to 900, the more likely a borrower is to repay. Knowing this, traditional bankers gladly accept high numbers, accept mediocre numbers as long as they can charge enough points and high enough interest, and reject low numbers.

The score most commonly used by lenders is known as a FICO. Although the exact formula for determining a score is not known, this is an approximate breakdown of how the score is determined:

- **Payment history – 35 percent .** This includes late payments, collection payments, bankruptcies, and so forth. The more recent these events, the harder they are on the score.

- **Outstanding debt – 30 percent.** This includes any debt: car loans, mortgages, and unsecured debt such as credit cards.

- **Length of credit history – 15 percent.** Newbies to the credit world do not have a history to check and therefore get a lower credit rating.

- **Number of inquiries on the credit report – 10 percent.** Having lots of inquiries makes it look as if the borrower is in some kind of financial trouble or is getting too heavily in debt.

- **Types of credit held – 10 percent.** How much debt is secured? How much is unsecured? What are the loans for?

Let's look at each of these in the context of private mortgage lending. The payment history is the most relevant to you. Being late with other payments may be an indicator that the borrower will be late with yours. However, don't jump to conclusions. Late payments, bankruptcies, and judgments can happen for a number of reasons.

Is it an issue of income versus expenses? That might truly affect you. But in many cases, this type of issue arises due to a recent divorce or unpaid medical bills resulting from an accident or illness. It could also be caused by a recent layoff. A bankruptcy due to a divorce shows up in the same way on a credit report as a bankruptcy due to having more expenses than income! Therefore, as a private mortgage lender, you have the option to find out the reasons behind the score.

Having too much outstanding debt is another big "no-no" in the traditional lending world. And it may truly be a sign that keeps you from wanting to lend. But, just as with late payment issues, outstanding debt issues may also be readily explainable.

Later in the book, you will learn that taking an equity loan on your home is a good way to find money for investment purposes. In fact, "borrowing" from a credit card at 6 percent and loaning out the money at 15 percent can also be a good strategy. Either of these strategies can make your outstanding debt look unfavorable even if you are financially sound.

The same kind of thing can be happening to your potential borrower. Many real estate investors show too much outstanding debt at any given time because they are in the business of buying and selling real estate. This does not make them poor candidates for loans! In fact, having the experience actually makes them better candidates for you.

The length of time with credit hinders those who have chosen to live without credit, young people who have yet to establish a credit record, and even women who have always had credit in their husbands' names. None of these issues directly affects the criteria you will use to determine if you wish to loan money to a borrower. At best, someone just establishing credit may not have a lot of experience, but if the other criteria are met, this should not really be an issue.

Those who deal in real estate or buy and sell cars or have any other reason to obtain several loans a year will find that their credit scores go down—even if they are making their payments on time! Why? Because each time these people apply for a loan, their credit reports are checked. And each time a credit report is checked, that inquiry is recorded. Too many inquiries, according to the lending industry, make you a bad risk. In actuality, it depends upon the reason for the inquiries.

The final category includes the type of credit held. Since you are going to be providing a mortgage loan that is secured by collateral, it really doesn't matter what types of loans your borrower has open. The biggest factors in your decision have much more to do with the property than with the borrower, and much more to do with the borrower's experience than with his or her credit score.

You now understand when to make a loan, and you understand that the bulk of your money will be earned through interest. In the next chapter, you will learn about the different types of mortgages, their interest structures, and other vehicles you can use when structuring your loan to provide you with even more return on your investment.

Case Study – Bob

Bob explains why he likes private mortgage investing and the different criteria on which to base your loan-to-value ratio:

I was in the stock market. In fact, I lost money in the market. It was always up and down and up and down. Since I have my own business, I just didn't have time to keep up with the market. It was too difficult to assess. That is why I got into private mortgages almost 20 years ago.

At first, I had most of my money in real property. I put any extra into private mortgages. It has been really beneficial for me. I've never had a foreclosure. I keep my loan-to-value at 65 to 70 percent. This makes things safe and keeps me covered in case of a real estate market fluctuation. The rates I earn and the ease of keeping up with the trends are a whole lot better than the stock market.

You do have to keep up with real estate market trends. In my area, the real estate market has gone crazy in the last few years—I would even say ridiculous. For me, this just means that I have to be careful when evaluating my loan-to-value ratio. For instance, if I am trying to keep my LTV at 65 percent, I want to be sure that I am loaning 65 percent of the real value of the home and not some inflated value. Sometimes I see a home appraised at $200,000, and I know that it is not really much more than $100,000. If I gave 65 percent based on the $200,000 appraisal, I would actually be handing the borrower more money than the home was really worth!

I'm very concerned about the appraisal. You don't want to get ahead of the appraisal. You can see the general prices in an MLS, but in a couple of weeks, they will jump up. That doesn't mean, however, that they will sell at that price. Be careful that you aren't looking at inflated appraisals. You need to watch it. For instance, I have a home that I could easily get appraised for what the other homes in the neighborhood are selling for. My home, however, does not have a pool and is smaller than the average home in the area. It shouldn't be appraised that high, but it would be. This is why you need to really look at the property and the properties around it.

When it comes to making a loan, I take whatever comes along, as long as the investment parameters are right. For instance, I have provided loans for undeveloped land, but to do so, I have only given 35 to 40 percent. Dealing with undeveloped land is more of a crapshoot. Then, there have been properties that seem great but the neighborhoods are terrible. I wouldn't put out a loan on a home in a terrible neighborhood for any interest rate. I simply do not want property in an undesirable area in case I should ever have to foreclose.

Luckily, I've never had to foreclose. The idea does concern me somewhat, but I know that my attorney can handle it with minimal effort on my part. In fact, most good mortgage brokers can also help you take care of it. It is not the worse [sic] thing that can happen as long as your LTV is good.

I've been asked whether I inspect all the properties that I lend on. My answer is "Yes, times five." You've got to do it. There are so many dishonest people out there. If you don't know your broker, you may find some fraudulent practices going on. For instance, you might be told of a $100,000 house and you plan to loan $50,000 on it. You look it up on the computer and it looks great. However, if you've been given the wrong legal description, you will be looking at the wrong house. The correct legal would show a trailer in a trailer park. That is a far cry from a single-family home on an acre lot! This won't happen if you go and have a look. Always be sure that what you are seeing physically is the same piece of property you sign for. Don't let anyone bait and switch.

Other things can occur too. For instance, I once was going to loan out on a $200,000 piece of property. I went out to the address, and it looked pretty good. However, something didn't seem right with the legal description. Then I realized what was going on. The piece of property was behind the one on the road. It had no road frontage at all—only an easement for egress/regress. That makes a big difference in the value of that property! The mortgage broker had not been out to the property, and the person needing the loan had glossed over the fact that there was no frontage. Avoid all of this by doing your homework!

I think that private mortgage investing is the best way to invest. You can take a million and put it out at 12 percent, and I guarantee that you can make $120,000 a year. In fact, I think that it would be just fine to invest everything you own this way.

The only problem I see is the tax rate. If the money you've invested is not in an IRA, then you can count on being taxed at 30 to 38 percent.

It is different with developments. With developments and projects, you can get Uncle Sam to give you tax cuts, but not at private mortgage investing. That seems unfair to me, since I am taking all the risk. However, it is the only problem I see with investing everything this way. And, truth be told, even with the taxes, you still make a heck of a lot more than normal investment vehicles. Getting a good accountant is really wise. They help you pay the least amount of taxes but keep you totally legal. You will know what I mean if you are ever audited.

I follow my own advice and invest everything this way. I use my IRA by going through Trust Administration Services in California. I was making 7 to 8 percent, and now I make 12 to 14 percent. And I don't have any concerns, because I have control of what I invest in. I keep my LTV to 65 percent and if I have to foreclose, then I have to foreclose. I would just turn it over to a lawyer, and it is done. The only issue I have with using my IRA is that I have to have the payments sent directly to the trustee in California. I really like seeing the payments and recording them instead of someone else doing it for me. If there is a problem, I may not know about it for ten days or so. However, that is the only drawback I see at all.

I also think that leveraging your home is a great idea. You are going to get at least 5 percent in your pocket on money that is simply sitting in your home. It is taxable income, but so is stock market income. And there is no long-term capital gain in a mortgage.

I am a firm believer in finding the right people to be on your team. For instance, it is really important to find a good broker, especially if you are new to real estate investing. The best way to find a good broker is by word-of-mouth. A broker can find out all the information you need to know about the property. This keeps you from having to do all the research yourself. Now, even with a good broker, I still inspect the property, but I don't have to do all of the legwork. By the time the broker brings a deal to me, I know that all I really have to do is go take a look.

Here is my word of caution: Do not deal with individuals. Individuals do not have to have a license and therefore do not have to follow any particular guidelines. If someone is out there being a broker without having a license, you are much more likely to find yourself getting into fraudulent deals.

As I said earlier, a good accountant is necessary. They keep you straight at the end of the year. And a good real estate lawyer is essential. I don't use them often, but when I have a question, I want to know that they know the answer. Remember, you want to speak to a real estate lawyer, not a divorce lawyer!

Here are a few other tips:

Escrow is something I have considered, but it is more of a pain than it is worth to me. Some people feel better about it as a safety precaution. I guess I just would rather contact them when it is due.

If you are going to partner with someone, make sure that they are trustworthy. There are several people with whom I would partner. There are several others, however, that I wouldn't touch with a 10-foot pole.

Any amount that you have to get started is better than that money sitting in the bank earning a measly 2 to 4 percent.

Always write in prepayment penalties. I typically go for 4 to 5 percent. This keeps me from having to move my money around as much.

It is like this: If you want to know about Hondas, you certainly wouldn't ask those questions at a Chevrolet dealer. The same holds true about private mortgage investing. Find those that know what they are doing.

CHAPTER 5

THE WORLD OF MORTGAGES, INTEREST RATES, AND FEES

FIXED-RATE VERSUS ADJUSTABLE-RATE MORTGAGES

When you provide a mortgage to a borrower, there are many different types from which to choose. Let's take a look at two of the most common ones.

Fixed-Rate Mortgages

This is the most common type of mortgage available. With a fixed-rate mortgage, you offer the borrower an unchanging interest rate for the entire life of the loan. For instance, if you determine that you are going to loan $100,000 at 12 percent for 3 years, then you will know exactly what your interest earnings will be each month over the life of the loan.

The good news is that you always know what you are

going to earn. This is also good if you believe that interest rates are falling, because you will be fixed at a higher rate. The downside is, if the rates increase, you are also still fixed. This means that your money will not be earning as much as it could be.

Determining what interest rate you will charge is based on the factors described in the previous chapter. The higher the risk, the higher the interest rate will be.

Adjustable-Rate Mortgages (ARMs)

With this type of mortgage, the interest rate is adjusted based on the changing market rates and economic trends. As a private mortgage lender, you might decide to offer this type of loan if you believe that interest rates are going to rise. In this way, you will not get stuck with a lower interest rate.

Keep in mind that you will want to put a "floor" on your interest rate, meaning that the interest rate will not go below a certain level. For instance, if you start with a 12 percent loan, you can state the conditions for increasing the interest rate, while also specifying that the interest will never drop below 12 percent.

ARMs are adjusted based on the terms of the loan. For short-term loans, you will want a shorter-term ARM. For instance, a 3-month ARM will adjust rates every 3 months, whereas a 3-year ARM will only adjust rates every 3 years. If you are only offering a 5-year loan, you do not want to create an ARM that only has the opportunity to adjust one time!

The interest rates for ARMs can be tied to 1-year Treasury bills, CDs, the prime rate, or another index. You will specify the index and then adjust your rate accordingly. Let's say that you are lending at 10 points above current $100,000 CD rates. If these rates go up 2 points, then the interest rate you charge the borrower will go up 2 points.

CONSTRUCTION LOANS

A construction loan is a short-term, nonpermanent loan for financing the cost of construction. Most construction loans last 6 to 9 months, but may last longer depending upon the complexity of the project. These loans are also "interest-only" loans, meaning that the borrower does not try to pay down the loan amount, but simply makes interest payments. The lender gets his or her entire investment back when the home is sold or when the builder gets a conventional loan.

As a lender, the best way to ensure the safety of your investment is to only lend out 50 percent of the current value of the project. For instance, if the lot is worth $30,000, you would advance only $15,000 to the builder. When the home is completed, you will have loaned out only 50 percent of the value of the completed home.

Many private investors like dealing with construction loans because:

- The bookkeeping is simple, since you are only

dealing with interest payments.

- You are working with a business as opposed to an individual. Typically, businesses will follow through on commitments. Additionally, they will have a track record so that you can assess the risks involved.

- The loan is short and the capital, along with the interest earned, can be put into another project quickly.

Builders like to deal with private lenders, because private lenders can get the money to them quickly. This is often an issue, since the builder wants to get started right away.

The downside is this: If a builder defaults on the loan, you will be left with an unfinished house. To get your investment out of the property, you will have to finish the home yourself and be involved in its sale. For those not experienced with the building side of real estate, this can seem daunting.

Here is what Matt Tabacchi had to say about this fear:

> "The majority of people who are building a house don't start building a house when they are broke or can't afford to. These are short-term loans. You are not giving a guy a loan to straighten him back out again. You are giving a guy a loan to make him better.

> "Most people building a house are very excited

from Day One to the end, because they can't wait to get into their new house. The only time that I have ever had delinquencies on construction loans are [sic] when I lend money directly to an inexperienced owner/builder who wants to build their house. That person usually doesn't know what they are doing. They think they can build this house for $100,000 when it takes $150,000. They run into all kinds of things they didn't know they were going to run into, because they don't do it every day.

"Usually when you do a construction loan, you want to make sure that a builder is involved. During that construction period, you get the interest on all the money starting Day One. So, if you are lending a guy $100,000 to build a house, you are putting $100,000 into the attorney's office's escrow account or title office's escrow account, and you are just releasing money as it goes. You get interest for the whole thing even if they are only taking $20,000 now. You get interest on everything until the house is complete.

"Construction loans are a little bit more work. When you have a construction loan, you have to look at the progress. The builder will give you a draw schedule — let's say five draws — you give him the first draw, and it is the clearing of the lot, the cement slab, the well, and a couple of other things. When he comes in for Draw No. 2, he needs to have paid receipts for what was done on Draw No. 1. When he comes to get Draw No. 3, he has to give paid receipts for Draw No. 2 (the frame, the truss, etc.) so that you know for a fact that he is truly making progress.

"I also recommend that you have your appraiser inspect the property. The cost of this inspection is passed on to the borrower. The appraiser is licensed to inspect these situations and has insurance that will help cover you if there were a fraudulent matter.

"You are building a brand-new house, and you are loaning at such a low LTV that by the time the house is complete, you're at a great LTV, and it is a brand-new house that is easily marketable."

Let's look at an example: If you lend on a single-wide out in the middle of the forest on 5 acres, there are only so many people who will want to live out there if your borrower defaults. If you are building a brand-new house and the borrower defaults, there are many people who will want that brand-new house.

If the borrower defaults, that doesn't mean that you aren't going to have the same builder finish the house. The process doesn't have to slow down at all. The builder is being paid by you. You are still going to continue to have the builder finish the house. It is not a lot of work for you. Then you foreclose and have a new house that you can sell for a great profit.

I asked Doug Brown, a private investor, about construction loans. He likes them and doesn't feel concerned about a builder defaulting:

> "I've had many construction loans and so far, no one has defaulted. But even if they did, I wouldn't be too worried. I know a bit about building and know that real estate in my area is booming. I will not have a problem getting the house finished and sold. If the real estate market began to slide, however, I might be a bit more cautious about construction loans."

Lending for construction purposes may be a good way to build up the amount of capital you have to invest in other projects. For instance, if you loan out $50,000 for construction at 14 percent for 9 months, you get the following payments:

Month	Principal Loaned	Payment
1	$12,500	$583.33
2	$12,500	$583.33
3	$20,000	$583.33
4	$25,000	$583.33
5	$25,000	$583.33
6	$30,000	$583.33
7	$35,000	$583.33
8	$45,000	$583.33
9	$50,000	$583.33

This gives you about $5,250 in 9 months. Now you will have $53,000 to lend. If you had put the same money into a regular loan for 3 years, you would not have the capital to reinvest as quickly.

FIRST AND SECOND MORTGAGES

A first mortgage is one that is registered first against the property. This mortgage has to be paid first in the event of sale or default. A second mortgage is the second loan against a piece of property. This means if the homeowner is forced into foreclosure, the second mortgage holder will receive no proceeds from the sale of the home until the first mortgage has been completely repaid.

What does this mean to you if you choose to make a loan for a second mortgage? Let's look at an example: You have loaned $10,000 on the second mortgage of a $100,000 house. The borrower has a first mortgage of $80,000. If the borrower stops making payments on the first mortgage, the house will go into foreclosure. And either the court or the trustee, depending upon the state, will sell the house.

Now, let's assume that the house only sells at auction for $60,000. The first mortgage will be paid off first. Since there is nothing extra, the holder of the second mortgage will get nothing.

Matt Tabacchi does not feel comfortable putting any of his investors into second mortgages. Here is what he has to say:

> "If you do a first mortgage and you don't do more than 65 percent of what that piece of property is worth, you cannot go wrong. You

just can't. When you start on second mortgages and loaning more than 65 percent, then you start getting into much greater risk."

Does this mean you should never make a second mortgage? No. It only means that you need to be more careful.

If you lend money for a second mortgage, your risks are greater. This means that you will do two things: Increase the interest rate, and decrease the loan-to-value ratio. As your risk goes up, your need to protect your investment will also increase.

AMORTIZATION TABLES

An amortization table is a document that shows you exactly how much the borrower is paying each month for the privilege of borrowing. It gives the required payment on each specified date and a breakdown of the payment, showing how much constitutes interest and how much constitutes repayment of principal.

There are four important components of an installment loan:

1. The **principal** or amount financed.

2. The **interest rate** or rate you are charging for the use of the money.

3. The **term** or amount of time for repayment.

4. The **monthly payment**, which is determined by the first three items.

The interest rate determines how much you are earning each month on the unpaid balance of the loan. The interest rate is usually specified in terms of an annual percentage rate, or APR. To get the monthly percentage rate, divide the APR by 12.

As an example, if you loaned $100,000 at 15 percent APR, at the end of the first month, you would earn $1,250 in interest alone. If the borrower only paid the cost of interest each month, he or she would be paying you $1,250 for life!

Of course, most loan structures require a payoff in a specific number of years. To accomplish this, the monthly payment must be greater than the monthly interest cost so that each month, part of the payment goes toward the principal of the loan. As the principal is reduced, the monthly interest cost is also reduced, and with a fixed payment each month, more of the payment is applied toward the principal of the loan.

To continue the example above: If, instead of $1,250, the borrower paid $1,500 the first month, $1,250 would go toward the interest and $250 would go toward the principal. The balance of the loan for the second month would be $99,750.

So the interest owed for the second month is $1,246.87. Therefore, the second payment of $1,500 contains $1,246.87 in interest, with $253.13 going toward the principal.

It should be pointed out that there are many different types of loans. An amortization table can be applied to unconventional as well as conventional loans. In all cases, it will show for each payment the amount going toward interest and the amount going toward principal. Now let's look at an actual amortization table. Here are the specifics for this table:

$100,000 principal; 15-year term; 10 percent interest rate

1	2	3	4	5	6
Year	Outstanding Loan Amount	Payment	Interest	Repayment of Principal	Remaining Balance
2000	$100,000	$13,147	$10,000	$3,147	$96,853
2001	96,853	$13,147	9,685	3,462	93,391
2002	93,391	$13,147	9,339	3,808	89,583
2003	89,583	$13,147	8,958	4,189	85,395
2004	85,395	$13,147	8,539	4,608	80,787
2005	80,787	$13,147	8,079	5,068	75,719
2006	75,719	$13,147	7,572	5,575	70,144
2007	70,144	$13,147	7,014	6,133	64,011
2008	64,011	$13,147	6,401	6,746	57,265
2009	57,265	$13,147	5,727	7,420	49,845
2010	49,845	$13,147	4,984	8,163	41,682
2011	41,682	$13,147	4,168	8,979	32,704
2012	32,704	$13,147	3,270	9,877	22,827
2013	22,827	$13,147	2,283	10,864	11,963
2014	11,963	$13,147	1,196	11,951	12

The table above has the following six columns:

Column 1 – The year of the loan. Since this example is for a 15-year loan, this column shows the 15 years.

Column 2 – The outstanding loan amount. In the first year, the borrower owes the entire $100,000. In the last year, he or she will owe $0.

Column 3 – The payment, which is determined by using a financial calculator.

Column 4 – The interest paid. This is based on the interest rate of 10 percent multiplied by the outstanding loan amount in Column 2.

Column 5 – The repayment of principal, which is the difference between the payment in Column 3 and the interest in Column 4.

Column 6 – The remaining balance. This is the difference between the outstanding loan amount and the repayment of principal.

See Appendix 2 for an example of a 30-year amortization schedule.

SIMPLE INTEREST VERSUS COMPOUND INTEREST

Simple interest is calculated on the original principal only. Accumulated interest from prior periods is not used in calculations for the following periods. Simple interest is normally used for a single period of less than a year, such as 30 or 60 days.

Compound interest is calculated each period on the original principal and all interest accumulated during past periods. Although the interest may be stated as a yearly rate, the compounding periods can be yearly, semiannually, quarterly, or even continuously.

You can think of compound interest as a series of back-to-back simple interest contracts. The interest earned in each period is added to the principal of the previous period to become the principal for the next period.

This table below shows the results of making a one-time investment of $10,000 for 30 years using 12 percent simple interest and 12 percent interest compounded yearly and quarterly.

TYPE OF INTEREST	PRINCIPAL PLUS INTEREST EARNED
Simple	$46,000.00
Compounded Yearly	$299,599.22
Compounded Quarterly	$347,109.87

Using an annual compounding method, the amount of interest earned in the first year is added to the principal at the end of the year. During the second year, interest is earned on the total and added to the principal at the end of the year and so on for each year of the loan.

When interest is compounded quarterly, the interest earned in the first quarter is added to the principal balance at the end of the quarter. An important point to remember is that the interest earned is one-quarter of the annual interest.

With monthly compounding, the interest earned in the first month (one-twelfth of the annual interest) is added to the balance at the end of the first month.

The calculation is the same for daily compounding. The amount of interest earned each day (1/365) is added to the principal balance.

There is even continuous compounding, which compounds by the hour of each day!

To see how these different compounding techniques would affect a loan, let's look at a $10,000 loan at 15 percent over 5 years:

COMPOUNDED	FUTURE VALUE
Yearly	$20.113.57
Quarterly	$20,881.52
Monthly	$21,071.81
Daily	$21,166.74
Continuously	$21,169.86

All other things being equal, compound interest has a larger effect as the time period increases and as the interest rate increases. If you want to learn how to calculate both simple and compound interest, the formulas are provided in Appendix 4.

Besides the actual repayment of principal and the payment of interest, there are other ways to make money on the lending process.

PREPAYMENT PENALTIES

By the time you decide to loan money to a real estate investor, you have put a lot of time and energy into the process. If you have negotiated a 3-year term, you have done so believing that you would not have to go through this process for this capital again for another 3 years. There are times, however, when the borrower decides to pay off the loan early. In order to "pay for" this inconvenience to you, you can establish prepayment penalties when you draw up the note.

In most cases, a prepayment penalty is a fee charged to a borrower who pays off a loan before it is due. In addition, payment penalties may also be assessed when excessive portions of the loan's principal balance (generally 20 percent or more) are paid in a single year.

Prepayment penalties for banks are often 6 months' worth of interest payments on 80 percent of the balance owed on the mortgage. Most private mortgage investors charge 1 to 2 percent of the initial loan amount.

Is 2 percent the highest penalty? According to Doug Brown, prepayment penalties can be much higher. He has seen them as high as 5 percent. Although the actual creditworthiness of the borrower will not typically keep you from loaning money, it will help you determine such things as interest rates and penalties. Doug states, "If you are concerned about their credit, you will want to have higher prepayment penalties."

POINTS ON THE BEGINNING OF THE NOTE

As a borrower obtains a mortgage, he or she will incur mortgage fees and costs associated with completing the mortgage. One of those costs is the "loan origination fee." The loan origination fee is usually a percentage of the loan amount, generally expressed as "points."

Each point is equal to 1 percent of the loan amount. For example, one point on a $150,000 loan would be $1,500. One-and-a-half points on the same loan amount would be $2,250. This payment is usually up front, in cash, at settlement.

As a lender, you can charge as many points as you want. However, you need to be careful to keep the loan from becoming *usurious*. This means that you are charging too much, and it is illegal. For more information on usury issues, see Chapter 13.

POINTS ON THE END OF THE NOTE

Besides adding points on the beginning of the note, you can also add points to the end of the note. This would be the same as the origination fee mentioned above, except that the fee, either in full or in part, would be deferred until the end of the loan.

If you have a borrower who needs more money up front, you might consider deferring any points until the end of the loan. You might also decide to put one point at the beginning and two at the end.

When asked about deferring points, Matt Tabacchi said:

> "I do not recommend doing that. It is a way to let the client get more money up front. This will only work for the investor if it doesn't matter if they get money up front or in the end. The

problem is that the borrowers don't understand the deferred process. I'm just not fond of this practice."

KEEPING YOUR FUNDS FULLY INVESTED

Obviously, it is important to keep your funds fully invested. Let's assume that you have $30,000 in an account that is earning 5 percent interest, compounded yearly. In 5 years, you would end up with $8,288.45 in interest.

Now let's assume that you find an investor who is in need of $27,000 for that 5-year period. You decide to give him or her a loan at 15 percent interest. You would have $3,000 still left in your account earning 5 percent interest, and you would have $27,000 earning 15 percent. All earned interest from the loan would be deposited into the interest-bearing account on a yearly basis. At the end of 5 years, you would have:

- $20,250 from the simple interest earned on the loan at 15 percent.

- $2,936.10 from the compounded interest on the $3,000 plus the yearly earned interest of $4,050 from the loan.

This is a total of $23,186.10 in interest earned.

Finally, let's see what happens when you lend out the entire $30,000 at 15 percent and on a yearly basis put the interest into an account bearing 5 percent:

- $22,500 from the simple interest earned on the loan at 15 percent.

- $2,365.34 from the yearly compounded interest on the $4,500 earned yearly on the loan.

This is a total of $24,865.34 in interest earned.

You can see that loaning out the full $30,000 instead of just $27,000 increases your earnings over the 5-year period by $1,679.24.

So how do you go about getting all of your money to work? Let's go back to the borrower who wants to borrow $27,000 at 15 percent. If the factors are all in your favor and the loan-to-value ratio is below 70 percent, you can offer the borrower an extra $3,000. He or she may have only asked for $27,000 but may very well be able to use the $30,000 and take you up on the offer. In this way, you have just earned at least an extra $1,600, with no extra effort on your part.

Case Study – April

Not everyone waits until they start thinking about retirement to invest. Here is what April, age 18, has to say about private mortgage investing:

I saw my dad and my aunt and uncle making great interest rates with private mortgage investing. I couldn't wait until I was 18 and I could do it too. Before I was 18, I worked for my family business and did some babysitting and things. Then, when I graduated from high school, most people gave me money. By the time I was 18, I had almost $10,000 saved.

I didn't save all of my money—I do like to spend. However, I've had a savings account since I was 10 years old. I was never very impressed with my money just sitting in the bank. In fact, it was a big deal if my interest was over a dollar! Trust me, it is much better with private mortgage investing!

Right now, I am doing a $10,000 loan deal with Matt Tabacchi from Allstate Mortgage Loans. (My dad helped me get to the $10,000 mark!) Matt and other brokers get these small loans all the time. Instead of earning just 2 percent in a savings account, I am earning 14 percent. That is a big deal! My eighteenth birthday was in August, and I got my first check in October. If I had kept my $10,000 in a savings account at 2 percent, I would have earned $200 by the time I turned 19. Instead, I invested in a private mortgage and will earn $1,400. The loan I am doing is for about 5 years. That means that I will have $17,000 to invest by the time I am 23.

I have decided to save all of my interest and when I get all of my principal back, I will reinvest. It is the smart thing to do at my age! If I can keep doing this every five years and add the interest I earned, I will have over $2 million by the time I am 68! Just imagine what it will be if I start adding other funds.

Especially for someone young like me, I think it is very important to find a broker that you can trust. At my age, I am not very knowledgeable about property values or investing, so trusting a broker is essential. I am learning, though, and I want to learn more as I go along. I am already learning how to keep track of my monthly earnings. I simply copy the check each month and put that information, along with a breakdown of the principal and the interest, into a folder.

I'm glad I started early. The feeling of getting a big check every month is fantastic. Much better than chuckling over a dollar's worth of interest!

FORECLOSURE AND HOW IT WORKS

Believe it or not, foreclosing on a loan is another way to earn some money! Since you have no more than 70 percent invested in the property, if it goes to foreclosure, you will then have the opportunity to sell it for closer to full value and increase your profits. This is one reason that you want to be sure that you have accurate appraisals.

Let's take a quick look at how foreclosures work.

Foreclosure is a process that allows you, the lender, to recover the amount owed on a defaulted loan by selling or taking ownership (repossession) of the property securing the loan. The foreclosure process begins when a borrower/owner defaults on loan payments, and the lender files a public default notice. The foreclosure process can end in one of four ways:

1. The borrower/owner pays off the default amount to reinstate the loan during a grace period determined by state laws. This grace period is also known as pre-foreclosure.

2. The borrower/owner sells the property to a third party during pre-foreclosure. The sale allows the borrower/owner to pay off the loan and avoid having a foreclosure on his or her credit history.

3. A third party buys the property at a public auction at the end of pre-foreclosure.

4. The lender takes ownership of the property, usually with the intent to resell. The lender can take ownership through an agreement with the borrower/owner during pre-foreclosure or by buying back the property at the public auction. These are also known as bank-owned properties.

Mortgage notes usually carry a grace period; a 15-day grace period is typical, but some are as short as 10 days. Many people "play the float," that is, delay through most of the grace period before making payment, and no one, including the lender, thinks very much about it.

The day after the grace period ends, however, you can start charging a late fee. The late fee is usually a percentage of the principal balance; 3 percent is typical. Once the 30-day mark has arrived, the borrower is in default. At this point, you can add collection costs to the late fees.

Laws regarding mortgage default and foreclosure differ from state to state, so understanding your state's rules and having a good attorney are necessary in any foreclosure process.

If the borrower is unable or unwilling to negotiate with you, then you will begin the foreclosure action. Now, in addition to late fees and collection fees, you will be charging the borrower legal fees as well.

First, you would order a foreclosure search, which

reveals all the debts related to the property, such as mechanic's liens, equity loans, utility company liens, and tax liens. Someone will have to pay all these debts, so you include them with the amount still due under the original mortgage.

Next, you will file a *lis pendens,* or notice of default (depending on the state you are in), with the state court. These legal procedures announce publicly that a creditor (you) is foreclosing on a debtor (the borrower). You will also serve the borrower with a copy of the complaint in the action, and if the borrower does not successfully contest it, then the court will appoint a referee, who is a neutral third party in charge of the sale of the property.

The referee will give notice of the sale of the property according to the requirements of state law. This means publishing a classified advertisement in a newspaper, usually in the local papers and in the largest and closest metropolitan daily, and posting a notice in the courthouse, or both. The advertisement might mention the date of the auction on which the property will be sold, or a separate advertisement might announce the date.

The law in most states gives the homeowner every opportunity to stop the process leading to foreclosure, right up to the minute that the auctioneer's gavel comes down and sometimes even beyond. In some states, there is a period after the foreclosure during which the homeowner can redeem the property (right of redemption).

At the auction, you will offer the property subject to a minimum bid, or *upset price.* If nobody submits a bid at least as high as the upset price, then you will withdraw the property and attempt to sell it through other means.

Here is what Matt Tabacchi says about foreclosures in Florida in simple terms:

> "I lend Jack money, and he doesn't pay me by the 10th of the month. At this point, he is charged a late fee. I give him a call or send him a letter. If 30 days goes [sic] by and he doesn't respond, I take his file with all the disclosures down to a local real estate attorney and ask them to process the loan for foreclosure proceedings.
>
> "The attorney will then send a demand letter to the client that says they are demanded to pay off the loan within 30 days. If not, the attorney will proceed with the foreclosure.
>
> "Once we get to that point, 99 percent of the time, the borrower is [able] to refinance and pay us back. Since we only loaned 65 percent, they will often be able to find someone. They don't want to lose their house.
>
> "If they don't pay off, you proceed with the foreclosure. That process will take a little bit of time to get through all of the proceedings. You don't have to do anything; the attorney does it all.

"Now it is time for the foreclosure sale. Let's say that your balance was $50,000 plus the attorney fees of $3,000, and all your interest and late charges is [sic] another $2,000. That is $55,000. When the house goes to auction at the courthouse, the attorney will not let it be sold for less than $55,000. That is another reason we stay within 65 percent LTV, because we want that cushion.

"Foreclosure works differently in different states. Check with your local mortgage broker to understand the laws of your state."

A FORECLOSURE EXAMPLE – NORTH CAROLINA

Let's take a look at a typical foreclosure in North Carolina to give you a feel for the process.

The borrower has gotten behind on payments. You, as the lender, send out at least one, and maybe two or three, demands for payment. Once you believe that the borrower either can't or won't pay the mortgage, you start the foreclosure process. In North Carolina, this is a court proceeding.

You send a letter that says you are exercising your right to accelerate the mortgage. This means that you are declaring the entire mortgage due. This is a necessary step in North Carolina that must be handled before proceeding with foreclosure. At this point, you can refuse to accept any partial payments. If you do accept partial payments, you may waive your right to proceed with foreclosure.

Next, you serve the borrower with a Notice of Foreclosure Hearing. This hearing gives you permission to sell the real property. As the lender, all you have to do is prove that the borrower is behind on the payments.

Once you get the go-ahead to put the real property up for sale, your foreclosing attorney will post and publish a Notice of Foreclosure Sale. A copy of the notice must be served on the borrower at least 20 days in advance of the sale.

The sale is then conducted in a public place. Anyone interested in buying the property comes to the sale and bids on the property. This highest bidder gets the property unless you determine that the amount is not enough to cover your investment. If this is the case, you have the option of using other methods to sell the property.

If the process is concluded at auction, the highest bidder must then pay a deposit in the amount of 10 percent of the bid price.

After the auction, there is a 10-day waiting period, called the *upset bid period,* during which the borrower is given a chance to pay off the entire mortgage (which almost never happens), and other people are given a chance to post higher bids for the property. In most cases, no higher bids are posted. Assuming this is the case, the sale is considered final at the end of the 10-day upset bid period.

Once the sale is final, the highest bidder pays the rest of the bid price and receives from the foreclosing attorney a deed that conveys title to the property.

The money received from the highest bidder is first applied to pay any outstanding property taxes, and then it is applied toward the debt owed to you.

ANOTHER FORECLOSURE EXAMPLE – UTAH

The foreclosure process in Utah normally begins when the borrower becomes delinquent. The term *delinquent* is loosely defined and depends upon the terms of the note or the type of loan. Typically, however, delinquency is considered to be three months in arrears, at which point the foreclosure process begins.

To begin the process, you appoint a trustee to record a notice of default with the county recorder of the county where the property is located. From the date of the recording of the notice of default, the borrower has three months to reinstate or pay off the loan.

If the loan is not reinstated during that period of time, you set a foreclosure sale date, send a notice of sale to the borrower, and post the notice on the property. Additionally, you post the notice at the county recorder's office of the county where the property is located and publish it in a newspaper having general circulation in the county.

The sale is held at the courthouse in the county where the property is located and is conducted by either your trustee or an attorney that represents your trustee. The opening bid on the property is set by you. The attorney conducting the foreclosure sale purchases the property on your behalf if no bid higher than the opening bid is presented. Otherwise, the property is sold to the highest bidder.

The highest bidder must present $5,000 to the trustee or attorney and remit the balance by noon the following day.

FORECLOSURE IN COLORADO

In Colorado, a loan may be considered in default after only 30 days. Once a loan is in default, foreclosure action can begin.

To begin foreclosure, you hire a foreclosure attorney. At this point, to stop the foreclosure, the borrower must pay all the back payments, late fees, and foreclosure costs. If done, this is said to *cure* the loan. The borrower's right to cure the loan ends 15 days before the auction.

The foreclosure attorney prepares and files the documents with the public trustee's office for the county where the property is located. When the public trustee receives the foreclosure documents from the lender's attorneys, the trustee schedules a public auction of the property 45 to 60 days in the future.

Your attorney must then schedule a Rule 120 Hearing to take place before the auction date. The judge may cancel this hearing if the borrower does not officially respond when given notice. The purpose of the hearing is to legally establish whether the lender has the right to foreclose on the property and sell it at the public auction.

Once the property is sold, the borrower has a 75-day redemption period. During this time, the borrower can still get the property back by paying off the bid, fees, taxes, insurance, and interest to the public trustee's office.

Since foreclosure is handled differently from state to state, it is very difficult to predict what you could encounter. That is why it is best to have a good real estate attorney to help you. See Chapter 13 for additional information concerning real estate attorneys and the foreclosure process.

CHAPTER 6

WAYS TO INVEST

There are three ways for a private mortgage investor to hold a loan. He or she can hold it personally, as part of a partnership, or use monies from a self-directed IRA. Let's look at the pros and cons of each method.

HOLDING THE NOTE PERSONALLY

This is the simplest way to hold a note. If you are in a state with a mortgage, you are named as the note holder. In states where a deed of trust is used, you are listed as the beneficiary.

When you hold the note personally, you take on all the profit and all the risk. Any taxes are your responsibility. Any capital gains are also your responsibility, and any losses incurred are incurred by you alone.

The good news is that you get to make all the decisions concerning the loan. You do not determine a loan amount or a percentage amount based on group consensus, but on your own judgment.

NOTE: This is not the same thing as preparing the note yourself rather than using a mortgage broker. In either case, you can decide to be the sole note holder.

Using Your Equity

If you hold the note personally, you will need the funds to do so. If you own a home, you are likely to have the funds you need in the form of equity.

People talk about the equity in their homes, but what is it? It is the percentage of the property you actually own. If you bought a $150,000 house, your equity is the amount you put down when you purchased plus any principal you have paid on your mortgage. Additionally, if your home has increased in value, you have that much more equity. When your mortgage is fully paid, your equity is 100 percent.

However, what good is it doing you if it is simply sitting in your home? Unless you sell the house, the equity does nothing for you. You can't spend equity or even invest it.

Rather than have equity sitting in a structure, you might consider taking out a home equity loan. Banks and finance companies often given favorable rates on home equity loans since real estate is perceived to be a very stable investment. Additionally, you can generally deduct the interest you pay. However, be sure to consult your tax advisor regarding the deductibility of interest.

Why would you borrow money to invest? It all has to do with the interest earned. With private mortgages, you can earn far more interest than you pay back in the equity loan. For instance, you may be able to get 16 percent on $50,000 and only have to pay 7 percent to your bank. This means that your equity is earning you 9 percent instead of sitting idly in your home.

Equity Line Versus Second Mortgage

What is the difference between an equity line and a second mortgage? This is often confusing because the terminology is confusing. A second mortgage is any loan that involves a second lien on the property.

The confusion started when second mortgages began to be structured as a line of credit and became known as *home equity loans* or *home equity lines of credit* (HELOC). These loans are adjustable-rate mortgages.

If you own your house free and clear and you want a line of credit secured by a mortgage, that loan is a HELOC, even though it is a first mortgage. Similarly, if you use a HELOC to refinance your first mortgage, the HELOC becomes a first mortgage. Otherwise, HELOCs are considered to be second mortgages.

SHARING A LOAN

As with other types of investments, private mortgages can be held by a group. In some ways, it is like the idea of mutual funds. Instead of one person investing all the money, a group of people pools its money to make investments.

Although this can be done simply by gathering together some friends, family, or investors, it is often in your best interest to form a partnership or corporation. Determine which is best for you by consulting with your accountant.

Hold the Note Through a Partnership

For many people, getting started in private mortgages is a big leap and one that they are not quite ready to fund on their own. They may also be concerned about taking on all the liability and responsibility associated with sole ownership. If you feel this way, then a partnership may be just right for you.

Limited partners invest in a company, but are not involved in the management of the business. They assume only limited liability and receive special tax privileges. Both general and limited partners are taxed at their personal rates on their shares of taxable income from the business. The limited partnership itself is not taxed.

The limited partnership is like a corporation in many respects. It allows people to invest in the business, but their liability is limited to the amount of their investment or as agreed in the limited partnership agreement.

If there is no partnership agreement, the income, losses, and gains are allocated in proportion to the partnership interests of each partner. Partners can agree among themselves as to how income, losses, and gains are divided among the partners. The partners then report the amounts allocated on their own income tax returns and pay tax accordingly.

You can either form your own limited partnership or join one that is already functioning as an investment partnership set up to invest in private notes. Forming your own company will be a difficult endeavor, and you will definitely need the help of a good lawyer. If you decide to go with an already-formed limited partnership, you will get the benefit of experienced management. In this way, you will not lose money while learning the ropes.

Either way, working with a limited partnership limits your control. If you see a good deal but the others in the partnership do not agree, the deal will not be made. Just as with holding the note personally, holding the note through a limited partnership has its pros and cons.

The first thing you want to consider is the partners. Are they financially strong? Are they trustworthy? Do they comprehend when an investment makes sense and when it doesn't? Keep in mind that just because these "partners" are friends or family does not automatically make the answers to any of these questions yes!

Once you determine that your partners are good, you have to evaluate the deal. What kind of ROI (return on investment) can you expect? Over what period of time? Does it sound too good to be true? Is the risk level acceptable to you? Do you have an exit strategy if you want to get out of the partnership? How long will this investment require that you be in the partnership?

Partnerships seem to work best when all sides have some experience, similar investment goals, are not dependent on the income to live, and have taken time to plan out a good partnership structure.

With a partnership, you need to have an agreement on how decisions are made. Will there be managing partners? How will deadlocks be resolved? The best way to develop a consistent approach to your investments is by drafting a written real estate partnership agreement with the help of an attorney. Be sure to have a partnership attorney who is separate from your own personal attorney. If there are ever any disputes or issues, you will want your own attorney to review the documents.

How will you stay abreast of the investments? What kind of meeting schedule or reporting schedule will there be?

Checklist of issues to be included in partnership agreement:

1. Purpose of forming the company and goals the company wants to achieve.

2. Partnership allocations.

3. Capital investment (initial contributions).

4. Value of the investments.

5. Legal ownership entity: corporation, LLC, LLP.

6. Management strategy for the partnership.

7. How and when to make partnership decisions.

8. How and when to make the decision to sell the investment or buy more.

9. How to decide on rent increases.

10. Do you need a managing partner?

11. Who is the managing partner?

    a. Term

    b. Removal of manager

    c. Authority of manager

    d. Power and actions of manager

    e. Compensation of manager

  f. Right to delegate

  g. Authority to convey property

  h. Standard of care

  i. Restrictions on the authority of the manager

  j. Indemnification

  k. Duty of loyalty

12. Tax issues.

  a. Who gets tax benefits?

  b. In which proportions?

  c. Who prepares the K-1 and by what date?

  d. How are accounting costs shared?

13. What happens when there is a cash shortfall?

14. Failure to pay contributions.

15. Loans by members.

16. Meetings.

17. Quorum.

18. How to allocate profits and losses.

19. Liability insurance.

20. Directors' insurance.

21. Life insurance and how the cost of the insurance is to be funded.

22. Liquidating distributions if and when the company is dissolved.

23. Books and records.

    a. Accounting period

    b. Fiscal year

    c. Banking

    d. Monthly reporting

    e. Tax returns

    f. Location of books and reports

24. Death or incompetence of a member.

    a. Will transfer

    b. Transfer to a permitted transferee

    c. Limited or unlimited power of appointment

    d. Sale of share to a partner (right of first refusal)

    e. Estate-planning transfers (review life insurance issues so that share disbursements are limited to the same number of parties; that is, shares go to wife not to the six children each with one portion of a vote).

25. Dispute resolution.

    a. Mediation

b. Arbitration

As you can see from the checklist, being involved in real estate partnerships is not easy, but careful planning will put you on the road to success.

Hold the Note Through an LLC

A *limited liability company* (LLC) is a business structure that fits somewhere between the partnership or sole proprietorship and the corporation. Like owners of partnerships or sole proprietorships, LLC owners report business profits or losses on their personal income tax returns; the LLC itself is not a separate taxable entity.

As with a corporation, however, all LLC owners are protected from personal liability for business debts and claims. This is what makes it limited liability. If your business owes money or faces a lawsuit, only the company assets are at risk.

It is very easy to organize an LLC. In most states, the only legal requirement is that you file "articles of organization" with your state's LLC filing office. Most states provide a fill-in-the-blank form that takes just a few minutes to prepare.

A few states require an additional step: Prior to filing your articles of organization, you must publish your intention to form an LLC in a local newspaper.

Although not a legal necessity, you will also want

to prepare an LLC operating agreement. This agreement states the rights and responsibilities of the LLC owners. If you don't create a written operating agreement, the LLC laws of your state will govern your LLC.

The operating agreement should cover:

- How profits are split up.

- How major business decisions are made.

- Procedures for handling the departure and addition of members.

The main difference between an LLC and a partnership is that LLC owners are not personally liable for the company's debts and liabilities. This means that creditors of the LLC usually cannot go after the owners' personal assets to pay off LLC debts. Partners, on the other hand, do not receive this limited liability protection unless they are designated as "limited" partners in their partnership agreement.

Also, owners of limited liability companies must file formal articles of organization with their state's LLC filing office, pay a filing fee, and comply with certain other state filing requirements before they open for business. By contrast, people who form a partnership don't need to file any formal paperwork and don't have to pay any special fees.

LLCs and partnerships are almost identical when it comes to taxation, however. In both types of businesses, the owners report business income or losses on their personal tax returns; the business itself does not pay tax on this money. In fact, LLCs and partnerships file the same informational tax return with the IRS (Form 1065) and distribute the same schedules to the business's owners (Schedule K-1, which lists each owner's share of income).

Hold the Note Through a Corporation

A corporation is very different from a partnership. It is a separate legal entity and is distinct from its members. There are two main types of corporations: the *C corporation* and the *S corporation.* Let's look at both.

The C Corporation

This is the typical corporation. Most standard businesses are C corporations, which:

- Pay taxes at their own corporate income tax rates.

- File corporate taxes using IRS Form 1120.

- Are controlled by a board of directors that is elected by the shareholders.

- Conduct day-to-day activities through officers and employees. The authority to do so is delegated by the directors.

- Are owned by shareholders, which do not

have power in day-to-day operations. They do, however, have the power to appoint and remove directors.

- Are guided by the board of directors, which is responsible for the long-term management and policy decisions of the corporation.

- Are run by corporate officers who are elected by the board of directors and are responsible for conducting the day-to-day operational activities of the corporation.

- May often offer their employees unique fringe benefits.

- Are required to hold annual meetings. Corporate minutes of the meetings must be taken, officers must be appointed, and shares must be issued to shareholders.

- Are generally taxed on their own profits; then, any profits paid out in the form of dividends are taxed again to the recipient as dividend income at the individual shareholder's tax rate.

The S Corporation

An S corporation begins its existence as a C corporation. However, after the corporation has been formed, it may elect S corporation status by submitting IRS Form 2553 to the Internal Revenue Service.

Once this filing is complete, the corporation is taxed as a partnership or sole proprietorship rather than as a separate entity.

To qualify for S corporation status, the corporation must:

- Maintain only one class of stock.

- Maintain a maximum of 75 shareholders.

- Be comprised solely of shareholders who are individuals, estates, or certain qualified trusts, who consent in writing to the S corporation election.

- Not have a shareholder who is a nonresident alien.

- Complete and file IRS Form 1120 to report its annual income to the IRS each year.

Owners who want the limited liability of a corporation and the "pass-through" tax treatment of a partnership will often make the S corporation election. In most cases, corporations that would benefit from S corporation status are those that plan to distribute the majority of earnings to their shareholders in the year in which those earnings are realized.

The Differences Between LLCs and S Corporations

There are a number of additional benefits of an LLC, taxed as an S corporation, over the traditional straight S corporation form of business organization. These additional tax benefits include the ability to have:

- More than 75 business owners.

- A nonresident alien as an owner.

- A corporation or a partnership as an owner.

- More than 80 percent ownership in a separate corporate entity.

- Disproportionate ownership—ownership percentages that are different from each respective owner's investment in the business.

- Flow-through business-loss deductions in excess of each respective owner's investment in the business.

- Owners and members who are active in the management of the business without losing their limited personal liability exposure.

As you can see, there are many different considerations when determining a business entity for your private mortgage investing activities. Check with your accountant to find the one that is right for you.

Hold the Note Through a Tenancy in Common

Another way to hold a note is through a tenancy in common (TIC). A TIC is created when two or more people are legally granted interest in the same property. The interest need not be equal or created at the same time as in joint tenancy. If one of them dies, the others do not automatically own the deceased's interest, as they would in a joint tenancy. The interest of the deceased passes to his or her heirs.

Advantages: The primary advantage of a tenancy in common is that it's easy to move investors in and out of the investment group while doing 1031 exchanges — and to preserve 1031 exchanges for those leaving.

Disadvantages: The key disadvantage is that each tenant in common is *fully liable personally* for all debts, lawsuits, and so forth, regarding the property, since tenancies in common are treated as general partnerships.

HOLDING NOTES IN A SELF-DIRECTED IRA

When you think of a self-directed IRA, you typically think of money markets, mutual funds, stocks, and bonds. Few people think of real estate; however, it is well within the IRS guidelines.

Funding private mortgages can be an excellent way to grow your retirement account. And for those who have seen stocks sliding and account balancing crumbling, private mortgages with 10 to 16 percent returns look like a great alternative.

The biggest issue is finding an IRA trustee willing to work with real estate and private mortgages. They do exist, but not every self-directed IRA trustee understands or wants to be involved in private mortgages.

IRAs are typically promoted by financial services companies without the expertise to provide truly self-directed plans. These same companies also have no incentive to develop such programs due to their own financial motivations. Prior to the Internet, people had few choices. Now, however, average investors have more accessibility to companies providing true self-directed IRAs, and the idea of investing in real estate is spreading quickly.

The next chapter focuses solely on how to use your self-directed IRA in this manner.

CHAPTER 7

GETTING THE MOST FROM YOUR IRA

IRA investor interest in real estate has increased recently, as dramatic stock market declines have prompted investors to look for ways to diversify IRA investment risk. Let's look now at the ins and outs of using your IRA for private mortgage loans.

WHY USE IRA FUNDS FOR PRIVATE MORTGAGES?

The key to self-direction is the flexibility to place any legal investment in your IRA. Providing private mortgages allows you to invest outside the typical financial securities. It also allows real estate investors to invest in an asset that they know and understand.

Tax law changes in 2002 made your self-directed IRA much more flexible. Most significantly, you have newer opportunities to consolidate investments, and you can make more contributions to qualified plans.

Fully self-directed plans allow you, the investor, to select the investment on your own. Self-directed plan administrators may be located via an Internet search. A list of those willing to work with private mortgages is available in Appendix 5.

Any type of investment real estate can qualify for IRA investment, including apartment buildings, office buildings, and motels. The choice is yours. The power of a self-directed IRA is the ability to put your retirement funds into an investment that you can see, select, control, and understand.

Many financial experts would lead you to believe that financing real estate inside an IRA is too complex. That is a complete myth. If you use an IRA LLC, it is exactly the same as any other real estate transaction. And, just as with other investments, you can also pool resources and form a partnership.

There are differences, however. For instance, you cannot write off depreciation on your real estate investment, since you are getting your tax break up front. An IRA is a tax-exempt entity, so there are no deductions to take.

ESTABLISHING A SELF-DIRECTED IRA

Among the many investment options available, real estate is often overlooked. Few people are aware that opening a self-directed IRA creates a world of investment choices.

Any real estate investment made with an IRA must be obtained by establishing a self-directed traditional or Roth IRA. These self-directed IRAs have a trustee in the form of an IRA custodian, an IRA administrator, or an IRA advisor. These trustees charge a setup fee and annual fees for their efforts.

Initial fees vary widely. They can be as little as $50 to as much as $1,500. The same applies to the annual fees, which range from $200 to $500 or more. These fees are dependent upon the type of trustee and what he or she does for you—the more the trustee does, the more it costs you.

IRA custodians do the least amount of work for you and, therefore, charge the smallest fees. Advisors, on the other hand, help you to find properties and investors, help with all the paperwork and legalese, and much more, thus charging you far more for their involvement in your account.

As with all investments, be sure to understand the process and check out the IRA custodian. Check out the company with the Better Business Bureau and your state's attorney general's office. By all means, do not sign any paperwork before you understand it. If you find it confusing, take it to your lawyer.

While any form of IRA allows for real estate

investment, there are other pros and cons to consider when choosing the account type that's best for you:

- **A traditional IRA** lets you deduct annual contributions (currently set at $3,000, or $3,500 if you're age 50 or older) from your income. However, once you begin withdrawing money, those funds will be taxed as regular income.

- **A Roth IRA** allows you no deduction on your current contributions (again, $3,000), but does allow you to withdraw funds tax-free. If you expect to buy a real estate investment in an IRA and hold it for a long period, this is probably your best option, particularly if the property increases in value over that period.

- **A SEP-IRA** is designed for self-employed individuals and small companies. You can contribute up to 25 percent of your compensation, or $40,000, whichever is less. However, keep in mind that if you have employees, you must make contributions for them as well. This option is a great alternative for real estate practitioners who can make the higher contributions, because they can build up funds more rapidly to purchase properties. Withdrawals from a SEP-IRA are treated in the same way as those of a traditional IRA for tax purposes.

Trust Administration Services offers this chart to help you determine which IRA would be best for you:

	May Be Suitable For	Features	Eligibility Requirements	Plan Contribution Limits	Distributions	Deadline to Set Up/Contribute
Regular IRA	Wage-earning individuals who want to save for retirement Non-employed spouses who file a joint tax return	Earnings accumulate tax deferred Contributions may be tax deductible Can be used in conjunction with any retirement plan	Must be under age 70 ½ to contribute Must have earned compensation during the year	Annual contributions of up to $3,000, or 100% of compensation, whichever is less [1] Non-employed spouses may also contribute up to $3,000 per year $500 catch-up contributions for age 50+	Distributions taken prior to age 59 ½ may be subject to a 10% federal tax penalty, in addition to ordinary income tax, unless rolled over within 60 days [2] Minimum distributions required at age 70 ½	Tax filing deadline not including extensions (usually April 15th)
Rollover IRA	Individuals who are about to receive a qualified plan or 403(b) distribution, and who want to defer taxes on the distribution Retirement plan distributions received by surviving spouse may also be rolled over	Earnings accumulate tax deferred A direct rollover from a qualified plan or 403(b) enables the participant to avoid the 20% federal tax withholding	None	None	Same as regular IRA	If the distribution is received by the participant (or surviving beneficiary), it must be rolled over within 60 days of receipt
Roth IRA	Wage-earning individuals who want to save for retirement Non-employed spouses who file a joint tax return	Tax-free growth and distribution of assets (provided certain conditions are met) Contributions, which are non-deductible, may be made even after age 70 ½ Can be used in conjunction with any retirement plan	Must have adjusted gross income (AGI) below $110,000 if single and $160,000 for joint filers Phased out when AGI is $95,000 - $110,000 for single and $150,000 - $160,000 for joint filers	After-tax contributions of up to $3,000, or 100% of compensation, whichever is less [1] Non-employed spouses may also contribute up to $3,000 per year $500 catch-up contributions for age 50+	Tax-free distribution events; [3] Account established at least five calendar years and - Attainment of age 59 ½ - Permanent disability - First time home purchase ($10,000 lifetime cap) - Death No minimum distributions required at age 70 ½	Tax filing deadline not including extensions (usually April 15th) Contributions only permitted for tax year 1998 and later

	May Be Suitable For	Features	Eligibility Requirements	Plan Contribution Limits	Distributions	Deadline to Set Up/Contribute
Roth Conversion IRA	Individuals with IRAs who do not expect to take withdrawals for at least five years	Tax-free growth and distribution of assets (provided certain conditions are met)	Adjusted gross income (AGI) below $100,000 to convert a regular IRA to a Roth Conversion IRA[4] Married couples filing separately are not eligible	No limits SEP-IRA and SIMPLE-IRAs (after two years) may also be converted	Same tax-free distribution events as Roth IRA	The year the distribution from the regular IRA occurs determines the tax year of the conversion
Education IRA	Individuals who want to save for a child's postsecondary education	Earnings accumulate tax-free provided the distributions are used for the intended	Contributors must have adjusted gross income (AGI) below $110,000 if single and $200,000 for joint filers Phased out when AGI is $95,000 - $110,000 for single and $190,000 - $200,000 for joint filers	After-tax contributions of up to $2,000 per child under age 18	Penalty-free distribution events: - Postsecondary education expenses of named child - All money in the account distributed for postsecondary education expenses or transferred to another Education IRA of a family member by the time the named child attains age 30	December 31st of the current year Contributions only permitted for tax year 1998 and later

[1] No more than $3,000 may be contributed between a regular IRA and Roth IRA combined.

[2] Distributions taken prior to age 59 ½ will generally be subject to a 10% federal tax penalty unless it is: (i) "rolled over" within 60 days of receipt, (ii) a timely removal of excess contribution, (iii) due to death or permanent disability, (iv) a series of substantially equal payments over single or joint life expectancy, or (v) used for a first home purchase (lifetime cap - $10,000), postsecondary education for the investor or dependent, deductible medical expenses or for certain unemployed individuals, medical insurance payments.

[3] Distributions that do not meet the tax-free distribution events are potentially taxable. Potentially taxable distributions are first made from amounts contributed/converted, and taken from earnings (see note 2 for exceptions to the 10% federal tax penalty).

[4] "Conversion" income is not included in the $100,000 AGI limit.

MAKING IRA INVESTMENTS THROUGH A LIMITED PARTNERSHIP

You can make your IRA investments personally or through a limited partnership. There are reasons that making IRA investments through a partnership is advantageous, including:

1. Your IRA's funds will be in the entity's name, making it easier to get cashier's checks for foreclosures or tax-lien auctions.

2. Real estate closings can be done more efficiently and require less explanation to the title company.

3. Your assets will be better protected.

Check with your CPA or tax advisor on the local, state, and federal tax implications of the entity you want your IRA to invest in. You will need a lawyer familiar with the prohibited transaction rules of Section 4975, as well as the plan assets regulations of ERISA.

BUYING FOREIGN PROPERTIES THROUGH YOUR IRA

Did you know that you can buy foreign properties through your IRA? It is true. There is nothing in the IRS Code that keeps anyone from purchasing property outside the United States. However, many custodians will not allow foreign real estate investment purchases.

These custodians often don't feel comfortable because

the property isn't visible. They can't ask a trusted real estate agent to take a look. How can you get around this? Find yourself a custodian who:

- Allows you to write your own checks, reducing the transaction costs.

- Allows you to make your own investment decisions.

- Has a low, flat-rate custodial fee.

Additionally, you will want to have your IRA in the form of a limited partnership. In this way, you will be protected from any possible litigation.

ENSURING THE TAX-DEFERRED STATUS OF THE ACCOUNT

One reason you should check your investments with a CPA who knows retirement planning law is so that you can keep your IRA's tax-deferred status. Make one simple mistake, and you may find yourself owing taxes on large portions of what you thought was nontaxable income. Combined penalties and income taxes can range from 15 percent to more than 100 percent of the real estate's value.

The first big rule is that the entire transaction has to flow through your IRA. Any money needed must be obtained from the IRA and not from you personally. Otherwise, you have jeopardized the tax-free status.

Another rule concerns the title. If the title is put in your name, you will not then be able to "sell" it to your IRA.

Then there are proceeds. When you get paid the interest each month, that money has to go straight to the IRA account. That interest can be reinvested in real estate or invested in other assets — as long as it stays within the IRA.

FOLLOWING IRS GUIDELINES

Properties included in IRAs cannot be the investor's personal residence or purchased from immediate family. Believe it or not, this does not include your siblings, just your parents, children, and grandchildren.

The IRS allows you to use the land or building, but not while it's in your IRA. For instance, you could buy a retirement home, rent it to someone else, put the rental income in your IRA, and, when you retire, take the house as a distribution. Then you could move in. In addition:

- You may not personally own the property purchased by your plan. It has to be owned by your IRA.

- You must ensure that your intended purchase is not a prohibited transaction. A prohibited transaction involves the improper use of your IRA or qualified plan holdings by you or any disqualified person. A disqualified person is any member of your immediate family (except siblings), employers, certain partners, fiduciaries, and other categories specified in the IRS Code. What does this mean? Find a good advisor, because IRS laws can be tricky.

- It must be for investment purposes only.

- Your business may not lease, or be located in or on, any part of the property while it's in your plan.

Once again, understand that using your IRA for real estate purposes can be tricky due to IRS laws. Because the laws governing IRA transactions are so complicated, we suggest that you consult with an experienced real estate professional.

REAL ESTATE IRAS ARE PROTECTED FROM CREDITORS

When you hold your assets in a retirement fund, including a self-directed IRA, they are protected from creditors. Let's examine the rules.

ERISA protects assets held in qualified plans from legal processes as long as the plan document has the proper "anti-alienation" clauses. Additionally, ERISA keeps these plans from being liquidated during a bankruptcy. Typically, these plans are employment plans such as 401(k)s.

And there is more good news for IRAs. A recent case in the U.S. Supreme Court, *Rousey v. Jacoway* (April 2005), concluded that IRAs were "exempt from the reach of their creditors." Even better for IRA holders is that bankruptcy laws have been amended so that now, all IRAs are exempt from collectors if the IRA holder goes bankrupt.

For these reasons, it may be wise to hold real estate assets inside your IRA.

DISTRIBUTING YOUR PROPERTY

You can withdraw real estate from your IRA and use it as a residence or second home when you reach retirement age (age $59^1/_2$ or older for a penalty-free withdrawal). At that time, you can elect either to have the IRA sell the property or take an in-kind distribution of the property.

Under that arrangement, your IRA custodian assigns the title to the property to you. You will then have to pay income taxes on the current value of the property if it is held in a traditional IRA. If the property is held in a Roth IRA, you won't owe taxes at distribution. This makes a Roth IRA extremely attractive if you anticipate that your real estate investments will appreciate over time.

RISK VERSUS REWARD

IRA real estate investing differs from typical real estate investments because you don't get the depreciation benefits. Plus, if the IRA buys the property, you don't get the tax write-offs.

However, you do get the benefit of increased interest rates over the traditional stocks and bonds. Investing your IRA in real estate can better protect against loss of your principal while generating attractive return rates. Plus, you probably know more about what makes a good real estate investment than what stock will be hot next month.

Self-directed IRAs provide more flexibility to the investor. You can decide to buy a property and change your mind—without tax implications.

Now that you understand the money side of the equation, how do you find potential clients? Chapter 8 will give you many different methods to get your private mortgage investments rolling.

Case Study – Jean

Jean, a 73-year-old retired investor, had this
to say about investing in private mortgages:

Before I started investing in private mortgages,
I had all my money in IRA funds. My bank had
talked me into switching to another mutual find.
When the stock market crashed, so did my IRA. I lost
half of my investment and to this day, I have never gotten it back.
Luckily for me, my son had begun to invest in private mortgages,
and he talked me into giving it a try too. I didn't understand it in the
beginning, but I have a great broker and a great son. They explain
everything to me. For me, it has been a great investment plan these
last two years.

One thing that was a bit different about private mortgage investing
was how I used my IRA money. There are not too many places that
will be a trustee over an IRA that is going to be used for real estate
investing. They simply don't believe in this kind of investing. However,
my son recommended a great IRA trustee in California named Trust
Administration Services. This meant that I had to transfer my IRA
money to the new trustee. For me, this was a bit complicated, but
only because of all the paperwork. Remember, your IRA activity gets
reported to the government, so everything has to be done in a very
proper order. Trust Administration Services was able to answer all my
questions and helped me get through the paperwork. Now that my
money is there, it has been quite easy.

Except for my Social Security and my small pensions, I have all my
money in private mortgage investing. I feel very safe. In fact, I even
have the equity in my home working for me. My house is paid off,
but I have taken an equity loan for about one half of the value of my
home and am using that money to earn money. The only drawback to
using your home equity is that you do have to pay your own bank for
the equity loan even if your borrower is not paying you. For me, this

is not an issue. I know that my incoming finances will cover me if the borrower doesn't pay. I also know that the borrower will eventually pay, or I will foreclose. At that time, I get my money back. As I said, I feel very safe.

Prior to investing in private mortgages, I was very concerned about getting long-term [care] insurance. When you get older, elderly, you do think about being a burden on your kids. You wonder if you are going to lose all your money. Long-term [care] insurance is very expensive. Nonetheless, I wanted to know that I would be able to go into an assisted-living home or a nursing home if the need ever arose. The interest is substantial and reliable and will more than pay for an assisted-living facility. Not only that, but my principal will not be touched.

That means that this money can go to my kids. The added bonus is that I am saving about $12,000 a year on insurance premiums. Now, instead of worrying about the future and spending money on insurance, I do wonderful things—like take trips!

If I had to give one tip to someone just starting out, it would be to find a good broker. I am very lucky. I have a good broker AND a good son! A good broker is someone you have confidence in. A good broker is one that goes out of his way and visits the people that are borrowing the money. He knows the properties he is brokering. He knows you and your level of comfort with different situations. When you have a good broker, you know that you can trust him.

I use Matt Tabacchi of Allstate Mortgage Loans and Investments, Inc. He is excellent. Let me explain what makes Matt so good. I had a mortgage on a million-dollar horse farm. The borrower had only needed $130,000, so this was a really good deal for me. However, the borrower had stopped paying. It looked like I might have to foreclose. This wasn't too bad, since I knew that my loan-to-value ratio was excellent and that I was the primary investor. However, no one likes the idea of foreclosure. This is where Matt came in. He talked with the guy, and we restructured and he paid all of that interest for a year up front. I walked away with $52,000 in one day!

Matt understands real estate mortgages, and I know that I can trust him. Even if we had to go to foreclosure, I know that Matt has worked the mortgage in such a way that I will never lose my principal. He often works deals where I get points up front and points on the back end. That can be a few thousand dollars before I ever give them the mortgage.

I'm glad that I am out of regular investing. I looked at the paper every day. I was a nervous wreck. With private mortgage investing, the risk is a lot less. In fact, there really is no risk as long as you keep your loan-to-value ratio at no more than 50 percent and check out property. Investing in this way allows me to live the lifestyle I want. I can spend on trips, or I can stay home. Whatever I choose. If I want to buy something extravagant, I can do it. I used to worry a lot. Being from the Depression era, I still do worry a bit, but not like I used to!

CHAPTER 8

SELLING MORTGAGES AND NOTES

Almost every mortgage can be sold, even if the payments are not being made on a timely basis. But why would you want to buy and sell mortgages? For the same reason that you would want to offer private mortgages: The return on investment is incredible!

Let's take a look at buying and selling mortgages and why it may be right for you.

BUYING A DISCOUNTED MORTGAGE

Certain pieces of information become public knowledge when a home is sold. These items include:

1. Price

2. Taxes

3. Liens

4. Buyer's name

5. Seller's name

6. Amount of mortgage

7. Names of lenders

All of this information can be found at your county courthouse or the clerk's office.

Suppose that a house seller is asking $100,000 as the purchase price. A couple (we'll call them Mr. and Mrs. Goodcredit) comes by to look at the house. Both of the Goodcredits earn respectable incomes and have excellent credit and work histories. But the Goodcredits are shy of the last $5,000 for the down payment.

With mortgage rates at 10 percent, they ask the seller if she would be willing to take an interest-only mortgage for 8 years. In an interest-only mortgage, only the interest is paid during the term of the loan, and the full balance is paid at the maturity date. In this case, it means the Goodcredits would pay $500 per year for the next 8 years, then in the 8th year, pay off the full $5,000. Both the primary mortgage and this second mortgage would be recorded at the local courthouse or county clerk's office. In other words, the financing becomes a matter of public record.

Now here is where you come in. Go down to wherever real estate mortgages are recorded, and look for

properties that have two mortgages — the primary and

the secondary. The primary will usually be a financial institution, and the secondary is often an individual. Find about 20 of these situations, and write down the names of the second mortgage holders. Next, call them. And here's what you'll say:

> "Hello, Ms. Smith, my name is Jim Jones. I'm a real estate investor, and I understand that you hold a mortgage for $5,000 on the property located at 123 Anywhere Street here in Anytown. Is that true?"

> She'll reply, "Well, I don't know! Who are you anyway, and how do you know about any of that?"

> "Well, Ms. Smith, as I say, I'm a real estate investor, and I'm just wondering if you'd be willing to sell that mortgage. You see, I pay cash for these kinds of mortgages, and I wanted to offer to buy that mortgage from you for cash. Would that be of interest to you?"

> "Well, maybe, that depends on what you're offering."

> "Well, I would be willing to buy the mortgage at a discount. So I could offer you $3,000." *(Your offer should be between 60 and 75 percent of the loan in order to make a profit.)* "How does that sound?"

> *(Your success here relies on the possibility of one, or even both, of two conditions: 1) A lump sum of*

cash is currently more attractive to Ms. Smith; 2) payments over time have become more of a hassle for Ms. Smith, even if they'd in fact turn out to be more profitable.)

"Why yes, I think I may be interested."

"You know, Ms. Smith, what I'd like to do is meet with you at *your* attorney's office to show you my proposal."

(In this way, Ms. Smith can feel rock-solid that this is not a scam. Going to her own attorney will make her feel secure that you are who you say you are.)

Following is an illustration demonstrating a potential 30 percent return on this investment:

Face Value	$5,000
Purchase Price	$3,000
Term Balance	5 years
Original Interest Rate	10%
Monthly Cash Flow	$41.67
Annual Return	$500/$3,000 = 16.7%
Total Interest You Received	$2,500
Discount	$2,000
Total Profit	$4,500
Average Annual Return	($4,500/$3,000)/5 yrs = 30%

SELLING MORTGAGES

Let's look at another example. Let's say you find a property valued at $80,000. The seller is retiring, owns the place free and clear (no mortgages), and wants to buy a condo in Florida for $30,000. You suggest that he invest the balance of his equity into seasoned mortgages worth $50,000 and paying 10 percent interest, with monthly payments of about $500 per month to supplement his Social Security. This income will not affect his Social Security. He agrees.

Now, locate a mortgage with a $50,000 plus face value, at 10 percent interest, with monthly payments of at least $500. Offer the mortgage holder $35,000 cash, to be paid at closing. The note is to be placed in escrow along with a signed copy of the agreement (preferably notarized).

At closing, your bank (if YOU are buying the property) or your buyer's bank puts up the money for a first mortgage of 90 percent of the price, or $72,000. From this amount:

- You pay $35,000 for the note. The note seller goes home happy.

- You pay the seller of the property $30,000 cash and give him the $50,000 in mortgage(s). He goes home happy.

- There is $7,000 left "on the table." This belongs to you, along with $8,000 in equity in the property (the difference between the $72,000 mortgage and the $80,000 value).

If you bought and sold simultaneously at a double closing, you would walk away with $15,000 cash—in other words, the $7,000 left on the table and the $8,000 equity you sold to your buyer (his down payment).

FINDING THE NOTES

I stated earlier that all of the information concerning privately held notes can be found at the county courthouse. If you use this direct approach to finding mortgages, you will want to make the time spent at the courthouse worth your while.

First, you will need to be able to look at land records and get the information you need. Clerks at the courthouse will be able to help you do this.

Additionally, you will want to go to the courthouse on a regular basis. Initially, you will have to go through two or three years' worth of records. Once that is done, however, you will still need to check recent records on a regular basis. Doing this monthly will help you stay up to date and find the most recent notes.

However, if you don't want to do that kind of legwork, there are other options available to you. One is getting the information from a company that does all the research for you. They do this and then sell the information via book or microfilm. However, you can often find this information at your local library in the form of *The Lusk Report* or the *Redi-Data Report.*

Beyond the courthouse, what methods are available to you? Plenty!

Did you know that nearly one-third of all real estate transactions involve some kind of private financing? That means that for every ten people you know with real estate, three of them hold a note or know someone who holds a note! With numbers like these, networking is a key way of finding notes.

Those who hold private notes often are not aware that they can be sold. And even if they are aware, they do not know whom to sell to. They may feel quite stuck. It is in your best interests to let everyone in your circle, including the local restaurant owner and the man who pumps your gas, know that you buy and sell mortgages.

You can also find the information you need through real estate agents. They have access to past transactions through the MLS. If you do a search based on seller financing, you will get a great list of potential notes.

CONTACTING THE NOTE HOLDER

Once you have the information, you will need to contact the note holder. It is very likely that the note holder will not accept your proposal on the first round, especially if it is a new note. This does not mean that you should cross this person off your list.

Instead, keep good records and call him or her back at a later date. Things change. For instance, the note holder may be in need of cash or may grow tired of "playing bank."

Not only do you need to contact the note holder, but you need to give him or her a way to contact you. A good idea is to write a follow-up letter and suggest that this letter be put with the note. In this way, if things change, he or she will know whom to contact.

GETTING THE AGREEMENT

So what do you do if the note holder agrees to sell the note? First and foremost, you will need to get that agreement in writing. It should be signed and notarized by all parties involved.

Once you have the agreement, you have all the options available to you. You can go ahead with the purchase, or you can choose to abort the purchase. Without the written agreement, however, the note holder has that power.

AFTER THE AGREEMENT

Typically, the best way to make money is to not only buy the note, but then to go ahead and sell it. As soon as you have the agreement, you can begin to look for investors. Your investors will give you a proposal based on your verbal assessment of the note. However, before actual prices can be considered, documentation must be presented.

DOCUMENTATION

There are four different sets of documents that you need to be familiar with to buy and sell notes, including:

- The original real estate transaction documents.

- Documents created to evaluate the deal.

- Documents created to close the deal.

- Postclosing documents.

Let's take a look at each.

Original Documents

You need to see the promissory note. It is important that you see this note, since it is what you are actually purchasing! It will tell you the following things:

- Loan amount

- Payment amount

- Interest rates

- Financial terms

You also need to see either the mortgage or the deed of trust.

Finally, you need to see the settlement statement, also known as the HUD-1. The HUD-1 will tell you:

- The sale price.

- The legal description.

- The amount of the down payment.

- The details of any other financing.

- If there is title insurance and from where.

- The hazard insurance carrier and amount.

- The real estate agencies involved in the original transaction and their commissions.

- The property taxes.

Looking at these three documents will help you determine if you really want to go through with buying the note. If anything negative comes to light and you choose to abort the transaction, you need to contact the note holder in writing.

Evaluation Documents

Many of these documents are similar to the documents needed to determine if you are willing to provide a private mortgage. For instance, you need an appraisal of the property and, if it is a commercial property, you need to see the financial statements.

You should also see "senior debt instruments." These are any mortgages, deeds, and the like, that are first in line in case of foreclosure. Additionally, you should know the status of these debt instruments. For instance, knowing that the first mortgage is in default would make a huge difference in whether you choose to buy the second mortgage note! This information is available at the courthouse.

Finally, you will need an *estoppel affidavit*. This is an affidavit sent to the note payer. Through this affidavit, they will confirm the note terms, conditions, and the current status of the note. Be sure to send this with return receipt requested as proof that the letter was sent.

Closing Documents

Closing documents depend upon what you plan to do with the note. If you are keeping the note, there will be one set. If you plan to sell the note immediately, there will be a different set.

If you sell the note immediately, you will have what is known as a *double closure,* and you will need two of everything—one with you as the buyer of the note and another with you as the seller of the same note. You will also want to be sure that your purchase assignment is recorded before your buyer's assignment.

Postsale Documents

If you are keeping the note, you will want to be immediately added to the insurance policy as the loss payee. In this way, you will be paid if something happens to the property.

You will also need to send a letter letting the payer

know that you are the new note holder. At this time, you should instruct the payer on where to send the payments. You will also send the payer the letter from the former note holder that authorizes this transaction.

If you are a second note holder, you will also need to contact the senior note holders and let them know you are now a junior note holder. Ask them to inform you if there is ever a problem with the first note.

The postsale documents when you sell the note immediately are really simple: Cash the check!

Although different from investing in private mortgages, buying and selling mortgage notes is another way to create an investment vehicle that provides you with high-interest yields. Additionally, you can buy and sell mortgage notes using some of the same strategies found in this book, including using IRA investments, partnerships, and corporations.

CHAPTER 9

FINDING POTENTIAL BORROWERS

THE RIGHT BORROWERS

You have money to invest, and now it is time to find borrowers. Before thinking about how to do that, you need to define what the right borrower looks like.

This is partially done when you consider your loan parameters, since you know that you are looking for borrowers with experience. Borrowers with experience are far more likely to succeed in the proposed deal. They are not as likely to be caught off guard if something doesn't go exactly as planned. They are far more likely to have backup exit strategies.

However, having experience isn't enough. Someone once said, "You can have 20 years of experience or the same experience 20 times." In other words, has your borrower merely been in the business a long time, or has he or she been continually learning and growing while in the business? You definitely want to find someone who shows a good track record, or compensate for his or her lack of experience with your LTV ratio, interest rate, or both.

One way to determine whether your investors are experienced is to ask around. Ask for references, and then check up on them. Go to the courthouse, and see how many deals they've completed. Check to see if they have any lawsuits against them.

What are some caution signs? You may want to forgo doing business with someone who:

- Won't give you any references.

- Doesn't want you to get an appraisal.

- Doesn't want you to see the property.

- Won't get together all the necessary paperwork.

If you have started to work with someone who seems to be hiding something, it's not too late to back out. It's better to be safe than sorry. Only do deals that adequately protect you and your money.

WHO ARE THE BEST BORROWERS?

Borrowers come in all shapes and sizes. They can be first-time homebuyers, developers, speculators, and real estate investors. For the purpose of private mortgage investing, you will probably want to stick with real estate investors — *experienced* real estate investors.

Why are real estate investors best for you? Let's take a look at a few of the reasons:

Real estate investors are looking for short-term loans. Landlords and homeowners are typically looking for 15- to 30-year loans, and you simply do not want to have your money tied up that long.

- Real estate investors are not "one-time shots." In other words, investors tend to buy many pieces of property each year—often 30 or more. This means that you only have to find a few good investors rather than a new one for each deal.

- Real estate investors are not looking for loans above about 70 percent, because they are buying the property at reduced rates. Homeowners, on the other hand, often need 80 percent or more. Developers need to borrow more than the current value of the property, since they only have raw land and still need to build on it. Supplying only 70 percent of the value of the property makes the loan a far safer investment.

- Real estate investors are willing to pay a higher interest rate to get what they need when they need it. This translates into more profit for you.

There is no doubt that real estate investors should be the bulk of your business. That is not to say that you will never loan to a landlord, a homeowner, or a developer, but you will find that you make more profit with less worry when you use mostly real estate investors.

ARE THERE ENOUGH "BEST BORROWERS" OUT THERE?

You might be wondering if there are really enough real estate investors needing private funding. The answer is a resounding yes.

Let's take a look at some statistical proof. According to the National Real Estate Investors Association, investors accounted for 23 percent of all home sales in 2004 for a total of 1.9 million homes!

Additionally, according to the same survey, there are over 10 million Americans who have at least one piece of investment property. Even if only 10 percent meet the qualifications of the "best borrower," there are still 1 million real estate investors to choose from.

In other words, the potential national demand for private mortgages is in the *billions* of dollars each year! The possibilities are endless.

NETWORK

Networking can and should play an important part in your search for real estate investors. However, the investors are spread out all over your community (and the United States). It is not like you can just walk up to the "investor section" of town and pick someone out of the group.

To network effectively, you will need to build a database of acquaintances as well as professionals. To do this, you'll have to use personal contacts, investment professionals, industry and local organizations, libraries, media, and the Internet.

Friends and Acquaintances

There is a strong possibility that you already know potential investors. They could be relatives or friends or perhaps people you know from church. They may not meet all the qualifications of the "perfect" borrower, but, then again, they just might! And you'll never know until you tell them what you do.

Just as you may be surprised to learn that church-going acquaintances also invest in real estate, they may be just as surprised to find out that you have money to invest in such endeavors. So stop being surprised, and tell the world what you do.

Local Investment Clubs

Go to a local real estate investing club. They are full of informative speakers and active investors who would gladly pay you for your services. It is pretty easy to find an investment club. Simply check for club listings in the phone book or on the Internet, and ask others in the real estate field.

Once you find a local club, join. A good club will have several hundred members with a large body that is active for the monthly meetings. Joining, although it will cost you, provides you with many benefits, such as discounts on computer research and legal paper subscriptions, as well as discounts on rehab items such as tile flooring.

When you go to the meeting, be sure to take your business cards — this is a networking event! Whenever you get the chance, let others in this group know what you are doing. You should easily leave a meeting with four or five possible borrowers.

Additionally, there is usually a back table where you can put your information. You might decide to leave a flyer that lets potential borrowers know that you are looking for a deal. Most often, the wholesalers have lists of properties there and will put you on their fax-out sheets for weekly updates.

Using the Internet

The Internet is a great tool for finding real estate investors both locally and nationally. One way is to go to Google and type in "real estate investors." This will bring up over 2 million different results. You may also try "finding private lenders," and then contact those sites as potential lenders. Finally, you can create your own Web site stating that you are a private mortgage investor.

Mortgage Brokers, Realtors, and Appraisers

Even if you don't have a local investment club, you can still get to know those involved in the real estate business in your area. Since you are not in direct competition with these business professionals, they might be willing to provide you with leads, and you could do the same for them. Keep in mind that networking needs to work both ways to benefit all involved.

HOLD A PRESENTATION

You might decide to gather together a large group of potential investors and hold a presentation. Here are the benefits of doing so:

Leveraging your time: You save time by talking to more than one person at a time. You also save time by talking only to those who are prequalified. For instance, you can let them know from the outset that unless they have a specific amount to invest, the presentation is not for them.

Attractive meeting location: It is true that you could hold a presentation in your office, but if it's like most offices, it is cramped and full of paperwork. Holding a presentation or luncheon allows you to have a nicer venue.

Controlled atmosphere: The meeting location provides a place where you are in control of the situation. You won't have to worry about telephones ringing, dogs barking, or children screaming.

Answer everyone's questions at once: People often ask questions that you haven't thought to answer.

Not only that, some people don't want to show what they don't know by asking a question. So, if someone asks, they all learn. With a group, everyone gets educated at once.

No pressure: Even when you are as careful as possible, a one-on-one meeting can come across as a high-pressure event. With a relaxed presentation, people can listen without the pressure. It is important not to put anybody on the spot.

Professional presentation: Since you will be presenting to a large group, you are more likely to really work on the presentation. This will help your pitch be top-notch.

Linger: Since it is not a high-pressure event, people will linger afterwards, asking more questions. Those who linger may very well turn out to be your next investors.

USE BIRD DOGS

Some private mortgage investors hire "bird dogs." These are people who go out and hunt up leads for you, and you provide them with a fee for each lead whether a deal materializes or not. Since this will save you time, and since time is money, you won't feel guilty about the referral fee—especially when you realize the interest you are generating.

LOOK FOR ADS AND FLIERS

There are people out there with real estate that they want to sell quickly. You see their ads all the time in the local paper:

GOT HOUSES? MUST SELL?
Fast Cash!

Call them, and let them know that you are a private mortgage investor. They may need your help on a deal, or they may know of a real estate investor looking for a good private loan.

Don't be shy; ask anyone and everyone regarding area real estate investors, and before long, you will be connected with successful investors.

CHAPTER 10

VERIFYING PROPERTY INFORMATION

When you decide to become a private mortgage originator, you take on the responsibility of due diligence: assessing and verifying the investment according to the parameters set. If you have decided to go it alone, all of the information gathering will be entirely up to you.

If you go with a mortgage broker, a good portion of the due diligence will be up to the broker. However, at least initially, you will want to verify at least some of the paperwork. As you develop a relationship with the broker, you will have to do less and less due diligence paperwork, but never give it up completely. You should always have firsthand information concerning your investments.

THE APPRAISAL

The very first item of business when carrying out due

diligence is the appraisal and subsequent report. This needs to be a complete report, using the following three methods:

1. Market approach

2. Income approach

3. Cost approach

Of these approaches, the market approach is the one of most concern. However, getting all three will help determine the accuracy. If either the cost or income approach is lower than the market approach, use the lowest one to determine the maximum LTV ratio.

You can have an appraiser do this for you, or you can learn to do the appraisals yourself. Either way, you should understand the different appraisal approaches and what they tell you, as well as the different ways to get comparable sales (comps).

The Market Approach

In the market approach, the value of the property is determined by recent sales of comparable properties in that market. For the best results, you will want to get at least four comps to determine the market appraisal portion of the report.

There are really three different methods of getting comps:

1. Doing your own research.

2. Using service companies.

3. Accessing the MLS.

When you do your own research, you can go to the courthouse (which is time consuming), check newspaper listings (not all localities list sales information), check tax appraisal districts (often undervalued and useless), use Internet searches (often outdated) or, by far the best way, know the neighborhood.

The longer you are in the investment business, the more you will realize the property values of particular neighborhoods. You can also learn about specific neighborhoods and communities by talking with Realtors, attending open houses, viewing floor plans, and so forth. Once you've done this enough in a particular area, you can get a feel for the value of the house just by driving by.

You may want to check out service companies that provide sales data from your area. As Internet technology grows, getting up-to-date information online gets easier and easier.

If you choose to go the Internet route, do not simply accept online companies' comps as accurate. Do a bit of your own legwork to check their figures. Once you have determined that they are correct, you will only have to spot-check properties occasionally. Also, remember that not all online databases are updated regularly. Be sure to find a site that updates regularly—the more regularly the better.

Finally, you can gain access to the Multiple Listing Service (MLS). Having this access is invaluable. If you don't have direct access to the MLS, you can often find someone in the real estate market who does and who will do searches for you for a fee. Instead of asking for a comp, ask for the data sheets and determine your own comp values.

It is better, however, if you can gain access to the MLS yourself. To do so, you could become a Realtor or obtain an associate membership. Whether you can access the MLS without a real estate license varies from area to area.

If you don't have a license or can't get an associate membership, you can always develop a good working relationship with someone who does. You might want to contact a Realtor who specializes in commercial properties. Why? He or she doesn't need to use the MLS daily like a residential Realtor does, and that will give you easier access to it.

Once you get at least four comps, you can then determine the market value of the property.

The Income Approach

As with the market approach, the income approach also requires four comps—rental comps—to determine the value. In order for your appraisal to be valid, you must be able to find similar properties in the neighborhood for rent, know the operating expenses associated with those rents, and have vacancy and collection loss data. You will also need to get their sales prices. You will probably not be able to get all the information for each comp property, but you will need sufficient information to determine the "typical" numbers for your property.

ANNUAL PROPERTY OPERATING DATA			
Property Address: **Date:** **Prepared by:**			
INCOME	**$**	**%**	Comments
Gross Scheduled Rent Income			
Other Income			
TOTAL GROSS INCOME			
VACANCY & CREDIT ALLOWANCE			
GROSS OPERATING INCOME			
EXPENSES			
Accounting			
Advertising			
Insurance (Fire & Liability)			
Janitorial Service			
Lawn/Snow			
Legal			
Licenses			
Miscellaneous			
Property Management			

ANNUAL PROPERTY OPERATING DATA			
Repairs & Maintenance			
Resident Superintendent			
Supplies			
Taxes			
Real Estate			
Personal Property			
Payroll			
Other			
Trash Removal			
Utilities			
Electricity			
Fuel Oil			
Gas			
Sewer and Water			
Telephone			
Other			
TOTAL EXPENSES			
NET OPERATING INCOME			

The Cost Approach

The cost approach involves estimating the replacement value of a property as separate components—land and improvements. Here's how it works:

1. Estimate the value of the land as if vacant.

2. Estimate the replacement cost of the building.

3. Estimate the building's loss in value from depreciation.

4. Subtract the building's depreciation from the estimated replacement cost.

5. Calculate the value of the property by adding the estimated land value to the depreciated value of the building.

Once all three approaches have been assimilated, you need to review them, as well as understand the growth potential of the area. You also need to determine if the rental demand in that area truly exists. Once that is done, you can determine the appraisal value of the property.

However, getting an appraisal is not the end of your due diligence investigation. Next you will want to conduct a physical inspection of the property.

PHYSICAL INSPECTION

The appraisal won't tell you everything; nor should you trust a piece of paper. You definitely should conduct an inspection of the property and of the area in general. Here are a few of the things you should look for and consider:

Structural inspection: If the property appears to need repairs, you may want to consult a building inspector or contractor so that you can get estimates of repairs. You will want to note any large repairs that were not part of the appraisal so that you can adjust the appraisal value accordingly.

Handicap accessibility: If the property you are buying is a commercial property, you will want to be sure that it complies with the handicap accessibility requirements under the ADA.

Drainage and retaining walls: Check both the condition and the design and look for any potential issues.

Roads: Check to see if the property has adequate access from the public street. Projected road improvements could significantly change the desirability of the property.

Public transit: If the property has access to public transportation, it can increase the value of that property.

Wells: If water for a site is provided by an on-site well, quality/potability and quantity (that is, gallons per hour) need to be determined. In some instances, the output of the well may limit the permitted development of the property.

EXAMINE FINANCIAL DOCUMENTATION

If the property you are considering is either commercial or a multi-family rental property, you definitely want to see the financial documentation for that property. Keep in mind that you don't care about the financial situation of the borrower—just the financial situation of the property. Knowing this situation helps you determine whether or not to loan the money.

What kind of financial documentation do you want to see?

- Rent rolls.

- Leases.

- Current and past financial statements.

- Expense projections.

- Licenses.

- Contracts that affect the property.

- Estoppel certificates (no defaults, no prepaid rent, status of security deposits, and the like) from each of the tenants prior to closing.

APPRAISALS ARE SUBJECTIVE

Keep in mind that appraisals are subjective. It is unlikely that two appraisers will give you the same figures for the same reasons. Let's take a quick look at some of the factors that affect the appraiser's valuation. These are factors that are beyond the actual home and its appearance:

1. Local taxes.

2. Plat survey: size of lot, topography and landscape, easements.

3. Deed. (Is the title clear? Are there any deed covenants that would limit use or resale opportunities?)

4. List of improvements, especially to kitchen and bathrooms. (Do you have permits, if required, for the alterations?)

5. Homeowner warranties.

6. Value and condition of neighborhood houses.

7. Zoning of, and plans for, any nearby vacant land.

8. Age of neighborhood.

9. Ease of access to work, schools, shopping, and recreation.

10. Adequacy and cost of utilities.

11. Adverse influences (such as proximity to highways, high-tension wires, commercial areas).

12. Present and proposed assessments.

Additionally, the appraiser will consider the following:

- **Local supply and demand:** How many homes are for sale in the immediate neighborhood? How quickly are they being sold? What are the current market trends? What is the reason for the sale of this particular piece of property?

- **Economic conditions:** What is the economy like in the region? Are there currently strikes or plant closings? Have there been any recent rezonings, or are there any scheduled? Are any plants leaving the area? Are any coming into the area?

- **Politics:** What state and local government actions are affecting property values? Have any school bonds been passed or been recently proposed? Have there been any property reassessments? Are taxes on the rise?

Every time you have an investment opportunity, you will go through the due diligence process. Not doing so can cause you a lot of problems, but more important, can cost you a lot of money.

Case Study – Bud

Let's hear what Bud has to say about private mortgage investing, and, in particular, his feelings on the accuracy of appraisals:

I got started in private mortgage investing in 1982. I was in apartment buildings, and I sold out and met a mortgage broker. In all my 25 years, I have only lost on one building, and that was due to fraud. It taught me a valuable lesson: inspect everything!

I think that private mortgage investing is great. Why? Because you are in control. With stocks and bonds, you never really know what you have. You are relying totally on someone else's opinion. That is not true with real estate. Real estate is tangible. I can go out and see it for myself. It is stable. Every now and then, I do the more traditional real estate deals, but only if a good deal comes up. Private mortgage investing, however, is much better. You just can't pass it up.

Some people only like certain kinds of deals. For instance, some people only want commercial property, while others only want single-family dwellings. I am willing to look at just about anything from mobile homes to construction loans. I see every loan as an individual deal. As long as there is equity in the property, it has the potential for a good, solid investment.

This is where the appraisals come in. Appraisals are supposed to let you know how much equity is actually in the property. In general, however, I don't like most appraisals. Appraisers are doing a job, typically for the person wanting the loan. They will ask the borrower what they want to borrow and what the loan-to-value ratio needs to be, and somehow, they get a figure that is almost on the dot to what the borrower needs it to be. For instance, an appraiser, with the help of comps, can come up with a price of $50/foot for a 30-year-old mobile home. Some are pretty sneaky that way.

This is why I always check out the property myself. I even check out the non-local ones. After you are in business a while, you can almost look at a building and know what it is going to be. In addition to the property itself, it is all about location.

Let me share with you one deal that sounded good on paper but just wasn't good at all. There was an out-of-town piece of property with a $250,000 home on it. It was a new home, and the appraisal was very good. By the photos, I would have said it was a really good deal. But I drove the 60 miles to see the property. Everything within a mile and a half of this new house was junk. There were trailers in horrible condition and run-down, unkempt homes. It was terrible. The house itself was great, but the location was awful. Who [sic] would you be able to sell this house to if you had to foreclose? No one!

The appraiser had used comps from three miles out. It is true that homes three miles out would make this home appraise at a higher value. In this case, three miles was just too far. My advice: Go and see the neighborhood.

That doesn't mean that I won't do deals that are not local. I will do it if I know the area. However, if things out of town go bad, it does make foreclosure more difficult. When you are first getting started, I would suggest staying local.

Let's talk for a minute about taxes and insurance. Some people like to have it escrowed. I guess I can understand that, but I just don't like the hassle and the cost. Once you do escrowed monies, you have to have a special account. I prefer to handle it on my own. In fact, I tend to like to do most of my private mortgage investing "solo" with the exception of finding a good broker. I don't like investing in loans with others because of the hassle. I also don't feel the need for loan servicing companies. I like private mortgage investing because of the ease and the control. Once I start partnering with others, my control gets lost.

CHAPTER 11

INSURANCE TO KEEP YOUR INVESTMENT SAFE

*T**he different insurances required** for a mortgage loan are for your protection and are paid for by the borrower. You will be the beneficiary of any insurance protection. Here's what you need to know about title insurance and property insurance.

TITLE INSURANCE

Title insurance is a policy protecting against loss should the condition of title to land be other than as insured. The coverage continues in effect for as long as you have an interest in covered property, and the cost varies depending upon the value of the property. The cost, however, is not something for you to worry about, since it is up to the borrower to pay for this insurance.

You will want to get a Lender's Title Insurance Policy. These are also known as Loan Policies, and they cover the amount loaned to the lender. The amount of the policy decreases as the loaned amount is paid off. In the case of private mortgage interest-only loans, the amount of the policy will remain the same throughout the life of the loan.

These policies guarantee that the property belongs to the person on the title, that there are no undisclosed liens or encumbrances, and that there are no undisclosed payments on taxes due.

Let's consider a property that is worth $100,000, and you loaned $65,000 to the borrower. Your Lender's Title Insurance will only cover the $65,000 and not the full value of the property.

At the mere hint of a claim adverse to your title, you should contact your title insurer or the agent who issued your policy. Title insurance includes coverage for legal expenses that may be necessary to investigate, litigate, or settle an adverse claim.

Title insurance for both sides is necessary. Being the lender, you want lender's title insurance, and your borrowers should be required to pay for your coverage. This keeps you "safe."

Not all states require or even authorize title insurance. Check with a local real estate broker or real estate attorney to determine the laws and availability of title insurance in your area.

COMMON TITLE PROBLEMS

It is true that the title company will check out the title thoroughly before issuing title insurance, often as far back as 50 years. In about 25 percent of the cases, problems are found and fixed on the title before the insurance is issued.

Even so, there are still possible problems that can occur with the title after closing. Such problems include:

- Mistakes in the public record.

- Undisclosed heirs claiming to own the property.

- Forged deeds.

- Lack of competency, capacity, or legal authority of a party.

- Deed not joined in by a necessary party (co-owner, heir, spouse, corporate officer, or business partner).

- Undisclosed (but recorded) prior mortgage or lien.

- Undisclosed (but recorded) easement or use restriction.

- Erroneous or inadequate legal descriptions.

- Lack of a right of access.

- Fraud in connection with the execution of documents.

- Undue influence on a grantor or executor.

- False personation by those purporting to be owners of the property.

- Will not properly probated.

- Mistaken interpretation of wills and trusts.

- Conveyance by a minor.

- Birth of heirs subsequent to the date of the will.

- Deeds executed under expired or false power of attorney.

- Confusion due to similar or identical names.

- Dower or courtesy rights of ex-spouse or former owners.

- Delivery of deeds after the death of a grantor.

- Off-record matters, such as claims for adverse possession or prescriptive easement.

- Deed to land with buildings encroaching on land of another.

- Incorrect survey.

- Silent (off-record) liens (such as mechanic's or estate-tax liens).

- Preexisting violations of subdivision laws, zoning ordinances, or CC&Rs.

- Forced removal of improvements due to lack of

building permit.

• Postpolicy construction of improvements by a neighbor on insured land.

Title insurance offers you financial protection against all of these possible events. The title company will negotiate any settlements and pay the claims and legal fees.

For added security, lenders like Doug Brown and Matt Tabacchi often require 125 percent title insurance. This means that the borrower must have title insurance worth 125 percent of the current value of the property. When asked why, Doug stated:

> "It is a protection against inflation and rising real estate prices. Let's imagine for a moment that you have loaned money on a $100,000 piece of property. In the ensuing years, the property becomes worth $125,000. Now, let's assume that you are having to foreclose on the property and in the process, a title defect is found. You will only get the amount of money that the title insurance stated — not the true value of the property! Requiring that the borrower get 125 percent title insurance costs you nothing and can protect you against rising costs."

PROPERTY INSURANCE

Property insurance provides financial protection against the loss of, or damage to, real and personal property caused by a covered peril. Most of the time, fire and hazard insurance will protect against the most common cause of real property destruction. In the case of catastrophes such as fire, explosion, theft, or vandalism, property insurance helps cover your costs, whether they're to repair damaged property or replace what you've lost.

Events that do damage are known as perils or causes of loss and include weather-related events, such as lightning strikes or hail, or human causes, such as robbery or vehicular accidents. There are two types of policies available to cover perils: a named-perils policy, which covers losses resulting from only those perils the policy names, and an all-risk policy (also known as special form coverage), which offers coverage for all perils except those specifically named.

As a private mortgage lender, you would be better off with all-risk policies (which typically have higher premiums). The problem is that this type of insurance is extraordinarily expensive, and some properties will not qualify for it even if the borrower can afford to pay it. Therefore, you are likely to have to accept a named-perils policy that covers the main causes of damage like fire, windstorm, and so on.

NOTE: If the property is in a floodplain, you should demand that the borrower also get federal flood insurance.

Policies can pay out in one of two ways: replacement cost or actual cash value. If you are covered for the actual cost of replacing your property, this is known as a replacement-cost basis. The alternative, actual cash value (ACV) reimbursement, is based on the replacement cost minus physical depreciation of the lost or damaged property.

The premiums for ACV policies tend to be lower, since they usually pay out less, but the reimbursement could be inadequate if you actually need to replace items. Therefore, you are better off with replacement-cost insurance.

Insurance is not the only protection you need. You also have to worry about the language of the mortgage note and the deed of trust. For this, you need a good real estate attorney.

CHAPTER 12

MORE SAFETY MEASURES FOR THE PRIVATE LENDER

THE USE OF A FIREPROOF SAFE

It is important to keep your original note in a safe place, such as a safe-deposit box or a fireproof safe in your home. Make a photocopy to keep with your trust deed and other escrow papers.

There are two reasons for this precaution: First, the note is not recorded in the county recorder's office; the deed of trust is. If you lost your deed of trust, you could simply get another copy at the recorder's office.

Second, your note is a negotiable instrument, which means it can be endorsed on the back like a check. You wouldn't keep an uncashed check lying around, so think of your note as a check, and take good care of it.

DIRECT DEPOSIT/AUTOMATIC ELECTRONIC PAYMENTS

Some people feel more comfortable knowing that the payments are set up to automatically draft out of the borrower's account. This does not guarantee that the investor will be paid, but since it is an automatic draft, the borrower is more likely to have that covered.

Additionally, having an automatic payment setup is good for the borrower. Many people do not seem to recognize that paying bills late can damage their credit rating, according to a national poll by the Direct Deposit and Direct Payment Coalition. The survey found that 35 percent had been late with major credit card payments, 19 percent had been late on car-loan payments, and 17 percent were late with payments to gas station or department store accounts. Only about half of those polled, though, identified a negative impact on their credit rating when asked to name "any possible consequences of paying bills late."

Payment history generally carries more weight than any other element in determining your credit score, which lenders often rely on when deciding whether to give you a loan or other form of credit. About 35 percent of the FICO score is based on payment history, which includes details on both timely and late or missed payments.

If the borrower has a less-than-stellar credit rating, paying the investor on time for 12 months will give him or her a good track record. One way to be sure that the payments are on time is to set up an automatic draft.

ADDITIONAL COLLATERAL

Although not a typical practice with private mortgage investing, it is possible to ask for additional collateral besides the property when loaning out money. Perhaps the borrower needs money that amounts to a 75 percent LTV ratio but also owns another piece of property free and clear. You can write a loan agreement that has that second piece of property as collateral, thus making your LTV lower. Keep in mind that going above a 65 percent LTV can be an unwise decision in some cases, so unless you are experienced or really trust your broker, it is best to stay away from these kinds of deals.

REQUIRE A SURVEY

It is important to distinguish between a survey and an appraisal, both of which are charged to the borrower. An appraisal assists the investor in assessing the value of the property to determine whether a mortgage should be made and in what amount. Generally, the appraisal will analyze the condition of the house, its location, structural soundness, and comparable sales in the area.

A survey, on the other hand, goes to the question of the marketability of the house. The surveyor determines whether the house is within the property borders, whether there are any encroachments on the property by neighbors, and the extent to which any easements on the property may affect legal title.

It should be noted that the typical survey that most purchasers obtain when they go to closing is called a "house location" survey. Title insurance generally excludes coverage encroachments, overlaps, boundary line disputes, and any other matters that would be disclosed by an accurate survey and inspection of the premises. The title insurance industry takes the position that a house location survey is not an accurate survey and thus will reject many claims regarding boundary disputes. So, to make your title insurance as good as possible, it is best to require a survey.

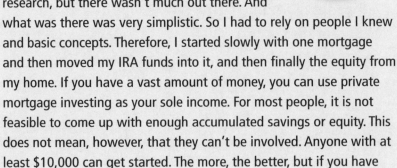

Case Study – Doug

Doug, who has been investing for five years and has gotten many others interested in the process, says:

I learned about private mortgage investing from my father-in-law. I tried to do a bit of research, but there wasn't much out there. And what was there was very simplistic. So I had to rely on people I knew and basic concepts. Therefore, I started slowly with one mortgage and then moved my IRA funds into it, and then finally the equity from my home. If you have a vast amount of money, you can use private mortgage investing as your sole income. For most people, it is not feasible to come up with enough accumulated savings or equity. This does not mean, however, that they can't be involved. Anyone with at least $10,000 can get started. The more, the better, but if you have

$10,000 sitting around without any immediate need, you can put it to work for 12 percent or more!

I firmly believe in using the equity in your home. Oh, I've heard people say that they are "earning" money since their home is increasing in value. But, in reality, how are you going to actually get at that equity without selling your home? The problem with selling is that you will need to live somewhere else, and you have to pay the escalated price to live somewhere else. By pulling out the equity—all the stuff that you never see and do very little for you—it can be put to work making money. Right now, you can borrow at 6 to 7 percent, thus making about 7 to 9 percent interest. Not only that, but your home is still increasing in value!

The risk, should the mortgage default to you, is that you have to continue making your payments. You have to be in enough of a financial situation to pay for up to 6 months if the loan defaults. If you can't, then stay away.

As far as the kind of land to invest in, it simply doesn't matter to me. I personally try to stay away from mobile homes since they are mobile. In other words, my investment could simply move away.

However, mobile homes are registered, just like a car, so this isn't too much of a concern. The critical thing is loan-to-value ratio and to be sure that the property is valued correctly.

I don't find most appraisals accurate, since it depends so much on who is doing the appraisal. If the appraisal is bank ordered, it leans to the bank. A homeowner's appraisal will lean toward the homeowner. Let me give you an example: I bought a commercial building about a year ago, and the appraisal was rushed through. The appraiser never went into the building. The appraisal was the exact amount of the sales contract. He just copied it. It was worth nearly $100,000 more. Appraisals are simply very subjective. And the hotter the real estate market, the more subjective the appraisals.

That is why I inspect most of my properties. I used to inspect all of them, but now I only inspect about 90 percent. This is because I trust my broker and know the area. I have always used Matt Tabacchi of Allstate Mortgage Loans and Investments, Inc. He is a great broker, because he goes a step further. He doesn't disappear once a deal has been brokered. If things go awry, he is there to help straighten them back out.

I don't worry much about the safety of my private mortgage investments. It is the safest investment vehicle I have ever encountered as long as you follow the parameters. Of course, I am someone who puts everything on the line every day. If you are a bit more concerned about safety, you can always escrow insurance and taxes, and have your payments direct-deposited to your bank. Everyone has different comfort levels. If you want to know that your money is under your pillow, then you have to do what you feel comfortable with.

Here are a few other tips I would like to share so that you can become a successful private mortgage investor:

- It is important to work with a broker. Dealing directly with clients would be difficult. Since the borrower pays his fees anyway, you simply can't lose!

- Don't do anything you aren't comfortable with.

- See each property personally.

- Keep your LTV below 70 percent. This makes everything secure, even in a foreclosure.

- Start small, and see how it goes.

CHAPTER 13

REAL ESTATE ATTORNEYS ARE WORTH THE PRICE

MORTGAGE NOTE AND DEED OF TRUST

If you were a dentist, you would work with drills and small mirrors. If you were a contractor, you would work with hammers and saws. As a private mortgage investor, you work with mortgage notes and deeds of trust. These are the tools with which you secure your loan, and just like a dentist using a faulty drill or a contractor using a faulty saw, a faulty note can have disastrous effects.

This is why it is absolutely necessary to have a real estate attorney — one who represents you — draw up these forms.

Whoever drafts the note initially should make sure it clearly states the names of both the borrower and the lender, contains the address of the property, the loan amount, the interest rate, any interest rate adjustment criteria, the payment schedule, and the minimum payment due on each payment date. It should also state when final payments are due, any penalty for late payments, whether there is a penalty for early payoff, and any other conditions imposed by the lender. The note must be signed and dated by the borrower. Since most private notes are individually tailored to a particular situation, there is no such thing as a "standard form" that is used.

Every state is different, so the wording will be different in each state. A competent real estate attorney will know these differences and be able to produce a document that works best for you.

Once again, you really should consider investing only in states that are lender-friendly. To be lender-friendly, a state should:

- Allow nonjudicial foreclosures.

- Not have laws that unfairly penalize lenders for minor errors or omissions.

- Not have laws that make lending money for a mortgage burdensome by insisting on too many disclosures or qualifications.

MORTGAGE RENEWALS

When you loan out money, you do so for a certain period of time. Most private mortgage loans are 360/120 loans if they are principal and interest. This means that the loan is amortized over 360 months (30 years) and that it balloons at 120 months (10 years). To balloon means that the entire principal that is owed at

10 years is due on that balloon date. If mortgage loans are interest-only, the typical loan is 5 years, with the principal due at the end of the 5-year period.

If you had a 360/180, you would know that the loan is amortized over 30 years and balloons at 15 years.

Let's just say we do a $100,000 loan at 360/60. That means that in 5 years, the borrower either has to pay us off, or refinance. Now, if the borrower paid for 5 years and paid perfectly, we have the opportunity to give him or her a mortgage renewal. Instead of calling the balloon due, we let the borrower ride. Whether you offer a mortgage renewal to the borrower is completely up to you. There is no right or wrong answer.

MORTGAGE COMMITMENT LETTER

This letter is simply an approval from the investor. Let's say that a broker sends Jack a loan package for a borrower who needs $100,000. If Jack agrees that he wants to do this loan, he will give the broker a mortgage commitment letter. This does not require Jack to follow through; he can put in provisions that he is agreeing based on the appraisal, the title search, and so forth. In this way, the broker can then commit to the borrower.

See Appendix 1 for a sample mortgage commitment letter.

DISCLOSURE FORMS

Disclosure forms are between the broker and the

borrower. However, as an investor, you will receive a copy of all these signed disclosure forms. This way, if you ever have an issue with the borrower, you have proof of what the borrower knew and what he or she signed.

For instance, one form that is signed shows that the borrower knows how much must be paid monthly, to whom, and where. This form also states the late charges and returned check fees and states that the insurance and taxes are the responsibility of the borrower.

Disclosures also show the borrower the interest rate to be paid and the number of payments that need to be made. The borrower will signify whether he or she is going to occupy the property, that he or she has not been coerced into taking insurance from a specific company, and that he or she received a copy of the *Consumer Handbook on Adjustable-Rate Mortgages.* And these are just a few of the different disclosures signed by the borrower.

Take a look at Appendix 2 to see some of the standard disclosure forms.

USURY LAWS

Something else you need to watch out for is state usury laws that affect mortgages. Each state is different, not only in the amount of maximum interest you can charge, but on what that interest is based on the particular kind and size of the loan. A chart is shown in Appendix 6 to give you an idea. Please keep in mind that these laws change regularly.

For instance:

The state's high court overturned a 2004 Illinois Appellate Court decision that the Illinois Interest Act applies to virtually all mortgages made in the state. The 1974 law bars lenders that charge interest greater than 8 percent from charging additional fees exceeding 3 percent of the principal.

Disagreeing with the Appellate Court, the Illinois Supreme Court ruled that federal law preempts the Illinois Interest Act. In effect, the state's usury law now no longer applies to any home loans.

In Florida, usury laws only affect property that is homesteaded — property that is the primary residence of the borrower. Even then, you can charge high interest rates as long as you stay within the limits and have the right legal forms signed.

It is very important that you have a real estate lawyer who knows the usury laws of the state in which you are investing.

FORECLOSURE

As with usury laws and wording on notes and deeds, foreclosures differ from state to state. A good attorney is crucial to understanding the laws of the states in which you will be lending.

Here are the three things you need to be concerned with when involved in a foreclosure:

- Judicial versus nonjudicial foreclosure.

- Time allowed before an auction can be held.

- Existence of redemption rights.

If you have loaned money in a judicial foreclosure state, you will have to go through a court hearing in order to auction the property. On the other hand, a nonjudicial state allows you to notify the borrower, wait the specified time, and then auction the property. This is a much cheaper and easier way to foreclose.

One major point regarding foreclosures executed in judicial foreclosure states is that as the mortgage holder, you are not allowed to make a profit on the foreclosure sale itself. All monies that the auction brings in, over the outstanding debt balance, are interlocked through the court and are supposed to be paid to junior/subordinate lien holders. After that, any remaining balance is supposed to go to the mortgagee.

States also differ on the time allowed to elapse before an auction can be held. For private mortgage investors, the shorter the time period, the better.

The right to redemption allows the borrower who was foreclosed upon to get his or her payments up to date; pay off any penalties, interest, and legal fees; and then redeem the property. Long redemption periods are more borrower-friendly than lender-friendly. It is best to lend money in states with short or nonexistent rights to redemption.

For state-by-state information on these policies, see Appendix 7.

FINDING A GOOD ATTORNEY

When selecting an attorney, you should ask for referrals from friends, business acquaintances, and other real estate investors After you select two or three real estate attorneys, you can get a list from **www.martindale.com** or **www.law.com** that shows their qualifications. You can also go to the courthouse in your area, check with the clerk there, ask to review cases in which those attorneys have been involved, and, most importantly, you can find out whether they won or lost their cases.

QUESTIONS TO ASK A PROSPECTIVE ATTORNEY

The important thing when choosing a real estate attorney is that you are comfortable with him or her and truly believe that the attorney can see things from your point of view. You need to have confidence that he or she will advise you correctly.

1. What experience do you have in creative real estate investing, such as private mortgage lending?

The attorney should understand and be open to creative real estate investing.

2. How much of your practice is in real estate?

Depending on your market size, it should be at least 30 to 50 percent. In smaller markets, there would be less need for an attorney to devote all of his or her practice to real estate.

3. Do you have other real estate investors as clients?

If so, ask if you can contact them for references.

4. What are your fees?

The size of the law firm is not an important factor, except larger firms usually charge more because of their overhead and are not as available to you as a smaller firm. Be careful of lowball quotes promising everything for an unreasonably low price. While some real estate attorneys are extremely competitive in price, it still holds true that you get what you pay for. The low-cost/high-volume attorneys are best for buyers and sellers who understand the real estate transaction.

5. Do you work with other real estate professionals?

The attorney should be able to recommend and refer you to other professionals, such as CPAs, mortgage brokers (for refinances), and so forth.

6. Are you familiar with closing practices in the geographic area involved?

Since each state, and sometimes localities within a state, have different real estate laws, this is a very important question.

CHAPTER 14

BOOKKEEPING AND TAXES

RECORDING A PAYMENT

Keeping a detailed, well-organized, and legible payment record showing the date each payment was received and a breakdown of the principal, interest, and late charge for each amount received is important to maintaining the value of your note.

If you ever decide to sell your note, you will be required to show the payment history to a prospective note buyer, so the note buyer can verify the payment patterns of the note payer.

If the payments on a seasoned note, which is a note with a payment history over an extended period, have been made consistently on time, the value of the note will be greater than if the payments have been late or delinquent, because the perceived risk of the note is lower.

Other benefits of keeping detailed records include:

- Ease of calculating taxes at the end of the year.

- Records to prove delinquency in case of foreclosure.

- Ability to calculate payoffs.

So just what do you need to record for each payment? Here are the main items:

- Amount of interest

- Amount toward principal

- Late fees

- Other fees

- Date of payment

SOFTWARE TO USE

There are a great many varieties of mortgage software programs available with a wide range of features and prices. Your best bet is to start light. Try one of the fast and simple programs; then trade up as you need to.

Chuck, a private mortgage investor and a mortgage broker, uses NoteSmith. According to the NoteSmith Web site at **www.notesmith.com**:

> The NoteSmith family of loan servicing software tracks notes, discounted notes, leases, rent, and other cash flows. Perfect for investors, loan companies, and not-for-profit organizations,

NoteSmith is affordable, easy to use, and fully featured. Used nationwide since 1988 and internationally since 1995, NoteSmith is designed for Windows 95, 98, ME, NT, 2000, and XP.

The NoteSmith family of loan servicing software is designed to perform all of the tracking activities for an investor in, or an originator of, mortgage notes, discounted notes, car loans, mobile home paper, rental property, and other cash flows. Choose the program that is right for you.

NoteSmith is designed for individual note investors. NoteSmith Pro has additional features for small loan companies, landlords, and investors with sophisticated needs. NoteSmith Net has the same feature set as NoteSmith Pro but is designed for multiple, simultaneous users on a local area network.

To see a demo of this product, you can go to:
www.notesmith.com/Download/NSDemo.pdf

For further information, you can contact:
PRINCETON INVESTMENTS, INC.
1112 Oakridge Drive
Suite 104-224
Ft. Collins, CO 80525
888-226-2486

Here are a number of other good mortgage software providers:

Utopia Originator (www.callutopia.com/utopia .html): Complete mortgage originator management software solution.

The Mortgage Office (www.callutopia.com/utopia .html): A complete suite of mortgage software products designed from the ground up to specifically address the needs of those who originate and service loans and mortgage pools. Its modular design includes a complete loan servicing and loan origination system, mortgage pool software, trust accounting, default services tracking, escrow administration, and more.

PipeLine Solutions (www.pipesoft.com): Complete loan processing software application with free demo download.

Dynatek's MORvision™ (www.dynatek.com): The industry's most advanced loan origination system, automating everything from point-of-sale and Web origination through processing, underwriting, closing, secondary tracking, and delivery.

Integra Software Solutions (www.integra-online .com): Comprehensive point-of-sale through postclosing and secondary marketing software for lenders interested in efficiencies gained from automating every step of your mortgage loan workflow.

Loan Administrator Pro (www.laproiq.com): LA Pro helps banks, finance companies, credit unions, CUSOs, business development authorities, micro lenders, and other lending organizations around the globe remain profitable and grow their business in an increasingly competitive environment. LA Pro easily integrates with existing general ledger systems as well as core processing, loan origination, and documentation software utilizing the latest data-sharing technology, including APIs and XML. With versions available on most popular databases, including MS Access and MS SQL Server, LA Pro can meet the loan servicing needs of lenders of all types and sizes and includes multicurrency capabilities as well as SBA reporting.

Twenty-First Century (www.21stcenturycompany .com/lsps.htm): New loan servicing software for Windows XP. Graphical point-and-click system with functions for interest accrual based on fixed and variable rates; customer statements and payment processing; delinquency reporting and customer notification; collection reports and inquiry display; complete loan account history from origination through payoff; payoff worksheet calculations with prepayment penalty options; late-charge assessment and payment reversals; and investor tracking with distribution payments and 1099 tax forms, interfaces to loan origination, general ledger system, Excel spreadsheets, report writers, and custom programs.

CALCULATING PAYOFFS

Mortgage payments are paid in arrears, that is, behind. Take a sample mortgage with an original balance of

$100,000, at 10 percent interest for 180 months. The monthly payments are $1,074.61. The interest accrues from the payment date until the next payment date.

So, to determine a payoff, you have to know the daily rate. A daily rate is figured by:

Original principal x the interest rate divided by 365

In this case, $100,000 x 10%/365 = $27.40 per day.

Once you know the daily rate, you can calculate the payoff using this formula:

Principal balance + days past payment x daily rate

Let's assume that the 60th payment was made, and the principal balance is $81,316.29. If the mortgage is paid off 10 days after the last payment due date, then the payoff would be:

$81,316.29 + (10 x $27.40) = $81,590.29

TAX DEDUCTIONS

Home-Based Business

One of the best ways to write off expenses toward your tax bill is to start a home-based business. If you have a full-time job in addition to having a home-based business, your deductions may exceed your home-based business income by thousands of dollars. That means that your home business would report a net loss for the year.

With a home-based business, you can deduct many

items on your taxes, such as computer equipment, books, and even travel. Be sure to consult your accountant before using any of the following strategies.

1. The standard charge for the first phone line into your house cannot be deducted. If you use your home phone for business, you can deduct only the extra business costs, for example, long-distance calls and call waiting. You'll also have to document your business use. Better idea: Get a separate business phone.

2. Document the business use of your personal car by keeping track of business miles driven and the purpose of each trip. Trips are deductible at the rate of 31 cents a mile, plus parking and tolls. You can also deduct a portion of your car-loan interest.

3. The deduction for transportation expenses may potentially reduce your net cash outlay for a car to less than half its cost. For example, let's see what happens if you're in the 31 percent tax bracket and bought a $6,000 car, using it solely for business purposes. You can claim the first $1,700 as a business expense and choose a 5-year depreciation schedule. If you drive 30,000 miles in the first year, your net cost for the acquisition drops to less than half. This is a

potential expense scenario:

Cost of car: $6,000
Minus election to expense:
$1,700 x .31 ($527)
Minus depreciation:
($6,000 – $1,700) x .20 [5 years]) x .31 ($267)
Thus, we get the net cost of the car.
Net cost of car: $5,206

Minus expenses:
30,000 miles @ 10 mpg = 3,000 gallons @ $1.70/
gal = $5,100
Repairs, oil, and upkeep: $900
Insurance: $1,210
Garage rent, license, registration: $750
Tolls, parking, interest on auto
loan, and the like ($6/day): $2,190

Add these up to get total expenses:
Total expenses: $10,150
Your tax savings at your marginal rate are:
Tax savings ($10,150 x .31): $3,146.50

And your final net cost totals:
Final net cost ($5,206 – $3,146.50): $2,059.50

While the above numbers have been simplified, what I want you to recognize is that your car can be a valuable source of tax-saving dollars. If you have a car that is used 75 percent of the time for business, everything related to that car would be 75 percent deductible. That would include your new CD player and the dice you hang on your rearview mirror.

Focus on our objective here. If you can convert personal expenses into business expenses and you're in the 28 percent tax bracket, you have, in effect, created a 28 percent discount on the cost of anything that qualifies as a business expense. Suddenly, that item that was too pricey at $100 becomes a bargain at $72 ($100 – $28). The trick, as with many tax strategies, is to get the government to help lower your overall costs.

4. Business conventions are tax-deductible, but not for your spouse unless he or she is employed by the business and has a legitimate reason for being there.

5. If you combine a business trip with a vacation, the travel cost can't be written off unless the trip's primary purpose is business. If you do some business, however, you can deduct a pro rata portion of your hotel bill and meals, plus direct expenses such as taxi fares.

Let's say you took a trip from New York to London primarily for business purposes. You were away from home from July 20 through July 29 and spent three days vacationing and seven days conducting business (including two travel days). Suppose your airfare was $500 and your meals and lodging amounted to $75 per day. You could deduct 70 percent of your transportation expenses (seven out of ten days) and $75 per day for seven business days, since you were away from home for more than seven days, and more than 25 percent (three out of ten days) of your time was devoted to business. Remember that only 50 percent of your meals would be deductible.

6. Your home office can be a room or a portion of a room, but it must be used exclusively and regularly as your primary place of business. There's zero write-off for an office that doubles as the dining room table.

The size of the deduction depends on the percentage of floor space used. If your office takes up, say, 10 percent of your house, you can write off 10 percent of your mortgage interest or rent; real estate taxes; homeowner's insurance; home maintenance such as house painting; the bills for heat, water, electricity, and trash removal; and a home security system. You also can depreciate your office space.

There's a limit, however. Most home-office write-offs can't exceed your net business expenses. So you get much less if your business isn't profitable. The exception: You're still allowed write-offs for real estate taxes and mortgage interest. Unused deductions can be carried forward to future years.

7. You can hire your spouse, then set up a medical reimbursement plan for your employees and their families. You can't cover yourself directly, but you can be covered as a member of your spouse's family. The plan doesn't require you to buy insurance. Instead, you reimburse—and deduct from your taxes—your employees' out-of-pocket medical and dental bills. This works for most small businesses, but not for S corporations.

8. Each employee can put as much as $3,000 a year into a tax-deferred individual retirement account. By paying your spouse $3,000, you can jointly put $6,000 away. Children may owe no taxes on as much as $4,700 ($7,700 if they have an IRA).

9. Take advantage of higher-contribution retirement plans available to self-employed people—up to $35,000 in certain Keogh plans.

10. Convert your business to an S corporation to reduce self-employment taxes. As business income rises, consider changing to a C corporation to take advantage of additional fringe benefits.

Depreciation

Depreciation is a convention of accounting and tax laws. It is the gradual, mandatory expensing of improvements to real estate over the life of those improvements.

The rules for depreciation usually bear no relationship to the market value of the same real estate. The property can actually be appreciating in value while you are depreciating the asset on your tax return.

Depreciation can be thought of as non-cash expense of real property. This non-cash expense can reduce current taxable income, while not reducing actual income. Depreciation is allowed in real estate investing.

Other Real Estate Deductions

- Real estate taxes and mortgage interest on an investment property are fully tax deductible.

- Operating expenses, such as utilities, insurance, repairs, and condominium common charges, are deductible.

- Rental fees paid to brokers are deductible, although they must be spread out over the life of the loan.

TAX CONSIDERATIONS

Taxes are an integral part of successful real estate investing, and they often make the difference between a positive cash flow and a negative one. Know the tax situation, and see how it can be manipulated to your advantage. It is a good idea to consult a tax advisor.

Even though you should consider tax laws, keep in mind that the tax code is constantly changing, and a good investment is a good investment regardless of the tax code. Be sure to find an accountant who is well-versed with the constantly evolving tax code.

Rental Property

1. If you spend a majority of your time in the real property businesses, meeting the one-half personal services and 750-hour tests, rental real estate losses are no longer passive per se. If the taxpayer materially participates in each rental real estate activity, losses are fully deductible. If not, even though the taxpayer is a real estate professional, losses are passive and deductible only up to $25,000 (if MAGI is less than $100,000).

2. You generally must include in your gross income all amounts you receive as rent. Rental income is any payment you receive for the use or occupation of property. Expenses of renting property can be deducted from your gross rental income. You generally deduct your rental expenses in the year you pay them.

3. Report rental income on your return for the year you actually or constructively receive it. Include advance rent in your rental income in the year

you receive it regardless of the period covered or the method of accounting you use.

4. If your tenant pays any of your expenses, the payments are rental income. You must include them in your income. You can deduct the expenses if they are deductible rental expenses.

5. If you receive property or services, instead of money, as rent, include the fair market value of the property or services in your rental income. If the services are provided at an agreed-upon or specified price, that price is the fair market value unless there is evidence to the contrary.

6. If you have any personal use of a vacation home or other dwelling unit that you rent out, you must divide your expenses between rental use and personal use.

S Corporation

In general, an S corporation does not pay a tax on its income. Instead, its income and expenses are passed through to the shareholders, who then report these items on their own income tax returns.

If you are an S corporation shareholder, your share of the corporation's current-year income or loss and other tax items is taxed to you whether or not you receive any amount. The S corporation should send you a copy of Schedule K-1 (Form 1120S) showing your share of the S corporation's income, credits, and deductions for the tax year. You must report your distributive share of the S corporation's income, gain, loss, deductions, or credits on the appropriate lines and schedules of your Form 1040.

Investment Clubs

Generally, an investment club is treated as a partnership for federal tax purposes unless it chooses otherwise. In some situations, however, it is taxed as a corporation or a trust.

Tax Reporting for Note Holders

The amount of interest received each year by the seller or note holder must be reported on Schedule B of Form 1040. This is a very simple process if the note holder has an amortization schedule for the loan, which summarizes the interest portion of each payment received.

A portion of the principal received each year must also be reported on Schedule D of Form 1040 (and supporting Form 6251 for Installment Sales). This is not as simple as the tax reporting for interest.

The total amount of the gain on the sale is called the *realized gain*. Realized gain is the net sales price less the cost. The amount of the realized gain that is reported each year on the note holder's tax return is called *recognized gain*.

The amortization schedule shows the amount of interest and principal reduction for each payment and the yearly totals.

Tax reporting for partial sales and split-funded sales is somewhat more complicated than for a full sale. You should consult your tax advisor for the tax reporting method for these types of sales.

As you can see, it is very important to have an amortization schedule for your note.

1031 Tax-Deferred Exchange

A 1031 tax-deferred exchange allows you to roll over all of the proceeds received from the sale of an investment property into the purchase of one or more other like-kind investment properties. At closing, proceeds are transferred to a third party — called a facilitator or qualified intermediary — who holds them until they are used to acquire the new property. A 1031 exchange is often referred to as a Starker exchange.

With a 1031, capital gains taxes are deferred if all of the exchange funds are used to purchase like-kind investment property. The deferment is like getting an interest-free loan on the tax dollars you would have owed for a cash sale. More equity is retained, and that helps you move into properties of higher value each time you perform a 1031 exchange.

A 1031 exchange is possible when you sell real estate held for investment purposes. It cannot be used for the sale of your personal residence.

Exchanged properties must be like-kind. For a real

estate exchange, this means real property for real property, but not necessarily land for land or a rental house for another rental house. *"In a like-kind exchange, both the property you give up and the property you receive must be held by you for investment or for productive use in your trade or business." – IRS*

Take a look at the IRS rules for specific information about what types of properties qualify as like-kind.

Proceeds not used to purchase new investment property are taxed as a cash sale.

Selling Too Many Too Quickly

One problem with selling too many properties too quickly is that the IRS could say that your real estate business is your trade, subject to ordinary income and self-employment taxes.

Self-employment tax, a Social Security and Medicare tax primarily for individuals who work for themselves, is similar to the Social Security and Medicare taxes withheld from the paycheck of most employees. The self-employment tax rate costs you 15.3 percent of your profits (however, this may provide retirement benefits.)

Another common issue is selling a property too quickly. To take advantage of the low 15 percent capital-gains tax rate, you must keep the investment property for at least a year before selling. If you sell before a year, your tax rate, the usual capital gains rate of 35 percent, could eat up a significant amount of your profits.

END-OF-YEAR LIST

If you or your company, corporation, partnership, or trust is in a trade or business, you receive mortgage interest incident to your trade or business, you receive interest payments from individuals, and these individuals paid you more than $600 in interest in a calendar year, you must:

a) Provide a Form 1098 by January 31 of each year to each individual who paid you at least $600 of mortgage interest in the last year.

b) You also must send a copy of the Form 1098 to the IRS along with the summary form 1096 by February 28.

Case Study – Chuck

I love private mortgage investing over other traditional investment vehicles. The stock market is up and down and must be checked daily. Not only that, it costs to trade. Tax liens require as much or more research than the stock market. Neither is terribly safe. The benefits of investing in private mortgages are that they are a very low-risk [investment], and the return on investment is much greater than normal. Private mortgages are great. They produce a great return on investment, with George Washington doing all the work.

My son entered the mortgage business ten years ago. We discussed private investing, and I started out with a small mortgage loan. I became addicted to the point of becoming a mortgage broker. I talked to my CPA, and not only did he agree it was worth pursuing, he also became a private investor.

Interest rates run between 12 and 15 percent, depending on the type of property and the credit rating of the borrower. Terms vary between interest-only, which is my preference, to 30-year amortization schedules. A 5- or 10-year balloon is usually included.

There are fees involved in private mortgage investing. The good part is that the borrower pays them. Fees include origination fees, inspection fees, lawyer fees, appraisals, and the like.

My favorite borrowers are Realtor/builders. They spend their own personal dollars on building the house, and I lend them money to finish it. These loans last 9 to 15 months, and they are interest-only. The investment stays intact, and the interest is great. In a word, they are easy—easy to service!

I have a borrower that [sic] I have been lending money to for 5 years. A couple of times, the money never left the title company. This means that I have my money working for me every day. I take the payoff and have it back out there making interest immediately. I highly recommend construction loans. However, I don't just do construction loans. Any and all real property is a candidate. However, the type of property determines the interest rate and terms that are offered to the borrower.

For the average person in or trying to get into the mortgage business, it is well worth the effort to find a brokerage firm you trust and are confident in. When a mortgage is paid off, I want those funds reinvested ASAP. This is where a good brokerage firm is a must. I have had funds change borrowers the same day, and I have not seen or touched the money. The bottom line is I did not lose a day of interest. Even so, I always, always, always personally look at the properties. I take pictures and research the area for my own personal investments. This is my policy, and I think it would be a good policy for anyone investing in private mortgages to adapt [sic].

There are many different things that can kill a loan, from lack of pride of ownership to finding out that the borrower lied on the application. This is where a good brokerage firm shines. The process starts when a client looking to borrow money approaches the broker. The broker takes a loan application and, from that point on, they start doing research. A good broker will do research until the day of closing. They will want to be sure they are giving true information to their investor. A good broker leans toward investor satisfaction since the investors are there for the long-term, and the borrowers are here for right now.

Besides having a good mortgage broker, title insurance is a must. No investment should be made without proper title work and documentation. Would you really lend money to your brother-in-law's brother with just a handshake and expect to get paid back? If you would, I have a bridge for sale at a fantastic price. One of the basic requirements is that the investor is the first mortgagee with clear and free title. The title company guarantees this with the title insurance. There is no reason to neglect this insurance, since it is at the borrower's expense. It is mandatory in some states, but not in all. So, if you live in a state where this is not mandatory, be sure to get it anyway!

As for what monies to invest, I think that using both IRA money and home equity can be great ideas. If the IRA is producing less than 12 percent, it makes sense to get that money into private mortgage investing, since the return is greater with the same or less risk. The paperwork is a bit more complicated; however, a good broker or attorney can get the job done.

You can also use money from your home equity. This is an individual decision and is determined by your level of investing knowledge and understanding [of] the risks involved. When you choose to use your home equity, even if the borrower does not make his or her payment on time, you must still make your payment. Since it is a bit more risky, it is not something I would recommend just starting out. You don't want to go so far out on a limb that if someone stubs a toe, you are in trouble.

How much should you start with? I started with a $10,000 loan that lasted 6 months. With the origination fee and interest, I received $700 profit. The original investment never left the title company. My broker reinvested this money at [a] higher interest rate. I was hooked. Crawl before you walk before you run is a good adage for beginners and is what I recommend.

The only other thing I would recommend is excellent bookkeeping. I use a software program called NoteSmith and keep handwritten ledger sheets on each account just in case my computer fails.

You simply can't go wrong with property—they don't make any more dirt. Even if you don't get into it at the right price today, down the road, it is going to get to the right price. Private mortgage investing is truly the way to watch your investments consistently increase.

CONNECTING THE DOTS ...

Now that you've read all 14 chapters, are you ready to test-drive private mortgage investing in your own portfolio? Chances are, you're raring to take the wheel and start raking in double-digit earnings in the safe, secure realm of private mortgages. As you shift from first gear into second and beyond, remember to keep the following points in mind:

Know your mortgage broker. The selection of your mortgage broker is probably the single most important decision you can make—especially at the outset of your private mortgage investing endeavors. Your broker is also in a position to refer you to a good accountant, appraiser, and real estate attorney.

Start small, increasing your capital outlay as you gain confidence and practical experience.

Diversify. Unless you have a huge amount of money to invest, you probably won't be able to live on your private mortgage interest. Think of private mortgage interest as supplemental income that fits neatly between your stock dividends and bond interest.

You don't have to go it alone. If you're more comfortable investing with a group, you can partner up with other like-minded investors in a number of partnership and corporate configurations.

Keep your finger in the pie. Be as "hands on" as you can. Drive by the property. Get to know the neighborhood. Learn to do your own appraisals. Become an expert at due diligence.

Keep your eyes on the prize. Concentrate on the property appraisal, rather than the borrower's credit score, and never forget the five all-important investment parameters!

Read and reread this book. Soon you'll know the most important precepts by heart, and your confidence will rise along with your income.

Last, but not least, there are hundreds of worthy borrowers out there who need your services. Many times, a little help from you, a private mortgage lender, can make a real difference in a real person's life. So feel good about what you're doing, and enjoy the ride!

FORMS

MORTGAGE NOTE – ALABAMA EXAMPLE

After Recording Return To:

[Space Above This Line For Recording Data]

MORTGAGE

DEFINITIONS

Words used in multiple sections of this document are defined below and other words are defined in Sections 3, 11, 13, 18, 20, and 21. Certain rules regarding the usage of words used in this document are also provided in Section 16.

A. **"Security Instrument"** means this document, which is dated, together with all Riders to this document.

B. **"Borrower"** is the mortgagor under this Security Instrument.

C. **"Lender"** is a organized and existing under the laws of _____.

Lender's address is _____.

Lender is the mortgagee under this Security Instrument.

D. **"Note"** means the promissory note signed by Borrower and dated

The Note states that Borrower owes Lender Dollars (U.S. $) plus interest. Borrower has promised to pay this debt in regular Periodic Payments and to pay the debt in full not later than

E. **"Property"** means the property that is described below under the heading "Transfer of Rights in the Property."

F. **"Loan"** means the debt evidenced by the Note, plus interest, any prepayment charges and late charges due under the Note, and all sums due under this Security Instrument, plus interest.

G. **"Riders"** means all Riders to this Security Instrument that are executed by Borrower. The following Riders are to be executed by Borrower [check box as applicable]:

- Adjustable Rate Rider
  ❏ Condominium Rider ❏ Second Home Rider

- Balloon Rider
  ❏ Planned Unit Development Rider
  ❏ Other(s) [specify]

- 1-4 Family Rider
  ❏ Biweekly Payment Rider

H. **"Applicable Law"** means all controlling applicable federal, state, and local statutes, regulations, ordinances, and administrative rules and orders (that have the effect of law) as well as all applicable final, non-appealable judicial opinions.

I. **"Community Association Dues, Fees, and Assessments"** means all dues, fees, assessments, and other charges that are imposed on Borrower or the Property by a condominium association, homeowners association, or similar organization.

J. **"Electronic Funds Transfer"** means any transfer of funds, other than a transaction originated by check, draft, or similar paper instrument, which is initiated through an electronic terminal, telephonic instrument, computer, or magnetic tape so as to order, instruct, or authorize a financial institution to debit or credit an account. Such term includes, but is not limited to, point-of-sale transfers, automated teller machine transactions, transfers initiated by telephone, wire transfers, and automated clearinghouse transfers.

K. **"Escrow Items"** means those items that are described in Section 3.

L. **"Miscellaneous Proceeds"** means any compensation, settlement, award of damages, or proceeds paid by any third party (other than insurance proceeds paid under the coverages described in Section 5) for: (i) damage to, or destruction of, the Property; (ii) condemnation or other taking of all or any part of the Property; (iii) conveyance in lieu of condemnation; or (iv) misrepresentations of, or omissions as to, the value and/or condition of the Property.

M. **"Mortgage Insurance"** means insurance protecting Lender against the nonpayment of, or default on, the Loan.

N. **"Periodic Payment"** means the regularly scheduled amount due for (i) principal and interest under the Note, plus (ii) any amounts under Section 3 of this Security Instrument.

O. **"RESPA"** means the Real Estate Settlement Procedures Act (12 U.S.C. §2601 et seq.) and its implementing regulation, Regulation X (24 C.F.R. Part 3500), as they might be amended from time to time, or any additional or successor legislation or regulation that governs the same subject matter. As used in this Security Instrument, "RESPA" refers to all requirements and restrictions that are imposed in regard to a "federally related mortgage loan" even if the Loan does not qualify as a "federally related mortgage loan" under RESPA.

P. **"Successor in Interest of Borrower"** means any party that has taken title to the Property, whether or not that party has assumed Borrower's obligations under the Note and/or this Security Instrument.

TRANSFER OF RIGHTS IN THE PROPERTY

This Security Instrument secures to Lender: (i) the repayment of the Loan, and all renewals, extensions, and modifications of the Note; and (ii) the performance of Borrower's covenants and agreements under this Security Instrument and the Note. For this purpose, Borrower irrevocably mortgages, grants, and conveys to Lender, with power of sale, the following described property located in the _____ of _____

[Type of Recording Jurisdiction]   [Name of Recording Jurisdiction]

which currently has the address of

[Street]

Alabama ("Property Address"):

[City]   [Zip Code]

TOGETHER WITH all the improvements now or hereafter erected on the property, and all easements, appurtenances, and fixtures now or hereafter a part of the property. All replacements and additions shall also be covered by this Security Instrument. All of the foregoing is referred to in this Security Instrument as the "Property."

BORROWER COVENANTS that Borrower is lawfully seized of the estate hereby conveyed and has the right to grant and convey the Property and that the Property is unencumbered, except for encumbrances of record. Borrower warrants and will defend generally the title to the Property against all claims and demands, subject to any encumbrances of record.

THIS SECURITY INSTRUMENT combines uniform covenants for national use and non-uniform covenants with limited variations by jurisdiction to constitute a uniform security instrument covering real property.

UNIFORM COVENANTS. Borrower and Lender covenant and agree as follows:

1. **Payment of Principal, Interest, Escrow Items, Prepayment Charges, and Late Charges.** Borrower shall pay when due the principal of, and interest on, the debt evidenced by the Note and any prepayment charges and late charges due under the Note. Borrower shall also pay funds for Escrow Items pursuant to Section 3. Payments due under the Note and this Security Instrument shall be made in U.S. currency. However, if any check or other instrument received by Lender as payment under the Note or this Security Instrument is returned to Lender unpaid, Lender may require that any or all subsequent payments due under the Note and this Security Instrument be made in one or more of the following forms, as selected by Lender: (a) cash; (b) money order; (c) certified

check, bank check, treasurer's check, or cashier's check, provided any such check is drawn upon an institution whose deposits are insured by a federal agency, instrumentality, or entity; or (d) Electronic Funds Transfer.

Payments are deemed received by Lender when received at the location designated in the Note or at such other location as may be designated by Lender in accordance with the notice provisions in Section 15. Lender may return any payment or partial payment if the payment or partial payments are insufficient to bring the Loan current. Lender may accept any payment or partial payment insufficient to bring the Loan current, without waiver of any rights hereunder or prejudice to its rights to refuse such payment or partial payments in the future, but Lender is not obligated to apply such payments at the time such payments are accepted. If each Periodic Payment is applied as of its scheduled due date, then Lender need not pay interest on unapplied funds. Lender may hold such unapplied funds until Borrower makes payment to bring the Loan current. If Borrower does not do so within a reasonable period of time, Lender shall either apply such funds or return them to Borrower. If not applied earlier, such funds will be applied to the outstanding principal balance under the Note immediately prior to foreclosure. No offset or claim which Borrower might have now or in the future against Lender shall relieve Borrower from making payments due under the Note and this Security Instrument or performing the covenants and agreements secured by this Security Instrument.

2. **Application of Payments or Proceeds.** Except as otherwise described in this Section 2, all payments accepted and applied by Lender shall be applied in the following order of priority: (a) interest due under the Note; (b) principal due under the Note; (c) amounts due under Section 3. Such payments shall be applied to each Periodic Payment in the order in which it became due. Any remaining amounts shall be applied first to late charges, second to any other amounts due under this Security Instrument, and then to reduce the principal balance of the Note.

If Lender receives a payment from Borrower for a delinquent Periodic Payment which includes a sufficient amount to pay any late charge due, the payment may be applied to the delinquent payment and the late charge. If more than one Periodic Payment is outstanding, Lender may apply any payment received from Borrower to the repayment of the Periodic Payments if, and to the extent that, each payment can be paid in full. To the extent that any excess exists after the payment is applied to the full payment of one or more Periodic Payments, such excess may be applied to any late charges due. Voluntary prepayments shall be applied first to any prepayment charges and then as described in the Note.

Any application of payments, insurance proceeds, or

Miscellaneous Proceeds to principal due under the Note shall not extend or postpone the due date, or change the amount, of the Periodic Payments.

3. **Funds for Escrow Items.** Borrower shall pay to Lender on the day Periodic Payments are due under the Note, until the Note is paid in full, a sum (the "Funds") to provide for payment of amounts due for: (a) taxes and assessments and other items which can attain priority over this Security Instrument as a lien or encumbrance on the Property; (b) leasehold payments or ground rents on the Property, if any; (c) premiums for any and all insurance required by Lender under Section 5; and (d) Mortgage Insurance premiums, if any, or any sums payable by Borrower to Lender in lieu of the payment of Mortgage Insurance premiums in accordance with the provisions of Section 10. These items are called "Escrow Items." At origination or at any time during the term of the Loan, Lender may require that Community Association Dues, Fees, and Assessments, if any, be escrowed by Borrower, and such dues, fees, and assessments shall be an Escrow Item. Borrower shall promptly furnish to Lender all notices of amounts to be paid under this Section. Borrower shall pay Lender the Funds for Escrow Items unless Lender waives Borrower's obligation to pay the Funds for any or all Escrow Items. Lender may waive Borrower's obligation to pay to Lender Funds for any or all Escrow Items at any time. Any such waiver may only be in writing. In the event of such

waiver, Borrower shall pay directly, when and where payable, the amounts due for any Escrow Items for which payment of Funds has been waived by Lender and, if Lender requires, shall furnish to Lender receipts evidencing such payment within such time period as Lender may require. Borrower's obligation to make such payments and to provide receipts shall for all purposes be deemed to be a covenant and agreement contained in this Security Instrument, as the phrase "covenant and agreement" is used in Section 9. If Borrower is obligated to pay Escrow Items directly, pursuant to a waiver, and Borrower fails to pay the amount due for an Escrow Item, Lender may exercise its rights under Section 9 and pay such amount and Borrower shall then be obligated under Section 9 to repay to Lender any such amount. Lender may revoke the waiver as to any or all Escrow Items at any time by a notice given in accordance with Section 15 and, upon such revocation, Borrower shall pay to Lender all Funds, and in such amounts, that are then required under this Section 3.

Lender may, at any time, collect and hold Funds in an amount (a) sufficient to permit Lender to apply the Funds at the time specified under RESPA, and (b) not to exceed the maximum amount a lender can require under RESPA. Lender shall estimate the amount of Funds due on the basis of current data and reasonable estimates of expenditures of future Escrow Items or otherwise in accordance with Applicable Law.

The Funds shall be held in an institution whose deposits are insured by a federal agency, instrumentality, or entity (including Lender, if Lender is an institution whose deposits are so insured) or in any Federal Home Loan Bank. Lender shall apply the Funds to pay the Escrow Items no later than the time specified under RESPA. Lender shall not charge Borrower for holding and applying the Funds, annually analyzing the escrow account, or verifying the Escrow Items, unless Lender pays Borrower interest on the Funds and Applicable Law permits Lender to make such a charge. Unless an agreement is made in writing or Applicable Law requires interest to be paid on the Funds, Lender shall not be required to pay Borrower any interest or earnings on the Funds. Borrower and Lender can agree in writing, however, that interest shall be paid on the Funds. Lender shall give to Borrower, without charge, an annual accounting of the Funds as required by RESPA.

If there is a surplus of Funds held in escrow, as defined under RESPA, Lender shall account to Borrower for the excess funds in accordance with RESPA. If there is a shortage of Funds held in escrow, as defined under RESPA, Lender shall notify Borrower as required by RESPA, and Borrower shall pay to Lender the amount necessary to make up the shortage in accordance with RESPA, but in no more than 12 monthly payments. If there is a deficiency of

Funds held in escrow, as defined under RESPA, Lender shall notify Borrower as required by RESPA, and Borrower shall pay to Lender the amount necessary to make up the deficiency in accordance with RESPA, but in no more than 12 monthly payments.

Upon payment in full of all sums secured by this Security Instrument, Lender shall promptly refund to Borrower any Funds held by Lender.

    4. **Charges; Liens**. Borrower shall pay all taxes, assessments, charges, fines, and impositions attributable to the Property which can attain priority over this Security Instrument, leasehold payments or ground rents on the Property, if any, and Community Association Dues, Fees, and Assessments, if any. To the extent that these items are Escrow Items, Borrower shall pay them in the manner provided in Section 3.

Borrower shall promptly discharge any lien which has priority over this Security Instrument unless Borrower: (a) agrees in writing to the payment of the obligation secured by the lien in a manner acceptable to Lender, but only so long as Borrower is performing such agreement; (b) contests the lien in good faith by, or defends against enforcement of the lien in, legal proceedings which in Lender's opinion operate to prevent the enforcement of the lien while those proceedings are pending, but only until such proceedings are concluded; or (c) secures from the holder of the lien an agreement satisfactory to Lender subordinating the lien to this Security Instrument. If

Lender determines that any part of the Property is subject to a lien which can attain priority over this Security Instrument, Lender may give Borrower a notice identifying the lien. Within 10 days of the date on which that notice is given, Borrower shall satisfy the lien or take one or more of the actions set forth above in this Section 4.

Lender may require Borrower to pay a one-time charge for a real estate tax verification and/or reporting service used by Lender in connection with this Loan.

   5. **Property Insurance.** Borrower shall keep the improvements now existing or hereafter erected on the Property insured against loss by fire, hazards included within the term "extended coverage," and any other hazards including, but not limited to, earthquakes and floods, for which Lender requires insurance. This insurance shall be maintained in the amounts (including deductible levels) and for the periods that Lender requires. What Lender requires pursuant to the preceding sentences can change during the term of the Loan. The insurance carrier providing the insurance shall be chosen by Borrower subject to Lender's right to disapprove Borrower's choice, which right shall not be exercised unreasonably. Lender may require Borrower to pay, in connection with this Loan, either: (a) a one-time charge for flood zone determination, certification, and tracking services; or (b) a one-time charge for flood zone determination and certification services and subsequent charges each time remappings or similar changes occur which reasonably might affect

such determination or certification. Borrower shall also be responsible for the payment of any fees imposed by the Federal Emergency Management Agency in connection with the review of any flood zone determination resulting from an objection by Borrower.

If Borrower fails to maintain any of the coverages described above, Lender may obtain insurance coverage, at Lender's option and Borrower's expense. Lender is under no obligation to purchase any particular type or amount of coverage. Therefore, such coverage shall cover Lender, but might or might not protect Borrower, Borrower's equity in the Property, or the contents of the Property, against any risk, hazard, or liability and might provide greater or lesser coverage than was previously in effect. Borrower acknowledges that the cost of the insurance coverage so obtained might significantly exceed the cost of insurance that Borrower could have obtained. Any amounts disbursed by Lender under this Section 5 shall become additional debt of Borrower secured by this Security Instrument. These amounts shall bear interest at the Note rate from the date of disbursement and shall be payable, with such interest, upon notice from Lender to Borrower requesting payment.

All insurance policies required by Lender and renewals of such policies shall be subject to Lender's right to disapprove such policies, shall include a standard mortgage clause, and shall name Lender as mortgagee and/or as an additional loss payee. Lender shall have the right to hold the policies and renewal certificates.

If Lender requires, Borrower shall promptly give to Lender all receipts of paid premiums and renewal notices. If Borrower obtains any form of insurance coverage, not otherwise required by Lender, for damage to, or destruction of, the Property, such policy shall include a standard mortgage clause and shall name Lender as mortgagee and/or as an additional loss payee.

In the event of loss, Borrower shall give prompt notice to the insurance carrier and Lender. Lender may make proof of loss if not made promptly by Borrower. Unless Lender and Borrower otherwise agree in writing, any insurance proceeds, whether or not the underlying insurance was required by Lender, shall be applied to restoration or repair of the Property, if the restoration or repair is economically feasible and Lender's security is not lessened. During such repair and restoration period, Lender shall have the right to hold such insurance proceeds until Lender has had an opportunity to inspect such Property to ensure the work has been completed to Lender's satisfaction, provided that such inspection shall be undertaken promptly. Lender may disburse proceeds for the repairs and restoration in a single payment or in a series of progress payments as the work is completed. Unless an agreement is made in writing or Applicable Law requires interest to be paid on such insurance proceeds, Lender shall not be required to pay Borrower any interest or earnings on such proceeds. Fees for public adjusters, or other third parties, retained by Borrower shall not be paid out of the insurance proceeds and shall be the sole obligation of Borrower. If the restoration or repair is not economically feasible or Lender's security would be lessened, the insurance proceeds shall be applied to the sums secured by this Security Instrument, whether or not then due, with the excess, if any, paid to Borrower. Such insurance proceeds shall be applied in the order provided for in Section 2.

If Borrower abandons the Property, Lender may file, negotiate, and settle any available insurance claim and related matters. If Borrower does not respond within 30 days to a notice from Lender that the insurance carrier has offered to settle a claim, then Lender may negotiate and settle the claim. The 30-day period will begin when the notice is given. In either event, or if Lender acquires the Property under Section 22 or otherwise, Borrower hereby assigns to Lender (a) Borrower's rights to any insurance proceeds in an amount not to exceed the amounts unpaid under the Note or this Security Instrument, and (b) any other of Borrower's rights (other than the right to any refund of unearned premiums paid by Borrower) under all insurance policies covering the Property, insofar as such rights are applicable to the coverage of the Property. Lender may use the insurance proceeds either to repair or restore the Property or to pay amounts unpaid under the Note or this Security Instrument, whether or not then due.

6. **Occupancy.** Borrower shall occupy, establish,

and use the Property as Borrower's principal residence within 60 days after the execution of this Security Instrument and shall continue to occupy the Property as Borrower's principal residence for at least one year after the date of occupancy, unless Lender otherwise agrees in writing, which consent shall not be unreasonably withheld, or unless extenuating circumstances exist which are beyond Borrower's control.

7. **Preservation, Maintenance, and Protection of the Property; Inspections.** Borrower shall not destroy, damage or impair the Property, allow the Property to deteriorate, or commit waste on the Property. Whether or not Borrower is residing in the Property, Borrower shall maintain the Property in order to prevent the Property from deteriorating or decreasing in value due to its condition. Unless it is determined pursuant to Section 5 that repair or restoration is not economically feasible, Borrower shall promptly repair the Property if damaged to avoid further deterioration or damage. If insurance or condemnation proceeds are paid in connection with damage to, or the taking of, the Property, Borrower shall be responsible for repairing or restoring the Property only if Lender has released proceeds for such purposes. Lender may disburse proceeds for the repairs and restoration in a single payment or in a series of progress payments as the work is completed. If the insurance or condemnation proceeds are not sufficient to repair or restore the Property, Borrower is not relieved of Borrower's

obligation for the completion of such repair or restoration.

Lender or its agent may make reasonable entries upon and inspections of the Property. If it has reasonable cause, Lender may inspect the interior of the improvements on the Property. Lender shall give Borrower notice at the time of or prior to such an interior inspection specifying such reasonable cause.

8. **Borrower's Loan Application.** Borrower shall be in default if, during the Loan application process, Borrower or any persons or entities acting at the direction of Borrower or with Borrower's knowledge or consent gave materially false, misleading, or inaccurate information or statements to Lender (or failed to provide Lender with material information) in connection with the Loan. Material representations include, but are not limited to, representations concerning Borrower's occupancy of the Property as Borrower's principal residence.

9. **Protection of Lender's Interest in the Property and Rights Under this Security Instrument.** If (a) Borrower fails to perform the covenants and agreements contained in this Security Instrument, (b) there is a legal proceeding that might significantly affect Lender's interest in the Property and/or rights under this Security Instrument (such as a proceeding in bankruptcy, probate, for condemnation or forfeiture, for enforcement of a lien which may attain priority over this Security Instrument, or to

enforce laws or regulations), or (c) Borrower has abandoned the Property, then Lender may do and pay for whatever is reasonable or appropriate to protect Lender's interest in the Property and rights under this Security Instrument, including protecting and/or assessing the value of the Property, and securing and/or repairing the Property. Lender's actions can include, but are not limited to: (a) paying any sums secured by a lien which has priority over this Security Instrument; (b) appearing in court; and (c) paying reasonable attorneys' fees to protect its interest in the Property and/or rights under this Security Instrument, including its secured position in a bankruptcy proceeding. Securing the Property includes, but is not limited to, entering the Property to make repairs, change locks, replace or board up doors and windows, drain water from pipes, eliminate building or other code violations or dangerous conditions, and have utilities turned on or off. Although Lender may take action under this Section 9, Lender does not have to do so and is not under any duty or obligation to do so. It is agreed that Lender incurs no liability for not taking any or all actions authorized under this Section 9.

Any amounts disbursed by Lender under this Section 9 shall become additional debt of Borrower secured by this Security Instrument. These amounts shall bear interest at the Note rate from the date of disbursement and shall be payable, with such interest, upon notice from Lender to Borrower requesting payment.

If this Security Instrument is on a leasehold, Borrower

shall comply with all the provisions of the lease. If Borrower acquires fee title to the Property, the leasehold and the fee title shall not merge unless Lender agrees to the merger in writing.

10. **Mortgage Insurance.** If Lender required Mortgage Insurance as a condition of making the Loan, Borrower shall pay the premiums required to maintain the Mortgage Insurance in effect. If, for any reason, the Mortgage Insurance coverage required by Lender ceases to be available from the mortgage insurer that previously provided such insurance and Borrower was required to make separately designated payments toward the premiums for Mortgage Insurance, Borrower shall pay the premiums required to obtain coverage substantially equivalent to the Mortgage Insurance previously in effect, at a cost substantially equivalent to the cost to Borrower of the Mortgage Insurance previously in effect, from an alternate mortgage insurer selected by Lender. If substantially equivalent Mortgage Insurance coverage is not available, Borrower shall continue to pay to Lender the amount of the separately designated payments that were due when the insurance coverage ceased to be in effect. Lender will accept, use, and retain these payments as a non-refundable loss reserve in lieu of Mortgage Insurance. Such loss reserve shall be non-refundable, notwithstanding the fact that the Loan is ultimately paid in full, and Lender shall not be required to pay Borrower any interest or earnings on such loss reserve. Lender can no longer

require loss reserve payments if Mortgage Insurance coverage (in the amount and for the period that Lender requires) provided by an insurer selected by Lender again becomes available, is obtained, and Lender requires separately designated payments toward the premiums for Mortgage Insurance. If Lender required Mortgage Insurance as a condition of making the Loan and Borrower was required to make separately designated payments toward the premiums for Mortgage Insurance, Borrower shall pay the premiums required to maintain Mortgage Insurance in effect, or to provide a non-refundable loss reserve, until Lender's requirement for Mortgage Insurance ends in accordance with any written agreement between Borrower and Lender providing for such termination or until termination is required by Applicable Law. Nothing in this Section 10 affects Borrower's obligation to pay interest at the rate provided in the Note.

Mortgage Insurance reimburses Lender (or any entity that purchases the Note) for certain losses it may incur if Borrower does not repay the Loan as agreed. Borrower is not a party to the Mortgage Insurance.

Mortgage insurers evaluate their total risk on all such insurance in force from time to time, and may enter into agreements with other parties that share or modify their risk, or reduce losses. These agreements are on terms and conditions that are satisfactory to the mortgage insurer and the other party (or parties) to these agreements. These agreements may require the mortgage insurer to make payments using any source of funds that the mortgage insurer may have available (which may include funds obtained from Mortgage Insurance premiums).

As a result of these agreements, Lender, any purchaser of the Note, another insurer, any reinsurer, any other entity, or any affiliate of any of the foregoing, may receive (directly or indirectly) amounts that derive from (or might be characterized as) a portion of Borrower's payments for Mortgage Insurance, in exchange for sharing or modifying the mortgage insurer's risk, or reducing losses. If such agreement provides that an affiliate of Lender takes a share of the insurer's risk in exchange for a share of the premiums paid to the insurer, the arrangement is often termed "captive reinsurance." Further:

a. Any such agreements will not affect the amounts that Borrower has agreed to pay for Mortgage Insurance, or any other terms of the Loan. Such agreements will not increase the amount Borrower will owe for Mortgage Insurance, and they will not entitle Borrower to any refund.

b. Any such agreements will not affect the rights Borrower has - if any - with respect to the Mortgage Insurance under the Homeowners Protection Act of 1998 or any other law. These rights may include the right to receive certain disclosures, to request and obtain cancellation of the Mortgage Insurance, to have the Mortgage Insurance terminated automatically, and/or to receive a refund of any Mortgage Insurance premiums that were unearned at the time of such cancellation or termination.

11. **Assignment of Miscellaneous Proceeds; Forfeiture.** All Miscellaneous Proceeds are hereby assigned to and shall be paid to Lender.

If the Property is damaged, such Miscellaneous Proceeds shall be applied to restoration or repair of the Property, if the restoration or repair is economically feasible and Lender's security is not lessened. During such repair and restoration period, Lender shall have the right to hold such Miscellaneous Proceeds until Lender has had an opportunity to inspect such Property to ensure the work has been completed to Lender's satisfaction, provided that such inspection shall be undertaken promptly. Lender may pay for the repairs and restoration in a single disbursement or in a series of progress payments as the work is completed. Unless an agreement is made in writing or Applicable Law requires interest to be paid on such Miscellaneous Proceeds, Lender shall not be required to pay Borrower any interest or earnings on such Miscellaneous Proceeds. If the restoration or repair is not economically feasible or Lender's security would be lessened, the Miscellaneous Proceeds shall be applied to the sums secured by this Security Instrument, whether or not then due, with the excess, if any, paid to Borrower. Such Miscellaneous Proceeds shall be applied in the order provided for in Section 2.

In the event of a total taking, destruction, or loss in

value of the Property, the Miscellaneous Proceeds shall be applied to the sums secured by this Security Instrument, whether or not then due, with the excess, if any, paid to Borrower.

In the event of a partial taking, destruction, or loss in value of the Property in which the fair market value of the Property immediately before the partial taking, destruction, or loss in value is equal to or greater than the amount of the sums secured by this Security Instrument immediately before the partial taking, destruction, or loss in value, unless Borrower and Lender otherwise agree in writing, the sums secured by this Security Instrument shall be reduced by the amount of the Miscellaneous Proceeds multiplied by the following fraction: (a) the total amount of the sums secured immediately before the partial taking, destruction, or loss in value divided by (b) the fair market value of the Property immediately before the partial taking, destruction, or loss in value. Any balance shall be paid to Borrower.

In the event of a partial taking, destruction, or loss in value of the Property in which the fair market value of the Property immediately before the partial taking, destruction, or loss in value is less than the amount of the sums secured immediately before the partial taking, destruction, or loss in value, unless Borrower and Lender otherwise agree in writing, the Miscellaneous Proceeds shall be applied to the sums secured by this Security Instrument whether or not the

sums are then due.

If the Property is abandoned by Borrower, or if, after notice by Lender to Borrower that the Opposing Party (as defined in the next sentence) offers to make an award to settle a claim for damages, Borrower fails to respond to Lender within 30 days after the date the notice is given, Lender is authorized to collect and apply the Miscellaneous Proceeds either to restoration or repair of the Property or to the sums secured by this Security Instrument, whether or not then due. "Opposing Party" means the third party that owes Borrower Miscellaneous Proceeds or the party against whom Borrower has a right of action in regard to Miscellaneous Proceeds.

Borrower shall be in default if any action or proceeding, whether civil or criminal, is begun that, in Lender's judgment, could result in forfeiture of the Property or other material impairment of Lender's interest in the Property or rights under this Security Instrument. Borrower can cure such a default and, if acceleration has occurred, reinstate as provided in Section 19, by causing the action or proceeding to be dismissed with a ruling that, in Lender's judgment, precludes forfeiture of the Property or other material impairment of Lender's interest in the Property or rights under this Security Instrument. The proceeds of any award or claim for damages that are attributable to the impairment of Lender's interest in the Property are hereby assigned and shall be paid to Lender.

All Miscellaneous Proceeds that are not applied to restoration or repair of the Property shall be applied in the order provided for in Section 2.

12. **Borrower Not Released; Forbearance By Lender Not a Waiver.** Extension of the time for payment or modification of amortization of the sums secured by this Security Instrument granted by Lender to Borrower or any Successor in Interest of Borrower shall not operate to release the liability of Borrower or any Successors in Interest of Borrower. Lender shall not be required to commence proceedings against any Successor in Interest of Borrower or to refuse to extend time for payment or otherwise modify amortization of the sums secured by this Security Instrument by reason of any demand made by the original Borrower or any Successors in Interest of Borrower. Any forbearance by Lender in exercising any right or remedy including, without limitation, Lender's acceptance of payments from third persons, entities or Successors in Interest of Borrower or in amounts less than the amount then due, shall not be a waiver of or preclude the exercise of any right or remedy.

13. **Joint and Several Liability; Co-signers; Successors and Assigns Bound.** Borrower covenants and agrees that Borrower's obligations and liability shall be joint and several. However, any Borrower who co-signs this Security Instrument but does not execute the Note (a "co-signer"): (a) is co-signing this Security Instrument only to mortgage, grant, and convey the co-signer's interest in the Property under the terms of this Security Instrument; (b) is not personally obligated to pay the sums secured by this Security

Instrument; and (c) agrees that Lender and any other Borrower can agree to extend, modify, forbear, or make any accommodations with regard to the terms of this Security Instrument or the Note without the co-signer's consent.

Subject to the provisions of Section 18, any Successor in Interest of Borrower who assumes Borrower's obligations under this Security Instrument in writing, and is approved by Lender, shall obtain all of Borrower's rights and benefits under this Security Instrument. Borrower shall not be released from Borrower's obligations and liability under this Security Instrument unless Lender agrees to such release in writing. The covenants and agreements of this Security Instrument shall bind (except as provided in Section 20) and benefit the successors and assigns of Lender.

14. **Loan Charges.** Lender may charge Borrower fees for services performed in connection with Borrower's default, for the purpose of protecting Lender's interest in the Property and rights under this Security Instrument, including, but not limited to, attorneys' fees, property inspection and valuation fees. In regard to any other fees, the absence of express authority in this Security Instrument to charge a specific fee to Borrower shall not be construed as a prohibition on the charging of such fee. Lender may not charge fees that are expressly prohibited by this Security Instrument or by Applicable Law.

If the Loan is subject to a law which sets maximum

loan charges, and that law is finally interpreted so that the interest or other loan charges collected or to be collected in connection with the Loan exceed the permitted limits, then: (a) any such loan charge shall be reduced by the amount necessary to reduce the charge to the permitted limit; and (b) any sums already collected from Borrower which exceeded permitted limits will be refunded to Borrower. Lender may choose to make this refund by reducing the principal owed under the Note or by making a direct payment to Borrower. If a refund reduces principal, the reduction will be treated as a partial prepayment without any prepayment charge (whether or not a prepayment charge is provided for under the Note). Borrower's acceptance of any such refund made by direct payment to Borrower will constitute a waiver of any right of action Borrower might have arising out of such overcharge.

15. **Notices.** All notices given by Borrower or Lender in connection with this Security Instrument must be in writing. Any notice to Borrower in connection with this Security Instrument shall be deemed to have been given to Borrower when mailed by first-class mail or when actually delivered to Borrower's notice address if sent by other means. Notice to any one Borrower shall constitute notice to all Borrowers unless Applicable Law expressly requires otherwise. The notice address shall be the Property Address unless Borrower has designated a substitute notice address by notice to Lender. Borrower

shall promptly notify Lender of Borrower's change of address. If Lender specifies a procedure for reporting Borrower's change of address, then Borrower shall only report a change of address through that specified procedure. There may be only one designated notice address under this Security Instrument at any one time. Any notice to Lender shall be given by delivering it or by mailing it by first-class mail to Lender's address stated herein unless Lender has designated another address by notice to Borrower. Any notice in connection with this Security Instrument shall not be deemed to have been given to Lender until actually received by Lender. If any notice required by this Security Instrument is also required under Applicable Law, the Applicable Law requirement will satisfy the corresponding requirement under this Security Instrument.

16. **Governing Law; Severability; Rules of Construction.** This Security Instrument shall be governed by federal law and the law of the jurisdiction in which the Property is located. All rights and obligations contained in this Security Instrument are subject to any requirements and limitations of Applicable Law. Applicable Law might explicitly or implicitly allow the parties to agree by contract or it might be silent, but such silence shall not be construed as a prohibition against agreement by contract. In the event that any provision or clause of this Security Instrument or the Note conflicts with Applicable Law, such conflict shall not affect other provisions of this

Security Instrument or the Note which can be given effect without the conflicting provision.

As used in this Security Instrument: (a) words of the masculine gender shall mean and include corresponding neuter words or words of the feminine gender; (b) words in the singular shall mean and include the plural and vice versa; and (c) the word "may" gives sole discretion without any obligation to take any action.

17. **Borrower's Copy.** Borrower shall be given one copy of the Note and of this Security Instrument.

18. **Transfer of the Property or a Beneficial Interest in Borrower.** As used in this Section 18, "Interest in the Property" means any legal or beneficial interest in the Property, including, but not limited to, those beneficial interests transferred in a bond for deed, contract for deed, installment sales contract or escrow agreement, the intent of which is the transfer of title by Borrower at a future date to a purchaser.

If all or any part of the Property or any Interest in the Property is sold or transferred (or if Borrower is not a natural person and a beneficial interest in Borrower is sold or transferred) without Lender's prior written consent, Lender may require immediate payment in full of all sums secured by this Security Instrument. However, this option shall not be exercised by Lender if such exercise is prohibited by Applicable Law.

If Lender exercises this option, Lender shall give

Borrower notice of acceleration. The notice shall provide a period of not less than 30 days from the date the notice is given in accordance with Section 15 within which Borrower must pay all sums secured by this Security Instrument. If Borrower fails to pay these sums prior to the expiration of this period, Lender may invoke any remedies permitted by this Security Instrument without further notice or demand on Borrower.

19. **Borrower's Right to Reinstate After Acceleration.** If Borrower meets certain conditions, Borrower shall have the right to have enforcement of this Security Instrument discontinued at any time prior to the earliest of: (a) five days before sale of the Property pursuant to any power of sale contained in this Security Instrument; (b) such other period as Applicable Law might specify for the termination of Borrower's right to reinstate; or (c) entry of a judgment enforcing this Security Instrument. Those conditions are that Borrower: (a) pays Lender all sums which then would be due under this Security Instrument and the Note as if no acceleration had occurred; (b) cures any default of any other covenants or agreements; (c) pays all expenses incurred in enforcing this Security Instrument, including, but not limited to, reasonable attorneys' fees, property inspection and valuation fees, and other fees incurred for the purpose of protecting Lender's interest in the Property and rights under this Security Instrument; and (d) takes such action as Lender may reasonably require to assure that Lender's

interest in the Property and rights under this Security Instrument, and Borrower's obligation to pay the sums secured by this Security Instrument, shall continue unchanged. Lender may require that Borrower pay such reinstatement sums and expenses in one or more of the following forms, as selected by Lender: (a) cash; (b) money order; (c) certified check, bank check, treasurer's check, or cashier's check, provided any such check is drawn upon an institution whose deposits are insured by a federal agency, instrumentality or entity; or (d) Electronic Funds Transfer. Upon reinstatement by Borrower, this Security Instrument and obligations secured hereby shall remain fully effective as if no acceleration had occurred. However, this right to reinstate shall not apply in the case of acceleration under Section 18.

20. **Sale of Note; Change of Loan Servicer; Notice of Grievance.** The Note or a partial interest in the Note (together with this Security Instrument) can be sold one or more times without prior notice to Borrower. A sale might result in a change in the entity (known as the "Loan Servicer") that collects Periodic Payments due under the Note and this Security Instrument and performs other mortgage loan servicing obligations under the Note, this Security Instrument, and Applicable Law. There also might be one or more changes of the Loan Servicer unrelated to a sale of the Note. If there is a change of the Loan Servicer, Borrower will be given written notice of the change which will state the name and address of the new

Loan Servicer, the address to which payments should be made and any other information RESPA requires in connection with a notice of transfer of servicing. If the Note is sold and thereafter the Loan is serviced by a Loan Servicer other than the purchaser of the Note, the mortgage loan servicing obligations to Borrower will remain with the Loan Servicer or be transferred to a successor Loan Servicer and are not assumed by the Note purchaser unless otherwise provided by the Note purchaser.

Neither Borrower nor Lender may commence, join, or be joined to any judicial action (as either an individual litigant or the member of a class) that arises from the other party's actions pursuant to this Security Instrument or that alleges that the other party has breached any provision of, or any duty owed by reason of, this Security Instrument, until such Borrower or Lender has notified the other party (with such notice given in compliance with the requirements of Section 15) of such alleged breach and afforded the other party hereto a reasonable period after the giving of such notice to take corrective action. If Applicable Law provides a time period which must elapse before certain action can be taken, that time period will be deemed to be reasonable for purposes of this paragraph. The notice of acceleration and opportunity to cure given to Borrower pursuant to Section 22 and the notice of acceleration given to Borrower pursuant to Section 18 shall be deemed to satisfy the notice and opportunity to take corrective action provisions of this Section 20.

21. **Hazardous Substances.** As used in this Section 21: (a) "Hazardous Substances" are those substances defined as toxic or hazardous substances, pollutants, or wastes by Environmental Law and the following substances: gasoline, kerosene, other flammable or toxic petroleum products, toxic pesticides and herbicides, volatile solvents, materials containing asbestos or formaldehyde, and radioactive materials; (b) "Environmental Law" means federal laws and laws of the jurisdiction where the Property is located that relate to health, safety, or environmental protection; (c) "Environmental Cleanup" includes any response action, remedial action, or removal action, as defined in Environmental Law; and (d) an "Environmental Condition" means a condition that can cause, contribute to, or otherwise trigger an Environmental Cleanup.

Borrower shall not cause or permit the presence, use, disposal, storage, or release of any Hazardous Substances, or threaten to release any Hazardous Substances, on or in the Property. Borrower shall not do, nor allow anyone else to do, anything affecting the Property (a) that is in violation of any Environmental Law, (b) which creates an Environmental Condition, or (c) which, due to the presence, use, or release of a Hazardous Substance, creates a condition that adversely affects the value of the Property. The preceding two sentences shall not apply to the presence, use, or storage on the Property of small quantities of Hazardous Substances that are generally recognized to be appropriate to normal residential uses and to maintenance of the Property (including, but not limited to, hazardous substances in consumer products).

Borrower shall promptly give Lender written notice of (a) any investigation, claim, demand, lawsuit, or other action by any governmental or regulatory agency or private party involving the Property and any Hazardous Substance or Environmental Law of which Borrower has actual knowledge, (b) any Environmental Condition, including but not limited to, any spilling, leaking, discharge, release, or threat of release of any Hazardous Substance, and (c) any condition caused by the presence, use, or release of a Hazardous Substance which adversely affects the value of the Property. If Borrower learns, or is notified by any governmental or regulatory authority, or any private party, that any removal or other remediation of any Hazardous Substance affecting the Property is necessary, Borrower shall promptly take all necessary remedial actions in accordance with Environmental Law. Nothing herein shall create any obligation on Lender for an Environmental Cleanup.

NON-UNIFORM COVENANTS. Borrower and Lender further covenant and agree as follows:

22. **Acceleration; Remedies.** Lender shall give notice to Borrower prior to acceleration following Borrower's breach of any covenant or agreement in this Security Instrument (but not prior to acceleration under Section 18 unless Applicable Law provides otherwise). The notice shall specify: (a) the default; (b) the action

required to cure the default; (c) a date, not less than 30 days from the date the notice is given to Borrower, by which the default must be cured; and (d) that failure to cure the default on or before the date specified in the notice may result in acceleration of the sums secured by this Security Instrument and sale of the Property. The notice shall further inform Borrower of the right to reinstate after acceleration and the right to bring a court action to assert the non-existence of a default or any other defense of Borrower to acceleration and sale. If the default is not cured on or before the date specified in the notice, Lender at its option may require immediate payment in full of all sums secured by this Security Instrument without further demand and may invoke the power of sale and any other remedies permitted by Applicable Law. Lender shall be entitled to collect all expenses incurred in pursuing the remedies provided in this Section 22, including, but not limited to, reasonable attorneys' fees and costs of title evidence.

If Lender invokes the power of sale, Lender shall give a copy of a notice to Borrower in the manner provided in Section 15. Lender shall publish the notice of sale once a week for three consecutive weeks in a newspaper published in County, Alabama, and thereupon shall sell the Property to the highest bidder at public auction at the front door of the County Courthouse of this County. Lender shall deliver to the purchaser Lender's deed conveying the Property. Lender or its designee may purchase the Property at any sale. Borrower covenants and agrees that the proceeds of the sale shall be applied in the following order: (a) to all expenses of the sale, including, but not limited to, reasonable attorneys' fees; (b) to all sums secured by this Security Instrument; and (c) any excess to the person or persons legally entitled to it.

23. **Release.** Upon payment of all sums secured by this Security Instrument, Lender shall release this Security Instrument. Borrower shall pay any recordation costs. Lender may charge Borrower a fee for releasing this Security Instrument, but only if the fee is paid to a third party for services rendered and the charging of the fee is permitted under Applicable Law.

24. **Waivers.** Borrower waives all rights of homestead exemption in the Property and relinquishes all rights of courtesy and dower in the Property.

BY SIGNING BELOW, Borrower accepts and agrees to the terms and covenants contained in this Security Instrument and in any Rider executed by Borrower and recorded with it.

Witnesses:

(Seal)

Borrower:

(Seal)

[Space Below This Line For Acknowledgment]

MORTGAGE COMMITMENT LETTER

CONDITIONAL FIRST MORTGAGE LOAN COMMITMENT:

- $660,000 gross loan, purchase price $1.1M
- 12.9% payable monthly, 3 years interest only
- 3 pts. deferred origination fee
- 5% pre-payment penalty
- Tax and insurance escrow
- Title policy 125% of mortgage amount
- $1,000 prepaid commitment fee
- 1 pt. to Financial Group
- $240,000 to be escrowed for interior remodeling

SUBJECT TO LENDER APPROVAL OF THE FOLLOWING:

- Attorney approval of all documents
- Adequate insurance coverage; Lender name on Windstorm, Hazard & Flood
- Survey
- Credit report
- Financial statement and current #1040
- Interior and exterior inspection
- Lender approval of draw schedule for remodeling
- Recorded parking easement

_____ _____

John J. Smith,   Date
president

This commitment expires
10 days from this date

LOAN PACKAGE FROM BROKER

NAMB - Mortgage Loan Origination Agreement
(Must be adapted to conform to applicable state law)

You, the applicant(s), agree to enter into this Mortgage Loan Origination Agreement with **ALLSTATE MORTGAGE LOANS & INVESTMENTS** as an independent contractor to apply for a residential mortgage loan from a participating lender with which we from time to time contract upon such terms and conditions as you may request or a lender may require. You inquired into mortgage financing with **ALLSTATE MORTGAGE LOANS & INVESTMENTS** on **05/08/06**. We are licensed as a "Mortgage Broker" under

Section 1. Nature of Relationship
In connection with this mortgage loan we are acting as an independent contractor and not as your agent. We will enter into separate independent contractor agreements with various lenders. While we seek to assist you in meeting your financial needs, we do not distribute the products of all lenders or investors in the market and cannot guarantee the lowest price or best terms available in the market.

Section 2. Our Compensation
The lenders whose loan products we distribute generally provide their loan products to us at a wholesale rate. The retail price we offer you – your interest rate, total points and fees – will include our compensation. In some cases. we may be paid all of our compensation by either you or the lender. Alternatively, we may be paid a portion of our compensation by both you and the lender. For example, in some cases, if you would rather pay a lower interest rate, you may pay higher up-front points and fees. Also, in some cases, if you would rather pay less up-front, you may be able to pay some or all of our compensation indirectly through a higher interest rate in which case we will be paid directly by the lender. We also may be paid by the lender based on (i) the value of the Mortgage Loan or related servicing rights in the market place or (ii) other services, goods or facilities performed or provided by us to the lender.

Mortgage Loan Originator
Company Name: **ALLSTATE MORTGAGE LOANS & INVESTMENTS**
Address: **809 N.E. 25TH AVE.**
City, State, Zip: **OCALA, FL 34470**
Phone:
Fax:
Broker or Authorized Agent: _____
$\qquad$ Date

Borrower(s)
Name(s):
Address:
City, State, Zip:

By signing below, applicant(s) acknowledge receipt of a copy of this signed Agreement.

Borrower: _____
$\qquad$ Date

Co-Borrower: _____
$\qquad$ Date

Uniform Residential Loan Application

This application is designed to be completed by the applicant(s) with the Lender's assistance. Applicants should complete this form as "Borrower" or "Co-Borrower," as applicable. Co-Borrower information must also be provided (and the appropriate box checked) when ☐ the income or assets of a person other than the Borrower (including the Borrower's spouse) will be used as a basis for loan qualification or ☐ the income or assets of the Borrower's spouse or other person who has community property rights pursuant to state law will not be used as a basis for loan qualification, but his or her liabilities must be considered because the spouse or other person has community property rights pursuant to applicable law and Borrower resides in a community property state, the security property is located in a community property state, or the Borrower is relying on other property located in a community property state as a basis for repayment of the loan.

If this is an application for joint credit, Borrower and Co-Borrower each agree that we intend to apply for joint credit (sign below):

_____   _____
Borrower   Co-Borrower

I. TYPE OF MORTGAGE AND TERMS OF LOAN		
Mortgage ☐VA ☐Conventional ☐Other (explain) **Applied for:** ☐FHA ☐USDA Rural Housing Service	Agency Case Number	Lender Case Number
Amount $	Interest Rate %	**Amoritization Type:** ☐Fixed Rate ☐Other (explain) ☐GPM ☐ARM (type)

II. PROPERTY INFORMATION AND PURPOSE OF LOAN	
Subject Property Address (city, street, state and ZIP)	Number of Units
Legal Description of Subject Property (attach description if necessary)	Year Built
Purpose of Loan ☐Purchase ☐Construction ☐Other (explain): ☐Refinance ☐Construction-Permanent	**Property will be:** ☐Primary Residence ☐Secondary Residence ☐Investment

Complete this line if construction or construction-permanent loan.

Year Lot Acquired	Original Cost	Amount Existing Liens	(a) Present Value of Lot	(b) Cost of Improvements	Total (a + b)
	$	$	$	$	$

Complete this line if this is a refinance loan.

Year Acquired	Original Cost	Amount Existing Liens	Purpose of Refinance	Describe Improvements ☐made ☐to be made	
	$	$		Cost: $	

Title will be held in what Name(s)	Manner in which Title will be held	Estate will be held in: ☐Fee Simple ☐Leasehold (show expiration date)
Title will be held in what Name(s)		

Borrower	III. BORROWER INFORMATION	Co-Borrower

Borrower's Name (include Jr. or Sr. if applicable) | Co-Borrower's Name (include Jr. or Sr. if applicable)

Social Security Number	Home Phone (include area code)	DOB (mm/dd/yyyy)	Yrs. School	Social Security Number	Home Phone (include area code)	DOB (mm/dd/yyyy)	Yrs. School

☐Married ☐Unmarried (include ☐Separated single, divorced, widowed)	Dependents (not listed by Co-Borrower) no.	ages	☐Married ☐Unmarried (include ☐Separated single, divorced, widowed)	Dependents (not listed by Co-Borrower) no.	ages

Present Address (street, city, state, ZIP) | Present Address (street, city, state, ZIP)

☐Own ☐Rent _____No. Yrs. | ☐Own ☐Rent _____No. Yrs.

Borrower	IV. EMPLOYEE INFORMATION	Co-Borrower

Name & Address of Employer ☐Self Employed	Yrs. on this job	Name & Address of Employer ☐Self Employed	Yrs. on this job
	Yrs. employed in this line of work/ profession		Yrs. employed in this line of work/ profession

If employed in current position for less than two years or if currently employed in more than one position, complete the following:

Name & Address of Employer ☐Self Employed	Dates (from-to)	Name & Address of Employer ☐Self Employed	Dates (from-to)
	Monthy Income $		Monthy Income $
Position/Title/Type of Business	Business Phone (include area code)	Position/Title/Type of Business	Business Phone (include area code)

V. MONTHLY INCOME AND COMBINED HOUSING EXPENSE INFORMATION						
Gross Monthly Income	Borrower	Co-Borrower	Total	Combined Monthly Housing Expense	Present	Present
Base Empl. Income*	$	$	$	Rent	$	
Overtime	$	$	$	First Mortgage (P&I)	$	$

V. MONTHLY INCOME AND COMBINED HOUSING EXPENSE INFORMATION (cont.)						
Gross Monthly Income	Borrower	Co-Borrower	Total	Combined Monthly Housing Expense	Present	Proposed
Bonuses	$	$	$	Other Financing (P&I)	$	$
Commissions	$	$	$	Hazzard Insurance	$	$
Dividends/ Interest	$	$	$	Real Estate Taxes	$	$
Net Rental Income	$	$	$	Mortgage Insurance	$	$
Other (before completing, see the notice in "describe other income," below)				Homeowners Assn. Dues		
				Other:		
Total	$	$	$	Total	$	$

* Self Employed Borrower(s) may be required to provide additional documentation such as tax returns and financial statements.

Describe Other Income   Notice: Alimony, child support, or separate maintenance income need not be revealed if the Borrower (B) or Co-Borrower (C) does not choose to have it considered for repaying this loan.

BC		Monthly Amount
		$
		$

V. ASSETS AND LIABILITIES

This Statement and any applicable supporting schedules may be completed jointly by both married and unmarried Co-Borrowers if their assets and liabilities are sufficiently joined so that the Statement can be meaningfully and fairly presented on a combined basis; otherwise, separate Statements and Schedules are required. If the Co-Borrower section was completed about a non-applicant spouse or other person, this Statement and supporting schedules must be completed about that spouse or other person also.

Completed ☐Jointly ☐Not Jointly

ASSETS Description	Cash or Market Value	Liabilities and Pledged Assets. List the creditor's name, address, and account number for all outstanding debts, including automobile loans, revolving charge accounts, real estate loans, alimony, child support, stock pledges, etc. Use continuation sheet, if necessary. Indicate by (*) those liabilities, which will be satisfied upon sale of real estate owned or upon refinancing of the subject property.		
Cash Deposit toward purchase held by:	$			
List checking and savings accounts below		LIABILITIES	Monthly Payment & Months Left to Pay	Unpaid Balance
Name and address of Bank, S&L, or Credit Union		Name and address of Company	$ Payment/Months	$
Acct. no.	$	Acct. No.		

V. ASSETS AND LIABILITIES (cont.)			
List checking and savings accounts below	**LIABILITIES**	**Monthly Payment & Months Left to Pay**	**Unpaid Balance**
Name and address of Bank, S&L, or Credit Union	Name and address of Company	$ Payment/Months	$
	Acct. No.		
Acct. no. $	Name and address of Company	$ Payment/Months	$
	Acct. No.		
Acct. no. $	Name and address of Company	$ Payment/Months	$
	Acct. No.		
Acct. no. $	Name and address of Company	$ Payment/Months	$
Stocks and Bonds (Company name/number & description)	Acct. No.		
Life insurance net cash value Face amount: $ $	Name and address of Company	$ Payment/Months	$
Subtotal Liquid Assets $			
Real Estate onwed (enter market value from schedule of real estate owned) $			
Vested interest in retirement fund $			
Net worth of business(s) owned (attach financial statement) $	Acct. no.		
Automobiles owned (make & year) $	Alimony/Child Support/Separate Maintenance Payments owed to:	$	
Other Assets (itemize) $	Job Related Expense (child care, union dues, etc.)	$	
	Total Monthly Payments	$	
Total Assets a. $	Net Worth (a minus) ►	Total Liabilities b.	$

V. ASSETS AND LIABILITIES (cont.)

Schedule of Real Estate Owned (If additional properties are owned, use continuation sheet.)

Property Address (enter **S** if sold, **PS** if pending sale or **R** if rental being held for income) ▼	Type of Property	Present Market Value	Amount of Mortages & Liens	Gross Rental Income	Mortgage Payments	Insurance, Maintenace, Taxes & Misc.	Net Rental Income
		$	$	$	$	$	$
		$	$	$	$	$	$
		$	$	$	$	$	$
	Totals	$	$	$	$	$	$

List any additional names under which credit has previously been received and indicate appropriate creditor name(s) and account number(s):

Alternate Name	Creditor Name	Account Number

VII. DETAILS OF TRANSACTION / VIII. DECLARATIONS

VII. DETAILS OF TRANSACTION		VIII. DECLARATIONS	Borrower		Co-Borrower	
a. Purchase price	$	If you answer "Yes" to any questions a through i, please use continuation sheet for explanation.	Yes	No	Yes	No
b. Alterations, improvements, repairs						
c. Land (if acquired separately)		a. Are there any outstanding judgments against you?	☐	☐	☐	☐
d. Refinance (incl. debts to be paid off)		b. Have you been declared bankrupt within the past 7 years?	☐	☐	☐	☐
e. Estimated prepaid items		c. Have you had property foreclosed upon or given title or deed in lieu thereof in the last 7 years?	☐	☐	☐	☐
f. Estimated closing costs		d. Are you a party to a lawsuit?	☐	☐	☐	☐
g. PMI, MIP, Funding Fee		e. Have you directly or indirectly been obligated on any loan which resulted in foreclosure, transfer of title in lieu of foreclosure, or judgment?	☐	☐	☐	☐
h. Discount (if Borrower will pay)		(This would include such loans as home mortgage loans, SBA loans, home improvement loans, educational loans, manufactured (mobile) home loans, any mortgage, financial obligation, bond, or loan guarantee. If "Yes," provide details, including date, name, and address of Lender, FHA or VA case number, if any, and reasons for the action.)				
i. Total costs (add items a through h)						
j. Subordinate financing						
k. Borrower's closing costs paid by Seller		f. Are you presently delinquent or in default on any Federal debt or any other loan, mortgage, financial obligation, bond, or loan guarantee?	☐	☐	☐	☐
l. Other Credits (explain)						

VII. DETAILS OF TRANSACTION		VIII. DECLARATIONS				
		If you answer "Yes" to any questions a through i, please use continuation sheet for explanation.	**Borrower**		**Co-Borrower**	
			Yes No		Yes No	
m. Loan amount (exclude PMI, MIP, Funding Fee financed)		g. Are you obligated to pay alimony, child support, or separate maintenance?	☐	☐	☐	☐
n. PMI, MIP, Funding Fee financed		h. Is any part of the down payment borrowed?	☐	☐	☐	☐
o. Loan amount (add m & n)		i. Are you a co-maker or endorser on a note?	☐	☐	☐	☐
p. Cash from/to Borrower (subtract j, k, l & o from i)		j. Are you a U.S. citizen?	☐	☐	☐	☐
		k. Are you a permanent resident alien?	☐	☐	☐	☐
		l. Do you intend to occupy the property as your primary residence? If "Yes," complete question m below.	☐	☐	☐	☐
		m. Have you had an ownership interest in a property in the last three years?	☐	☐	☐	☐
		(1) What type of property did you own—principal residence (PR), second home (SH), or investment property (IP)?	———		———	
		(2) How did you hold title to the home—solely by yourself (S), jointly with your spouse (SP), or jointly with another person (O)?	———		———	

IX. ACKNOWLEDGEMENT AND AGREEMENT

Each of the undersigned specifically represents to Lender and to Lender's actual or potential agents, brokers, processors, attorneys, insurers, servicers, successors and assigns and agrees and acknowledges that: (1) the information provided in this application is true and correct as of the date set forth opposite my signature and that any intentional or negligent misrepresentation of this information contained in this application may result in civil liability, including monetary damages, to any person who may suffer any loss due to reliance upon any misrepresentation that I have made on this application, and/or in criminal penalties including, but not limited to, fine or imprisonment or both under the provisions of Title 18, United States Code, Sec. 1001, et seq.; (2) the loan requested pursuant to this application (the "Loan") will be secured by a mortgage or deed of trust on the property described in this application;

Borrower's Signature	Date	Co-Borrower's Signature	Date
X		X	

IX. ACKNOWLEDGEMENT AND AGREEMENT

The following information is requested by the Federal Government for certain types of loans related to a dwelling in order to monitor the lender's compliance with equal credit opportunity, fair housing and home mortgage disclosure laws. You are not required to furnish this information, but are encouraged to do so. The law provides that a lender may not discriminate either on the basis of this information, or on whether you choose to furnish it. If you furnish the information, please provide both ethnicity and race. For race, you may check more than one designation. If you do not furnish ethnicity, race, or sex, under Federal regulations, this lender is required to note the information on the basis of visual observation and surname if you have made this application in person. If you do not wish to furnish the information, please check the box below. (Lender must review the above material to assure that the disclosures satisfy all requirements to which the lender is subject under applicable state law for the particular type of loan applied for.) (3) the property will not be used for any illegal or prohibited purpose or use; (4) all statements made in this application are made for the purpose of obtaining a residential mortgage loan; (5) the property will be occupied as indicated in this application; (6) the Lender, its servicers, successors or assigns may retain the original and/or an electronic record of this application, whether or not the Loan is approved; (7) the Lender and its agents, brokers, insurers, servicers, successors, and assigns may continuously rely on the information contained in the application, and I am obligated to amend and/or supplement the information provided in this application if any of the material facts that I have represented herein should change prior to closing of the Loan; (8) in the event that my payments on

IX. ACKNOWLEDGEMENT AND AGREEMENT (cont.)

the Loan become delinquent, the Lender, its servicers, successors or assigns may, in addition to any other rights and remedies that it may have relating to such delinquency, report my name and account information to one or more consumer reporting agencies; (9) ownership of the Loan and/or administration of the Loan account may be transferred with such notice as may be required by law; (10) neither Lender nor its agents, brokers, insurers, servicers, successors or assigns has made any representation or warranty, express or implied, to me regarding the property or the condition or value of the property; and (11) my transmission of this application as an "electronic record" containing my "electronic signature," as those terms are defined in applicable federal and/or state laws (excluding audio and video recordings), or my facsimile transmission of this application containing a facsimile of my signature, shall be as effective, enforceable and valid as if a paper version of this application were delivered containing my original written signature. Acknowledgement. Each of the undersigned hereby acknowledges that any owner of the Loan, its servicers, successors and assigns, may verify or reverify any information contained in this application or obtain any information or data relating to the Loan, for any legitimate business purpose through any source, including a source named in this application or a consumer reporting agency.

BORROWER ☐ I do not wish to furnish this information	**CO-BORROWER** ☐ I do not wish to furnish this information
Ethnicity: ☐Hispanic or Latino ☐Not Hispanic or Latino	**Ethnicity:** ☐Hispanic or Latino ☐Not Hispanic or Latino
Race: ☐American Indian or Alaska Native ☐Asian ☐Black or African American ☐Native Hawaiian or Other Pacific Islander ☐White		**Race:** ☐American Indian or Alaska Native ☐Asian ☐Black or African American ☐Native Hawaiian or Other Pacific Islander ☐White
Sex: ☐Female ☐Male	**Sex:** ☐Female ☐Male

IX. ACKNOWLEDGEMENT AND AGREEMENT (cont.)

To be Completed by Interviewer This application was taken by: ☐Face-to-face interview ☐Mail ☐Telephone ☐Internet	Interviewer's Name (print or type)	Name and Address of Interviewer's Employer
	Interviewer's Signature Date	
	Interviewer's Phone Number (incl. area code)	

Mortgage Brokerage Business Contract

(hereinafter called Borrower), employs
(hereinafter called Business) to obtain a mortgage loan commitment (hereinafter called Commitment) within days from the date hereof and acknowledges that Business cannot make loans or commitments or guarantee acceptance into specific programs, terms or conditions of any loan. However, Business may issue a rate lock-in or commitment on behalf of a lender to the Borrower.

I. PROPERTY:
Address:

Borrower's estimates of fair market value: $
Borrower's estimates of the balances on any existing mortgage loan: $

II. TERMS OF LOAN APPLICATION:
Loan Amount: $ Interest Rate: %   Loan Term/Due In: months   months
Monthly Payment: $
Loan Type: ☐ First Mortgage ☐ Second/Junior Mortgage

III. MORTGAGE BROKERAGE FEE
Business, in consideration of the Borrower's agreement to pay a mortgage brokerage fee along with actual costs incurred in connection with this loan, agrees to exert its best efforts to obtain a bona fide mortgage loan commitment in accordance with the terms (or better terms) and conditions set forth herein. The Business and its associates or employees shall be held harmless from any liability resulting from failure to obtain said loan commitment. Borrower hereby agrees to pay the actual costs as estimated herein and Borrower agrees to pay Business a mortgage brokerage fee of $ for obtaining the commitment. Additionally, Borrower acknowledges that Business may receive additional compensation from Lender based on the mortgage program and terms Borrower has engaged Business to obtain in securing the commitment and that Business will receive a sum in range of %   to   % of the total loan amount. This additional compensation, the exact amount of which will be disclosed at the time of closing, is part of the total brokerage fee due Business. In no event will the brokerage fee, additional compensation included, exceed the maximum fee permitted by the applicable state law.

IV. APPLICATION FEE
An application fee is charged for the initial cost of processing, verifying and preparing your loan package to submit to a lender for commitment, and will be credited against the amount the Borrower owes if closing occurs. This fee is ☐Refundable ☐Nonrefundable ☐Applicable to your closing costs at the time of the settlement of your loan. Business acknowledges the receipt of $ as an Application Fee.

V. DEPOSIT
Business acknowledge the deposit of $ will be used toward the costs incurred by the

Business, or by third party, on behalf of Borrower, to pay expenses necessary to secure the mortgage loan commitment. Actual costs incurred by the Business for items listed on Good Faith Estimate are non-refundable, even if the mortgage loan commitment is not received. In the event of default by the Borrower, Business is authorized to immediately disburse from the deposit all sums then due Business or any third party. The disbursement is not a waiver of any other sums due Business by Borrower, as more fully enumerated herein. Money retained by Business as the deposit shall be returned to the Borrower, within 60 days of disposition of the loan, in accordance with the following:

> (a) the services for which the money is expended are not performed.
> (b) the services for which the money is expended are performed, but there is an excess amount that would be paid as brokerage fee but this commitment is not obtained.

VI. SERVICES TO BE PROVIDED BY MORTGAGE BROKERAGE BUSINESS

In consideration for Business earning its fee, the services to be provided by Business are assembling information, compiling file, and completing credit application for borrower(s). Processing the application file includes verifying of information received and ordering vendor reports. Preparation and submission of completed file for conditional loan commitment between borrower(s) and lender. Incidental services necessary to obtain commitment including courier, express mail, photographs, telephone toll charges.

Applicant	Date	Mortgage Brokerage Business	License #
Applicant	Date	By	Date

Standards and Disclosures

COMMITMENT: Brokerage Business hereby agrees to act on behalf of Borrower to secure a mortgage loan commitment. Brokerage Business cannot guarantee acceptance into any particular loan program or promise that any specific loan terms or conditions will be obtained. Receipt of a mortgage loan commitment by Brokerage Business satisfies Brokerage Businesses obligation under the Mortgage Brokerage Business Contract and Good Faith Estimate of Borrower's Costs and the terms of this contract are deemed fulfilledupon receipt of the mortgage loan commitment. Brokerage Business cannot make a mortgage loan or a Mortgage Loan Commitment. A Commitment may, however, be passed through to the Borrower if received from a lender. The term "Commitment" shall mean a written or oral Commitment received by the Brokerage Business, unless otherwise agreed in writing between Brokerage Businessand Borrower. Upon demand by the Borrower, the Brokerage Business shall produce for the Borrower's inspection evidence of the mortgage loan commitment.

AGENCY; NON-LIABILITY FOR LENDER'S ACTS: Borrower acknowledges that Brokerage Business is acting as an 'agent on behalf of the Borrower in securing a mortgage commitment pursuant to this Agreement. Borrower acknowledges that Brokerage Business shall not be responsible for any errors of the Lender or Investor nor for any term or condition of the loan documentation that may be contrary to any or federal law. Brokerage Business shall not be responsible for any nonperformance of a commitment or mortgage by any Lender or Investor.

LITIGATION: In the event of any litigation arising out of this Agreement, Brokerage Business shall be entitled to all costs incurred, including attorney's fees, whether before trial, at trial, on appeal, or in any other administrative or quasi-judicial proceedings.

ADDITIONAL CLAUSES: If not precluded by the provisions of this Agreement, any loan commitment and loan obtained by Brokerage Business may contain such additional clauses or provisions as the Lender may request including but not limited to, nonassumable clauses, late fee clauses and prepayment penalties.

TIME FOR PAYMENT: Unless otherwise agreed between Brokerage Business and Borrower, mortgage brokerage fee shall be due and payable in full upon delivery to the Borrower of mortgage loan commitment from the Lender or Investor, or may be paid at closing, if agreed to by Brokerage Business.

DECISION: In applying for this loan, Borrower acknowledges that Borrower has reviewed his personal and financial situation and that it is in Borrower's best interest to proceed with the loan. Borrower further acknowledges that Borrower has not relied on the advice of the Mortgage Brokerage Business or its colleagues as to wisdom of doing so.

GOOD FAITH ESTIMATE OF COSTS: The estimated costs stated may be expressed as a range of possible costs and can be charged only when such costs have actually been incurred in connection with securing the loan or loan commitment. Actual costs incurred for items which include, but are not limited to, express mail fees, long distance calls and photographs will be paid by Borrower unless otherwise stated herein.

TITLE: Borrower represents and warrants that he is the fee simple title holder to the property described in this Agreement and there are no liens, judgements, unpaid taxes or mortgages which will effect title to the property except Borrower agrees to pay all costs necessary to clear any defect if status of the title differs from the representation made herein.

DEFAULT: If commitment is secured and title is not found to be good, marketable and insurable by the attorney or title company acting for the lender, or the Borrower refuses to execute and deliver the documents required by the lender, or in any other way fails to comply with this Agreement, or if for any reason the loan referred to herein cannot be closed through no fault of the Brokerage Business, Borrower acknowledges that the full brokerage fee has been earned by Brokerage Business and agrees to immediately pay same plus any and all costs incurred on Borrower's behalf.

commitment and loan obtained by Brokerage Business may contain such additional clauses or provisions as the Lender may request including but not limited to, nonassumable clauses, late fee clauses and prepayment penalties.

TIME FOR PAYMENT: Unless otherwise agreed between Brokerage Business and Borrower, the mortgage brokerage fee shall be due and payable in full upon delivery to the Borrower of mortgage loan commitment from the Lender or Investor, or may be paid at closing, if agreed to by Brokerage Business.

DECISION: In applying for this loan, Borrower acknowledges that Borrower has reviewed his personal and financial situation and that it is in Borrower's best interest to proceed with the loan. Borrower further acknowledges that Borrower has not relied on the advice of the Mortgage Brokerage Business or its colleagues as to wisdom of doing so.

GOOD FAITH ESTIMATE OF COSTS: The estimated costs stated may be expressed as a range of possible costs and can be charged only when such costs have actually been incurred in connection with securing the loan or loan commitment. Actual costs incurred for items which include, but are not limited to, express mail fees, long distance calls and photographs will be paid by Borrower unless otherwise stated herein.

TITLE: Borrower represents and warrants that he is the fee simple title holder to the property described in this Agreement and there are no liens, judgements, unpaid taxes or mortgages which will effect title to the property except Borrower agrees to pay all costs necessary to clear any defect if status of the title differs from the representation made herein .

DEFAULT: If commitment is secured and title is not found to be good, marketable and insurable by the attorney or title company acting for the lender, or the Borrower refuses to execute and deliver the documents required by the lender, or in any other way fails to comply with this Agreement, or if for any reason the loan referred to herein cannot be closed through no fault of the Brokerage Business, Borrower acknowledges that the full brokerage fee has been earned by Brokerage Business and agrees to immediately pay same plus any and all costs incurred on Borrower's behalf.

DISCLOSURE: Borrower acknowledges that Brokerage Business has advised him any existing business relationship Brokerage Business has with any vendor. Borrower also acknowledges that Lender may require certain preapproved vendors be used exclusively for services required by this agreement. Brokerage Business has no business relationship with any vendor except as may be listed on attached Provider Relationship form.

SEVERABILITY OF CLAUSES CONTAINED HEREIN: In the event that any part or portion of this Agreement is held invalid or unlawful through any administrative, quasi-judicial, or judicial proceeding, the invalidity or illegality thereof shall not effect the validity of this Agreement as a whole and the other provisions and terms contained herein shall remain in full force and effect as if the illegal or invalid provision had been eliminated.

_____	_____	_____	_____
Applicant	Date	Applicant	Date

Federal Truth in Lending Disclosure Statement

Creditor: Borrower(s):   Account Number:

Annual Percentage Rate The cost of your credit as a yearly rate	Finance Charge The dollar amount the credit will cost you	Amount Financed The amount of credit provided to you or on your behalf	Total of Payments The amount you will have paid after you have made all payments as scheduled

Your payment schedule will be:

Number of Payments	Amount of Payments	When Payments are Due

Variable rate: ☐ If checked, your load contains a variable rate feature. Disclosures about the variable rate feature have been provided to you earlier.

Demand Feature: ☐ If checked, this obligation has a demand feature.

Insurance: You may obtain property insurance from anyone you want that is acceptable to the creditor.
☐ If checked, you can get insurance through Your Favorite Mortgage Corporation. You will pay $ _____ for 12 months hazard insurance coverage. You will pay $ _____ for 12 months flood insurance coverage.

Security: You are giving a security interest in _____ property located at
_____

Assignment of brokerage account and pledge of securities Personal property: stocks and lease

Assignment of life insurance policy   Other:

Late Charges: If a payment is late, you will be charged 5.000% of the payment.

Prepayment: If you pay off early, you ☐ may ☐ will not have to pay a penalty. You ☐ may ☐ will not be entitled to a refund of part of the finance charge.

Assumption: Someone buying your house ☐ may, subject to conditions, be allowed to ☐ cannot assume the remainder of the mortgage on the original terms.

See your contract documents for any additional information about nonpayment, default, and required repayment in full before the scheduled date, prepayment refunds and penalties and assumption policy.

ACKNOWLEDGMENT

By signing below you acknowledge that you have received a completed copy of this Federal Truth in Lending Statement prior to the execution of any closing documents.

_____   _____
Borrower   Date

_____   _____
Borrower   Date

Definition of Truth in Lending Terms

ANNUAL PERCENTAGE RATE

This is not the Note rate for which the borrower applied. The Annual Percentage Rate (APR) is the cost of the loan in percentage terms taking into account various loan charges of which interest is only one such charge. Other charges which are used in calculation of the Annual Percentage Rate are Private Mortgage Insurance or FHA Mortgage Insurance Premium (when applicable) and Prepaid Finance Charges (loan discount, origination fees, prepaid interst and other credit costs). The APR is calculated by spreading these charges over the life of the loan which results in a rate higher than the interest rate shown on your Mortgage/Deed of Trust Note. If interest was the only Finance Charge, then the interest rate and the Annual Percentage Rate would be the same.

PREPAID FINANCE CHARGES

Prepaid Finance Charges are certain charges made in connection with the loan and which must be paid upon the close of the loan. These charges are defined by the Federal Reserve Board in Regulation Z and the charges must be paid by the borrower. Non-inclusive examples of such charges are: Loan origination fee, "Points" or Discount, Private Mortgage Insurance or FHA Mortgage Insurance, Tax Service Fee. Some loan charges are specifically excluded from the Prepaid Finance Charge such as appraisal fees and credit report fees.

Prepaid Finance Charges are totaled and then subtracted from the Loan Amount (the face amount of the Deed of Trust/Mortgage Note). The net figure is the Amount Financed as explained below.

FINANCE CHARGE

The amount of interest, prepaid finance charge and certain insurance premiums (if any) which the borrower will be expected to pay over the life of the loan.

AMOUNT FINANCED

The Amount Financed is the loan amount applied for less the prepaid finance charges. Prepaid finance charges can be found on the Good Faith Estimate. For example if the borrower's note is for $100,000 and the Prepaid Finance Charges total $5,000 the Amount Financed would be $95,000. The Amount Financed is the figure on which the Annual Percentage Rate is based.

TOTAL OF PAYMENTS

This figure represents the total of all payments made toward principal, interest and mortgage insurance (if applicable).

PAYMENT SCHEDULE

The dollar figures in the Payment Schedule represent principal, interest, plus Private Mortgage Insurance (if applicable). These figures will not reflect taxes and insurance escrows or any temporary buydown payments contributed by the seller.

Disclosure Notices

Borrower(s):	Property Address:

( ) Occupancy Statement
This is to certify that I/we do not intend to occupy the subject property as my/our primary residence. I/We hereby certify under penalty of U.S. Criminal Code Section 1010 Title 18 U.S.C., that the above statement submitted for the purpose of obtaining mortgage insurance under the National Housing Act is true and correct.

Fair Credit Reporting Act
An investigation will be made as to the credit standing of all individuals seeking credit in this application. The nature and scope of any investigation will be furnished to you upon written request made within a reasonable period of time. In the event of denied credit due to an unfavorable consumer report, you will be advised of the identity of the Consumer Reporting Agency making such report and of right to request within sixty (60) days the reason for the adverse action, pursuant to provisions of section 615(b) of the Fair Credit Reporting Act.

Equal Credit Opportunity Act
The Equal Credit Opportunity Act prohibits creditors from discriminating against credit applicants on the basis of race, color, religion, national origin, sex, marital status, age (provided the applicant has the capacity to enter into a binding contract); because all or part of the applicant's income derives from any public assistance prgram; or because the applicant has in good faith exercised any right under the Consumer Credit Protection Act. Income which you receive as alimony, child support, or separate maintenance need not be disclosed to this creditor unless you choose to rely on such sources to qualify for the loan. Income from these and other sources, including part-time or temporary employment, will not be discounted by this lender because of your sex or marital status. However, we will consider very carefully the stability and probable continuity of any income you disclose to us. The Federal Agency that administers compliance with this law concerning this creditor is:

( ) Right to Financial Privacy Act
I/We acknowledge that this is notice to me/us as required by the Right to Financial Privacy Act of 1978 that the Veterans Administration (in the case of a VA Loan) or Department of Housing and Urban Development in the case of an FHA Loan has a right of access to financial records held by financial institutions in connection with the consideration or administration of assistance to me/us. Financial records involving my/our transactions will be available to the VA (in the case of a VA loan) or in HUD (in the case of an FHA loan) without further notice or authorization but will not be disclosed or released to another government agency or department without my/our consent, except as required or permitted by law.

( ) Information Disclosure Authorization
I/We hereby authorize you to release to **ALLSTATE MORTGAGE LOANS & INVESTMENTS** for verification purposes, information concerning:
- ( ) Employment History, dates, title(s), income, hours worked, etc.
- ( ) Banking (checking & savings) account of record
- ( ) Mortgage loan rating, (opening date, high credit, payment amount, loan balance and payment)
- ( ) Any information deemed necessary in connection wth consumer credit report for real estate transaction

This information is for the confidential use of this lender in compiling a mortgage loan credit report. A copy of this authorization may be deemed to be the equivalent of the original and may be used as a duplicate original.

(   ) Anti-Coercion Statement

The insurance laws of this state provide that the lender may not require the applicant to take insurance through any particular insurance agent or company to protect the mortgaged property. The applicant, subject to the rules adopted by the Insurance Commissioner, has the right to have tthe insurance placed with an insurance agent or company of his choice, provided the company meets the requirements of the lender. The lender has the right to designate reasonable financial requirements as to the company and the adequacy of the coverage.

I have read the foregoing statement, or the rules of the Insurance Commissioner relative thereto, and understand my rights and priveleges and those of the lender relative to the placing of such insurance. I have selected the following agencies to write the insurance covering the property described above:

(   ) Flood insurance Notification

Federal regulations require us to inform you that the property used as security for this loan is located in an area identified by the U.S. Secretary of Housing & Urban Development as having special flood hazards and that in the event of damage to the property caused by flooding in a federally-declared disaster, federal disaster relief assistance, if authorized, will be available for the property.

At the closing you will be asked to acknowledge your receipt of this information. If you have any questions concerning this notice, kindly contact your loan officer.

Important: Please notify your insurance agent that the "loss payee" clause for the mortgagee on both the hazard and flood insurance must read as follows, unless otherwise advised:

(   ) Consumer Handbook on Adjustable Rate Mortgages

I/We hereby acknowledge receipt from **ALLSTATE MORTGAGE LOANS & INVESTMENTS** of a copy of the book titled "Consumer Handbook on Adjustable Rate Mortgages" published by the Federal Reserve Board and the Federal Home Loan Bank Board which is provided in addition to other required adjustable rate mortgage disclosures.

I/We hereby certify that ilw have read the Notices set forth above and fully understand all of the above.

Borrower	Date
Borrower	Date
Borrower	Date
Borrower	Date

Notice to Borrower

Pursuant to the Florida Fair Lending Act

It you obtain this high-cost home loan, the lender will have a mortgage on your home. You could lose your home and any money you have put into it if you do not meet your obligations under the loan.

Mortgage loan rates and closing costs and fees vary based on many factors, including your particular credit and financial circumstances, your employment history, the loan-tovalue requested, and the type of property that will secure your loan. The loan rate and fees could also vary based upon which lender or broker you select. As a borrower, you should shop around and compare loan rates and fees.

You should also consider consulting a qualified independent credit counselor or other experienced financial adviser regarding the rates, fees, and provisions of this mortgage loan before you proceed. You should contact the United States Department of Housing and Urban Development for a list of credit counselors available in your area.

You are not required to complete this agreement merely because you have received these disclosures or have signed a loan application.

Borrowing for the purpose of debt consolidation can be an appropriate financial management tool. However, if you continue to incur significant new credit card charges or other debts after this high-cost home loan is closed and then experience financial difficulties, you could lose your home and any equity you have in it if you do not meet your mortgage loan obligations.

Remember that property taxes and homeowners' insurance are your responsibility. Not all lenders provide escrow scrviccs for thcsc payments. You should ask your lender about these services.

Also, your payments on existing debts contribute to your credit rating. You should not accept any advice to ignore your regular payments to your existing creditors.

_____   _____

Borrower   Date

_____   _____

Borrower   Date

Borrower's Certification & Authorization

Certification

The undersigned certify the following:

1. I/We have applied for a mortgage loan from **ALLSTATE MORTGAGE LOANS & INVESTMENTS** In applying for the loan,

   I/We completed a loan application containing various information on the purpose of the loan, the amount and source of the downpayment, employment and Income information, and assets and liabilities. I/We certify that all of the information is true and complete. I/We mad no misrepresentations In the loan application or other documents, nor did I/We omit any pertinent information.

2. I/We understand and agree that **ALLSTATE MORTGAGE LOANS & INVESTMENTS** reserves the right 10 change the mortgage loan review process to a full documentation program. This may include verifying the information provided on the application with the employer and/or the financial institution.

3. I/We fully understand that it is a Federal crime punishable by fine or imprisonment, or both, to knowingly make any false statements when applying for this mortgage, as applicable under the provisions of Title 18, United States Code, Section 1014.

Authorization to Release Information

To Whom It May Concern:

1. I/We have applied for a mortgage loan from **ALLSTATE MORTGAGE LOANS & INVESTMENTS** As part ot the application process, **ALLSTATE MORTGAGE LOANS & INVESTMENTS** may verify information contained in my/our loan applicatio and in other documents required in connection with the loan, either before the loan is closed or as part of its quality control program.

2. I/We authorize you to provide to **ALLSTATE MORTGAGE LOANS & INVESTMENTS** and to any investor to whom **ALLSTATE MORTGAGE LOANS & INVESTMENTS** may sell my mortgage, any and all infonnation and documentation that they request. Such information includes, but is not limited to, employment history and income; bank, money market, and similar account balances; credit history; and copies of income tax returns.

3. **ALLSTATE MORTGAGE LOANS & INVESTMENT** any investor that purchases the mortgage may address this authorization to any party named in the loan application.

4. A copy of this authorization may be accepted as an original.

5. Your prompt reply to **ALLSTATE MORTGAGE LOANS & INVESTMENTS** or the Investor that purchased the mortgage is appreciated.

Borrower's Signature	Date	Social Security Number
Borrower's Signature	Date	Social Security Number

Notice to Applicant of Right to Receive Copy of Appraisal Report

Date:
Loan Number:
Property Address:

You have the right to receive a copy of the appraisal report to be obtained in connection with the loan for which you are applying, provided that you have paid for the appraisal. We must receive your written request no later than   days after we notify you about the action taken on your application or you withdraw your application. If you would like a copy of the appraisal report, contact:

ALLSTATE MORTGAGE LOANS & INVESTMENTS
809 N.E. 25TH AVE.
OCALA, FL 34470

_____   _____
Borrower   Date

_____   _____
Borrower   Date

_____   _____
Borrower   Date

_____   _____
Borrower   Date

Equal Credit Opportunity Act Notice

Property Address:	Loan Number:

The federal Equal Credit Opportunity Act prohibits creditors from discriminating against credit applicants on the basis of race, color, religion, national origin, sex, marital status, age (provided the applicant has the capacity to enter into a binding contract); because all or part of the applicant's income derives from any public assistance program; or because the applicant has in good faith exercised any right under the Consumer Credit Protection Act. The federal agency that administers compliance with this law concerning this creditor is:

Alimony, child support, or separate maintenance income need not be revealed if you do not wish to have it considered as a basis for reporting.

_____

Borrower   Date

_____

Co-Borrower   Date

The Housing Financial Discrimination Act of 1977
Fair Lending Notice

Property Address:	Lender: **ALLSTATE MORTGAGE LOANS** **& INVESTMENTS** **809 N.E. 25TH AVE.** **OCALA, FL 34470**
Property Address:	Date:

It is illegal to discriminate in the provision of or in the availability of financial assistance because of the consideration of:

1. Trends, characteristics or conditions in the neighborhood or geographic area surrounding a housing accommodation, unless the financial institution can demonstrate in the particular case that such consideration is required to avoid an unsafe and unsound business practice; or

2. Race, color, religion, sex, marital status, domestic partnership, national origin or ancestry.

It is illegal to consider the racial, ethnic, religious or national origin composition of a neighborhood or geographic area surrounding a housing accommodation or whether or not such composition is undergoing change, or is expected to undergo change, in appraising a housing accommodation or in determining whether or not, or under what terms and conditions, to provide financial assistance.

These provisions govern financial assistance for the purpose of the purchase, construction, rehabilitation or refinancing of one- to four-unit family residences occupied by the owner and for the purpose of the home improvement of any one- to four-unit family residence.

If you have any questions about your rights, or if you wish to file a complaint, contact the management of this financial institution or the Department of Real Estate at one of the following locations:

ACKNOWLEDGEMENT OF RECEIPT

I/We received a copy of this notice.

_____   _____
Borrower   Date

_____   _____
Co-Borrower   Date

Credit Authorization

1. To all consumer-reporting agencies and to all creditors and depositories of the undersigned: Please be advised that the undersigned, and each of them, has made application to:
   ALLSTATE MORTGAGE LOANS & INVESTMENTS
   requesting an extension of credit to the undersigned. Therefore, the undersigned, and each of them, hereby authorizes you to provide credit report and/or a disclosure to Lender or any agent or balance. The undersigned also authorizes you to disclose your deposit or credit experiences with the undersigned to Lender or to third parties.

2. In addition, the undersigned, and each of them, hereby authorizes Lender to disclose to any third party, or any agent or employee thereof, information regarding the deposit or credit experience with any of the undersigned.

3. A photographic or carbon copy of this authorization bearing a photographic or carbon copy of the signature(s) of the undersigned may be deemed to be equivalent to the original hereof and may be used as a duplicate original.

_____

Borrower   Date

_____

Co-Borrower   Date

PRIVATE MORTGAGE INVESTING

Notice to the Home Loan Applicant
Credit Score Information Disclosure

Borrower(s) Name and Address:	Lender Name and Address:

In connection with your application for a home loan, the lender must disclose to you the score that a credit bureau distributed to users and the lender used in connection with your home loan, and the key factors affecting your credit scores.

The credit score is a computer-generated summary calculated at the time of the request and based on information a credit bureau or lender has on file. The scores are based on data about your credit history and payment patterns. Credit scores are important because they are used to assist the lender in determining whether you will obtain a loan. They may also be used to determine what interest rate you may be offered on the mortgage. Credit scores can change over time, depending on your conduct, how your credit history and payment patterns change, and how credit-scoring technologies change.

Because the score is based on information in your credit history, it is very important that you review the credit-related information that is being furnished to make sure it is accurate. Credit records may vary from one company to another.

If you have questions about your credit score or the credit information that is furnished to you, contact the credit bureau at the address and telephone number provided with this notice, or contact the lender, if the lender developed or generated the credit score. The credit bureau plays no part in the decision to take any action on the loan application and is unable to provide you with specific reasons for the decision on a loan application.

If you have questions concerning the terms on the loan, contact the lender.

One or more of the following credit bureaus provided a credit score that was used in connection with your home loan application.

Credit Bureau #1

Phone:
Fax:
Model Used:
Range of Possible Scores: _____ to _____

Borrower

Name:_____ Score:_____ Date:_____
Key Factors: _____
_____
_____

Co-Borrower

Name:_____ Score:_____ Date:_____
Key Factors: _____
_____
_____

Notice to the Home Loan Applicant
Credit Score Information Disclosure

Credit Bureau #2

Phone:
Fax:
Model Used:
Range of Possible Scores: ____to____

Borrower

Name:_____Score:_____Date:_____
Key Factors: _____
_____
_____

Co-Borrower

Name:_____Score:_____Date:_____
Key Factors: _____
_____
_____

Credit Bureau #3

Phone:
Fax:
Model Used:
Range of Possible Scores: ____to____

Borrower

Name:_____Score:_____Date:_____
Key Factors: _____
_____
_____

Co-Borrower

Name:_____Score:_____Date:_____
Key Factors: _____
_____
_____

I/We have received a copy of this Credit Score Information Disclosure

_____   _____
Borrower   Date   Co-Borrower   Date

Experian	**Trans Union**	**Equifax Credit Information Services**
PO Box 2002	PO Box 1000	PO Box 740241
Allen, TX 75013	Chester, PA 19022	Atlanta, GA 30374
1-888-397-3742	1-800-888-4213	1-800-685-1111

RESPA Servicing Disclosure

Lender: Date:

NOTICE TO FIRST LIEN MORTGAGE LOAN APPICANTS: THE RIGHT TO COLLECT YOUR MORTGAGE LOAN PAYMENTS MAY BE TRANSFERRED. FEDERAL LAW GIVES YOU CERTAIN RELATED RIGHTS. IF YOUR LOAN IS MADE, SAVE THIS STATEMENT WITH YOUR LOAN DOCUMENTS. SIGN THE ACKNOWLEDGMENT AT THE END OF THIS STATEMENT ONLY IF YOU UNDERSTAND ITS CONTENTS.

Because you are applying for a mortgage loan covered by the Real Estate Settlement Procedures Act (RESPA) (12 U.S.C. Section 2601et. Seq.) you have certain rights under that Federal Law.

This statement tells you about those rights. It also tells you what the chances are that the servicing for this loan may be transferred to a different loan servicer. "Servicing" refers to collecting your principal, interest and escrow account payments, if any. If your loan servicer changes, there are certain procedures that must be followed. This statement generally explains those procedures.

Transfer Practices and Requirements

If the servicing of your loan is assigned, sold, or transferred to a new servicer, you must be given written notice of that transfer. The present loan servicer must send you notice in writing of the assignment, sale or transfer of the servicing not less than 15 days before the effective date of the transfer. The new loan servicer must also send you notice within 15 days after the effective date of the transfer. The present servicer and the new servicer may combine this information in one notice, so long as the notice is sent to you 15 days before the effective date of transfer. The 15 day period is not applicable if a notice of prospective transfer is provided to you at settlement. The law allows a delay in the time (no more than 30 days after a transfer) for servicers to notify you upon the occurrence of certain business emergencies.

Notices must contain certain information. They must contain the effective date of the transfer of the servicing of your loan to the new servicer, and the name, address, and toll-free or collect call telephone number of the new servicer, and toll-free or collect call telephone numbers of a person or department for both your present servicer and your new servicer to answer your questions. During the 60-day period following the effective date of the transfer of the loan servicing, a loan payment received by your old servicer before its due date may not be treated by the new loan servicer as late, and a late fee may not be imposed by you.

Complaint Resolution

Section 5 of RESPA (12 U.S.C. 2605) gives you certain consumer rights, whether or not your loan servicing is transferred. If you send a "qualified written request" to your servicer, your servicer must provide you with a written acknowledgment within 20 Business Days of receipt of your request. A "qualified written request" is written correspondence, other than notice on a payment coupon or other payment medium supplied by the servicer, which includes your name and account number, and the information regarding your request. Not later than 60 Business Days after receiving your request, your servicer must make any appropriate corrections to your account, or must provide you with a written clarification regarding any dispute. During this 60-Business Day period, your servicer may not provide information to a consumer reporting agency concerning any overdue payment related to such period or qualified written request.

A Business Day is any day in which the offices of the business entity are open to the public for carrying on substantially all of its business functions.

Damages and Costs

Section 6 or RESPA also provides for damages and costs for individuals or classes of individuals in circumstances where servicers are shown to have violated the requirements of that Section.

Servicing Transfer Estimates

1. The following is the best estimate of what will happen to the servicing of your mortgage loan:

   A. ☐ We may assign, sell or transfer the servicing of your loan while the loan Is outstanding. ☐ We are able to service your loan and we ☐ will ☐ will not ☐ haven't decided whether to service your loan.

   OR

   B. ☐ We do not service mortgage loans, ☐ and we have not serviced mortgage loans in the past three years. We presently intend to assign, sell or transfer the servicing of your mortgage loan. You will be informed about your servicer.

2. For all first lien mortgage loans that we make in the 12-month period after your mortgage loan is funded, we estimate that the percentage of mortgage loans for which we will transfer servicing is between:

   _____ (0 to 25%) or)None) _____26 to 50% _____51 to 75% ____(76 to 100%) or (All)

3. A. ☐ We have previously assigned, sold or transferred the servicing of first lien loans.

   OR

   B. ☐ This is our record of transferring the servicing of the first-lien mortgage loans we have made in the past:

Year	**Percentage of Loans Transferred** (rounded to nearest quartile—0, 25%, 50%, 75%, or 100%)
_____	_____%
_____	_____%
_____	_____%
_____	_____%

   This information ☐ does ☐ does not include assignments, sales or transfers to affiliates or subsidiaries.

Acknowledgment of Mortgage Loan Applicant(s)

I/We have read this disclosure form, and understand its contents, as evidenced by my/our signature(s) below. I/We understand that this acknowledgment is required as part of the mortgage loan application.

_____   _____

Borrower   Date   Borrower   Date

Monthly Amortization Schedule

PMT. #	YEAR	PMT. DATE	PAYMENT	PRINCIPAL	INTEREST	PMI	BALANCE
1	1	05/08/06	1,028.61	28.61	1,000.000	0.00	99,971.39
2	1	06/08/06	1,028.61	28.90	999.71	0.00	99,942.49
3	1	07/08/06	1,028.61	29.19	999.42	0.00	99,913.30
4	1	08/08/06	1,028.61	29.48	999.13	0.00	99,883.82
5	1	09/08/06	1,028.61	29.77	998.94	0.00	99,854.05
6	1	10/08/06	1,028.61	30.07	998.54	0.00	99,823.98
7	1	11/08/06	1,028.61	30.37	998.24	0.00	99,793.61
8	1	12/08/06	1,028.61	30.67	997.94	0.00	99,762.94
9	1	01/08/07	1,028.61	30.98	997.63	0.00	99,731.96
10	1	02/08/07	1,028.61	31.29	997.32	0.00	99,700.67
11	1	03/08/07	1,028.61	31.60	997.01	0.00	99,669.07
12	1	04/08/07	1,028.61	31.92	996.69	0.00	99,637.15
13	2	05/08/07	1,028.61	32.24	996.37	0.00	99,604.91
14	2	06/08/07	1,028.61	32.65	996.05	0.00	99,572.35
15	2	07/08/07	1,028.61	32.89	995.72	0.00	99,539.46
16	2	08/08/07	1,028.61	33.22	995.39	0.00	99,506.24
17	2	09/08/07	1,028.61	33.55	995.06	0.00	99,472.69
18	2	10/08/07	1,028.61	33.88	994.73	0.00	99,438.81
19	2	11/08/07	1,028.61	34.22	994.39	0.00	99,404.59
20	2	12/08/07	1,028.61	34.56	994.05	0.00	99,370.03
21	2	01/08/08	1,028.61	34.91	993.70	0.00	99,335.12
22	2	02/08/08	1,028.61	35.26	993.35	0.00	99,299.86
23	2	03/08/08	1,028.61	35.61	993.00	0.00	99,264.25
24	2	04/08/08	1,028.61	35.97	992.64	0.00	99,228.28
25	3	05/08/08	1,028.61	36.33	992.28	0.00	99,191.95
26	3	06/08/08	1,028.61	36.69	991.92	0.00	99,155.25
27	3	07/08/08	1,028.61	37.06	991.55	0.00	99,118.20
28	3	08/08/08	1,028.61	37.43	991.18	0.00	99,080.77
29	3	09/08/08	1,028.61	37.80	990.81	0.00	99,042.97
30	3	10/08/08	1,028.61	38.18	990.43	0.00	99,004.79
31	3	11/08/08	1,028.61	38.56	990.05	0.00	98,966.23
32	3	12/08/08	1,028.61	38.95	989.66	0.00	98,927.28
33	3	01/08/09	1,028.61	39.34	989.27	0.00	98,887.94
34	3	02/08/09	1,028.61	39.73	988.88	0.00	98,848.21
35	3	03/08/09	1,028.61	40.13	988.48	0.00	98,808.08
36	3	04/08/09	1,028.61	40.53	988.08	0.00	98,767.55
37	4	05/08/09	1,028.61	40.93	987.68	0.00	98,726.62
38	4	06/08/09	1,028.61	41.34	987.27	0.00	98,685.28
39	4	07/08/09	1,028.61	41.76	986.85	0.00	98,643.52
40	4	08/08/09	1,028.61	42.17	986.44	0.00	98,601.35
41	4	09/08/09	1,028.61	42.60	988.01	0.00	98,558.75
42	4	10/08/09	1,028.61	43.02	985.59	0.00	98,515.73
43	4	11/08/09	1,028.61	43.45	985.16	0.00	98,472.28
44	4	12/08/09	1,028.61 .	43.89	984.72	0.00	98,428.39
45	4	01/08/10	1,028.61	44.33	984.28	0.00	98,384.06
46	4	02/08/10	1,028.61	44.77	983.84	0.00	98,339.29
47	4	03/08/10	1,028.61	45.22	983.39	0.00	98,294.07
48	4	04/08/10	1,028.61	45.67	982.94	0.00	98,248.40
49	5	05/08/10	1,028.61	46.13	982.48	0.00	98,202.27
50	5	06/08/10	1,028.61	46.59	982.02	0.00	98,155.68
51	5	07/08/10	1,028.61	47.05	981.56	0.00	98,108.63
52	5	08/08/10	1,028.61	47.52	981.09	0.00	98,061.11
53	5	09/08/10	1,028.61	48.00	980.61	0.00	98,013.11
54	5	10/08/10	1,028.61	48.48	980.13	0.00	97,964.63
55	5	11/08/10	1,028.61	48.96	979.65	0.00	97,915.67

PMT. #	YEAR	PMT. DATE	PAYMENT	PRINCIPAL	INTEREST	PMI	BALANCE
56	5	12/08/10	1,028.61	49.45	979.16	0.00	97,866.22
57	5	01/08/11	1,028.61	49.95	978.66	0.00	97,816.27
58	5	02/08/11	1,028.61	50.45	978.16	0.00	97,765.82
59	5	03/08/11	1,028.61	50.95	977.66	0.00	97,714.87
60	5	04/08/11	1,028.61	51.46	977.15	0.00	97,663.41
61	6	05/08/11	1,028.61	51.98	976.63	0.00	97,611.43
62	6	06/08/11	1,028.61	52.50	976.11	0.00	97,558.93
63	6	07/08/11	1,028.61	53.02	975.59	0.00	97,505.91
64	6	08/08/11	1,028.61	53.55	975.06	0.00	97,452.36
65	6	09/08/11	1,028.61	54.09	974.52	0.00	97,398.27
66	6	10/08/11	1,028.61	54.63	973.98	0.00	97,343.64
67	6	11/08/11	1,028.61	55.17	973.44	0.00	97,288.47
68	6	12/08/11	1,028.61	55.73	972.33	0.00	97,232.74
69	6	01/08/12	1,028.61	56.28	972.33	0.00	97,176.46
70	6	02/08/12	1,028.61	56.85	971.76	0.00	97,119.61
71	6	03/08/12	1,028.61	57.41	971.20	0.00	97,062.20
72	6	04/08/12	1,028.61	57.99	970.62	0.00	97,004.21
73	7	05/08/12	1,028.61	58.57	970.04	0.00	96,945.64
74	7	06/08/12	1,028.61	59.15	969.46	0.00	96,886.49
75	7	07/08/12	1,028.61	59.73	968.86	0.00	96,826.74
76	7	08/08/12	1,028.61	60.34	968.27	0.00	96,766.40
77	7	09/08/12	1,028.61	60.95	967.66	0.00	96,705.45
78	7	10/08/12	1,028.61	61.56	967.05	0.00	96,643.89
79	7	11/08/12	1,028.61	62.17	966.44	0.00	96,581.72
80	7	12/08/12	1,028.61	62.79	965.82	0.00	96,518.93
81	7	01/08/13	1,028.61	63.42	965.19	0.00	96,455.51
82	7	02/08/13	1,028.61	64.05	964.56	0.00	96,391.48
83	7	03/08/13	1,028.61	64.70	963.91	0.00	96,326.76
84	7	04/08/13	1,028.61	65.34	963.27	0.00	96,261.42
85	8	05/08/13	1,028.61	66.00	962.61	0.00	96,195.42
86	8	06/08/13	1,028.61	66.66	951.95	0.00	95,128.76
87	8	07/08/13	1,028.61	67.32	961.29	0.00	96,061.44
88	8	08/08/13	1,028.61	68.00	960.51	0.00	95,993.44
89	8	09/08/13	1,028.61	68.68	959.93	0.00	95,924.76
90	8	10/08/13	1,028.61	69.36	959.25	0.00	95,855.40
91	8	11/08/13	1,028.61	70.06	958.55	0.00	95,785.34
92	8	12/08/13	1,028.61	70.76	957.85	0.00	95,714.58
93	8	01/08/14	1,028.61	71.46	957.15	0.00	95,643.12
94	8	02/08/14	1,028.61	72.18	956.43	0.00	95,570.94
95	8	03/08/14	1,028.61	72.90	955.71	0.00	95,498.04
96	8	04/08/14	1,028.61	73.63	954.98	0.00	95,424.41
97	9	05/08/14	1,028.61	74.37	954.24	0.00	95,350.04
98	9	06/08/14	1,028.61	75.11	953.50	0.00	95,274.93
99	9	07/08/14	1,028.61	75.86	952.75	0.00	95,199.07
100	9	08/08/14	1,028.61	76.62	951.99	0.00	95,122.45
101	9	09/08/14	1,028.61	77.39	951.22	0.00	95,045.06
102	9	10/08/14	1,028.61	78.16	950.45	0.00	94,966.90
103	9	11/08/14	1,028.61	78.94	949.67	0.00	94,887.96
104	9	12/08/14	1,028.61	79.73	948.88	0.00	94,808.23
105	9	01/08/15	1,028.61	80.53	948.08	0.00	94,727.70
106	9	02/08/15	1,028.61	81.33	947.28	0.00	94,646.37
107	9	03/08/15	1,028.61	82.15	946.46	0.00	94,584.22
108	9	04/08/15	1,028.61	82.97	945.64	0.00	94,481.25
109	10	05/08/15	1,028.61	83.80	944.81	0.00	94,397.45
110	10	06/08/15	1,028.61	84.64	943.97	0.00	94,312.81
111	10	07/08/15	1,028.61	85.48	943.13	0.00	94,227.33
112	10	08/08/15	1,028.61	86.34	942.27	0.00	94,140.99

PMT. #	YEAR	PMT. DATE	PAYMENT	PRINCIPAL	INTEREST	PMI	BALANCE
113	10	09/08/15	1,028.61	87.20	941.41	0.00	94053.79
114	10	10/08/15	1,028.61	88.07	940.54	0.00	93985.72
115	10	11/08/15	1,028.61	88.95	939.66	0.00	93876.77
116	10	12/08/15	1,028.61	89.84	938.77	0.00	93786.93
117	10	01/08/16	1,028.61	90.74	937.87	0.00	93696.19
118	10	02/08/16	1,028.61	91.65	936.96	0.00	93604.54
119	10	03/08/16	1,028.61	92.56	936.05	0.00	93511.98
120	10	04/08/16	1,028.61	93.49	935.12	0.00	93418.49
121	11	05/08/16	1,028.61	94.43	934.18	0.00	93324.05
122	11	06/08/16	1,028.61	95.37	933.24	0.00	93228.69
123	11	07/08/16	1,028.61	96.32	932.29	0.00	93132.37
124	11	08/08/16	1,028.61	97.29	931.32	0.00	93035.08
125	11	09/08/16	1,028.61	98.26	930.35	0.00	92936.82
126	11	10/08/16	1,028.61	99.24	929.37	0.00	92837.58
127	11	11/08/16	1,028.61	100.23	926.38	0.00	92737.35
128	11	12/08/16	1,028.61	101.24	927.37	0.00	92636.11
129	11	01/08/17	1,028.61	102.25	926.36	0.00	92533.86
130	11	02/08/17	1,028.61	103.27	925.34	0.00	92430.59
131	11	03/08/17	1,028.61	104.30	924.31	0.00	92326.29
132	11	04/08/17	1,028.61	105.35	923.26	0.00	92220.94
133	12	05/08/17	1,028.61	106.40	922.21	0.00	92114.54
134	12	06/08/17	1,028.61	107.48	921.15	0.00	92007.08
135	12	07/08/17	1,028.61	108.54	920.07	0.00	91898.54
136	12	08/08/17	1,028.61	109.62	918.99	0.00	91788.92
137	12	09/08/17	1,028.61	110.72	917.89	0.00	91678.20
138	12	10/08/17	1,028.61	111.83	916.78	0.00	91566.37
139	12	11/08/17	1,028.61	112.95	915.66	0.00	91453.42
140	12	12/08/17	1,028.61	114.08	914.53	0.00	91339.34
141	12	01/08/18	1,028.61	115.22	913.39	0.00	91224.12
142	12	02/08/18	1,028.61	116.37	912.24	0.00	91107.75
143	12	03/08/18	1,028.61	117.53	911.08	0.00	90990.22
144	12	04/08/18	1,028.61	118.71	909.90	0.00	90871.51
145	13	05/08/18	1,028.61	119.89	908.72	0.00	90751.62
146	13	06/08/18	1,028.61	121.09	907.52	0.00	90630.53
147	13	07/08/18	1,028.61	122.30	906.31	0.00	90508.23
148	13	08/08/18	1,028.61	123.53	905.08	0.00	90384.70
149	13	09/08/18	1,028.61	124.76	903.85	0.00	90259.94
150	13	10/08/18	1,028.61	126.01	902.60	0.00	90133.93
151	13	11/08/18	1,028.61	127.27	901.34	0.00	90006.66
152	13	12/08/18	1,028.61	128.54	900.07	0.00	89878.12
153	13	01/08/19	1,028.61	129.83	898.78	0.00	89748.29
154	13	02/08/19	1,028.61	131.13	897.48	0.00	89617.16
155	13	03/08/19	1,028.61	132.44	895.17	0.00	89484.72
156	13	04/08/19	1,028.61	133.76	894.85	0.00	89350.96
157	14	05/08/19	1,028.61	135.10	893.51	0.00	89215.86
158	14	06/08/19	1,028.61	136.45	892.16	0.00	89079.41
159	14	07/08/19	1,028.61	137.82	890.79	0.00	88941.59
160	14	08/08/19	1,028.61	139.19	889.42	0.00	88802.40
161	14	09/08/19	1,028.61	140.59	888.02	0.00	88661.81
162	14	10/08/19	1,028.61	141.99	886.62	0.00	88519.82
163	14	11/08/19	1,028.61	143.41	885.20	0.00	88376.41
164	14	12/08/19	1,028.61	144.85	883.76	0.00	88231.56
165	14	01/08/20	1,028.61	146.29	882.32	0.00	88085.27
166	14	02/08/20	1,028.61	147.76	880.85	0.00	87937.51
167	14	03/08/20	1,028.61	149.23	879.38	0.00	87788.28
168	14	04/08/20	1,028.61	150.73	877.88	0.00	87637.55
169	15	05/08/20	1,028.61	152.23	876.38	0.00	87485.32

PMT. #	YEAR	PMT. DATE	PAYMENT	PRINCIPAL	INTEREST	PMI	BALANCE
170	15	06/08/20	1,028.61	153.76	874.85	0.00	87331.56
171	15	07/08/20	1,028.61	155.29	873.32	0.00	87176.27
172	15	08/08/20	1,028.61	156.85	871.76	0.00	87019.42
173	15	09/08/20	1,028.61	158.42	870.19	0.00	86861.00
174	15	10/08/20	1,028.61	160.00	868.61	0.00	86701.00
175	15	11/08/20	1,028.61	161.60	867.01	0.00	86539.40
176	15	12/08/20	1,028.61	163.22	865.39	0.00	86376.18
177	15	01/08/21	1,028.61	164.85	863.76	0.00	86211.33
178	15	02/08/21	1,028.61	166.50	862.11	0.00	86044.83
179	15	03/08/21	1,028.61	168.16	860.45	0.00	85876.67
180	15	04/08/21	1,028.61	169.84	858.77	0.00	85706.83
181	16	05/08/21	1,028.61	171.54	857.07	0.00	85535.29
182	16	06/08/21	1,028.61	173.26	855.35	0.00	85362.03
183	16	07/08/21	1,028.61	174.99	853.62	0.00	85187.04
184	16	08/08/21	1,028.61	176.74	851.87	0.00	85010.30
185	16	09/08/21	1,028.61	178.51	850.10	0.00	84831.79
186	16	10/08/21	1,028.61	180.29	848.32	0.00	94651.50
187	16	11/08/21	1,028.61	182.09	846.52	0.00	84469.41
188	16	12/08/21	1,028.61	183.92	844.69	0.00	84285.49
189	16	01/08/22	1,028.61	185.75	842.86	0.00	84099.74
190	16	02/08/22	1,028.61	187.51	841.00	0.00	83912.13
191	16	03/08/22	1,028.61	189.49	839.12	0.00	83722.64
192	16	04/08/22	1,028.61	191.38	837.23	0.00	83531.26
193	17	05/08/22	1,028.61	193.30	835.31	0.00	83337.96
194	17	06/08/22	1,028.61	195.23	833.38	0.00	83142.73
195	17	07/08/22	1,028.61	197.18	831.43	0.00	82945.55
196	17	08/08/22	1,028.61	199.15	829.46	0.00	82746.40
197	17	09/08/22	1,028.61	201.15	827.46	0.00	82545.25
198	17	10/08/22	1,028.61	203.15	825.45	0.00	82342.09
199	17	11/08/22	1,028.61	205.19	823.42	0.00	82136.90
200	17	12/08/22	1,028.61	207.24	821.37	0.00	81929.66
201	17	01/08/23	1,028.61	209.31	819.30	0.00	81720.35
202	17	02/08/23	1,028.61	211.41	817.20	0.00	81508.94
203	17	03/08/23	1,028.61	213.52	815.09	0.00	81295.42
204	17	04/08/23	1,028.61	215.66	812.95	0.00	81079.76
205	18	05/08/23	1,028.61	217.81	810.80	0.00	80861.95
206	18	06/08/23	1,028.61	219.99	808.62	0.00	80641.96
207	18	07/08/23	1,028.61	222.19	806.42	0.00	80419.77
208	18	08/08/23	1,028.61	224.41	804.20	0.00	80195.36
209	18	09/08/23	1,028.61	226.66	801.95	0.00	79968.70
210	18	10/08/23	1,028.61	228.92	799.69	0.00	79739.78
211	18	11/08/23	1,028.61	231.21	797.40	0.00	79508.57
212	18	12/08/23	1,028.61	233.52	795.09	0.00	79275.05
213	18	01/08/24	1,028.61	235.86	792.75	0.00	79039.19
214	18	02/08/24	1,028.61	238.22	790.39	0.00	78800.97
215	18	03/08/24	1,028.61	240.60	788.01	0.00	78560.37
216	18	04/08/24	1,028.61	243.01	785.60	0.00	78317.38
217	19	05/08/24	1,028.61	245.44	783.17	0.00	78071.92
218	19	06/08/24	1,028.61	247.89	780.72	0.00	77824.03
219	19	07/08/24	1,028.61	250.37	778.24	0.00	77573.66
220	19	08/08/24	1,028.61	252.87	775.74	0.00	77320.79
221	19	09/08/24	1,028.61	255.40	773.21	0.00	77065.39
222	19	10/08/24	1,028.61	257.96	770.65	0.00	76807.43
223	19	11/08/24	1,028.61	260.54	768.07	0.00	76546.89
224	19	12/08/24	1,028.61	263.14	765.47	0.00	76283.75
225	19	01/08/25	1,028.61	265.77	762.84	0.00	76017.98
226	19	02/08/25	1,028.61	268.43	760.18	0.00	75749.55

PMT. #	YEAR	PMT. DATE	PAYMENT	PRINCIPAL	INTEREST	PMI	BALANCE
227	19	03/08/25	1,028.61	271.11	757.50	0.00	75,478.44
228	19	04/08/25	1,028.61	273.83	754.78	0.00	75,204.61
229	20	05/08/25	1,028.61	276.56	752.05	0.00	74,928.05
230	20	06/08/25	1,028.61	279.33	749.28	0.00	74,648.72
231	20	07/08/25	1,028.61	282.12	746.49	0.00	74,366.60
232	20	08/08/25	1,028.61	284.94	743.67	0.00	74,081.66
233	20	09/08/25	1,028.61	287.79	740.82	0.00	73,793.87
234	20	10/08/25	1,028.61	290.67	737.94	0.00	73,503.20
235	20	11/08/25	1,028.61	293.58	735.03	0.00	73,209.62
236	20	12/08/25	1,028.61	296.51	732.10	0.00	72,913.11
237	20	01/08/26	1,028.61	299.48	729.13	0.00	72,613.63
238	20	02/08/26	1,028.61	302.47	726.14	0.00	72,311.16
239	20	03/08/26	1,028.61	305.50	723.11	0.00	72,005.66
240	20	04/08/26	1,028.61	308.55	720.06	0.00	71,697.11
241	21	05/08/26	1,028.61	311.64	716.97	0.00	71,385.47
242	21	06/08/26	1,028.61	314.76	713.85	0.00	71,070.71
243	21	07/08/26	1,028.61	317.90	710.71	0.00	70,752.81
244	21	08/08/26	1,028.61	321.08	707.53	0.00	70,431.73
245	21	09/08/26	1,028.61	324.29	704.32	0.00	70,107.44
246	21	10/08/26	1,028.61	327.54	701.07	0.00	69,779.90
247	21	11/08/26	1,028.61	330.81	697.80	0.00	69,449.09
248	21	12/08/26	1,028.61	334.12	694.49	0.00	69,114.97
249	21	01/08/27	1,028.61	337.46	691.15	0.00	68,777.51
250	21	02/08/27	1,028.61	340.83	687.78	0.00	68,436.68
251	21	03/08/27	1,028.61	344.24	684.37	0.00	68,092.44
252	21	04/08/27	1,028.61	347.69	680.92	0.00	67,744.75
253	22	05/08/27	1,028.61	351.16	677.45	0.00	67,393.59
254	22	06/08/27	1,028.61	354.67	673.94	0.00	67,038.92
255	22	07/08/27	1,028.61	358.22	670.39	0.00	66,680.70
256	22	08/08/27	1,028.61	361.80	666.81	0.00	66,318.90
257	222	09/08/27	1,028.61	365.42	663.19	0.00	65,953.48
258	22	10/08/27	1,028.61	369.08	659.53	0.00	65,584.40
259	22	11/08/27	1,028.61	372.77	655.84	0.00	65,211.63
260	22	12/08/27	1,028.61	376.49	652.12	0.00	64,835.14
261	22	01/08/28	1,028.61	380.26	648.35	0.00	64,454.88
262	22	02/08/28	1,028.61	384.06	644.55	0.00	64,070.82
263	22	03/08/28	1,028.61	387.90	640.71	0.00	63,682.92
264	22	04/08/28	1,028.61	391.78	636.83	0.00	63,291.14
265	23	05/08/28	1,028.61	395.70	632.91	0.00	62,895.44
266	23	06/08/28	1,028.61	399.66	628.95	0.00	62,495.78
267	23	07/08/28	1,028.61	403.65	624.96	0.00	62,092.13
268	23	08/08/28	1,028.61	407.69	620.92	0.00	61,684.44
269	23	09/08/28	1,028.61	411.77	616.84	0.00	61,272.67
270	23	10/08/28	1,028.61	415.88	612.73	0.00	60,856.79
271	23	11/08/28	1,028.61	420.04	608.57	0.00	60,436.75
272	23	12/08/28	1,028.61	424.24	604.37	0.00	60,012.51
273	23	01/08/29	1,028.61	428.48	600.13	0.00	59,584.03
274	23	02/08/29	1,028.61	432.77	595.84	0.00	59,151.26
275	23	03/08/29	1,028.61	437.10	591.51	0.00	58,714.16
276	23	04/08/29	1,028.61	441.47	587.14	0.00	58,272.69
277	24	05/08/29	1,028.61	445.88	582.73	0.00	57,826.81
278	24	06/08/29	1,028.61	450.34	578.27	0.00	57,376.47
279	24	07/08/29	1,028.61	454.85	573.76	0.00	56,921.62
280	24	08/08/29	1,028.61	459.39	569.22	0.00	56,462.23
281	24	09/08/29	1,028.61	463.99	564.62	0.00	55,998.24
282	24	10/08/29	1,028.61	468.63	559.98	0.00	55,529.61
283	24	11/08/29	1,028.61	473.31	555.30	0.00	55,056.30

PMT. #	YEAR	PMT. DATE	PAYMENT	PRINCIPAL	INTEREST	PMI	BALANCE
284	24	12/08/29	1,028.61	478.05	550.56	0.00	54,578.25
285	24	01/08/30	1,028.61	482.83	545.78	0.00	54,095.42
286	24	02/08/30	1,028.61	487.66	540.95	0.00	53,607.76
287	24	03/08/30	1,028.61	492.53	536.08	0.00	53,115.23
288	24	04/08/30	1,028.61	497.46	531.15	0.00	52,617.77
289	25	05/08/30	1,028.61	502.43	526.18	0.00	52,115.34
290	25	06/08/30	1,028.61	507.46	521.15	0.00	51,607.88
291	25	07/08/30	1,028.61	512.53	516.08	0.00	51,095.35
292	25	08/08/30	1,028.61	517.66	510.95	0.00	50,577.69
293	25	09/08/30	1,028.61	522.83	505.78	0.00	50,054.86
294	25	10/08/30	1,028.61	528.06	500.55	0.00	49,526.80
295	25	11/08/30	1,028.61	533.34	495.27	0.00	48,993.46
296	25	12/08/30	1,028.61	538.68	489.93	0.00	48,454.78
297	25	01/08/31	1,028.61	544.06	484.55	0.00	47,910.72
298	25	02/08/31	1,028.61	549.50	479.11	0.00	47,361.22
299	25	03/08/31	1,028.61	555.00	473.61	0.00	46,806.22
300	25	04/08/31	1,028.61	560.55	468.06	0.00	46,245.67
301	26	05/08/31	1,028.61	566.15	462.46	0.00	45,679.52
302	26	06/08/31	1,028.61	571.81	456.80	0.00	45,107.71
303	26	07/08/31	1,028.61	577.53	451.08	0.00	44,530.18
304	26	08/08/31	1,028.61	583.31	445.30	0.00	43,946.87
305	26	09/08/31	1,028.61	589.14	439.47	0.00	43,357.73
306	26	10/08/31	1,028.61	595.03	433.58	0.00	42,762.70
307	26	11/08/31	1,028.61	600.98	427.63	0.00	42,161.72
308	26	12/08/31	1,028.61	606.99	421.62	0.00	41,554.73
309	26	01/08/32	1,028.61	613.06	415.55	0.00	40,941.67
310	26	02/08/32	1,028.61	619.19	409.42	0.00	40,322.48
311	26	03/08/32	1,028.61	625.39	403.22	0.00	39,697.09
312	26	04/08/32	1,028.61	631.64	396.97	0.00	39,065.45
313	27	05/08/32	1,028.61	637.96	390.65	0.00	38,427.49
314	27	06/08/32	1,028.61	644.33	384.28	0.00	37,783.16
315	27	07/08/32	1,028.61	650.78	377.83	0.00	37,132.38
316	27	08/08/32	1,028.61	657.29	371.32	0.00	36,475.09
317	27	09/08/32	1,028.61	663.86	364.75	0.00	35,811.23
318	27	10/08/32	1,028.61	670.50	358.11	0.00	35,140.73
319	27	11/08/32	1,028.61	677.20	351.41	0.00	34,463.53
320	27	12/08/32	1,028.61	683.97	344.64	0.00	33,779.56
321	27	01/08/33	1,028.61	690.81	337.80	0.00	33,088.75
322	27	02/08/33	1,028.61	697.72	330.89	0.00	32,391.03
323	27	03/08/33	1,028.61	704.70	323.91	0.00	31,686.33
324	27	04/08/33	1,028.61	711.75	316.86	0.00	30,974.58
325	28	05/08/33	1,028.61	718.86	309.75	0.00	30,255.72
326	28	06/08/33	1,028.61	726.05	302.56	0.00	29,529.67
327	28	07/08/33	1,028.61	733.31	295.30	0.00	28,796.36
328	28	08/08/33	1,028.61	740.65	287.96	0.00	28,055.71
329	28	09/08/33	1,028.61	748.05	280.56	0.00	27,307.66
330	28	10/08/33	1,028.61	755.53	273.08	0.00	26,552.13
331	28	11/08/33	1,028.61	763.09	265.52	0.00	25,789.04
332	28	12/08/33	1,028.61	770.72	257.89	0.00	25,018.32
333	28	01/08/34	1,028.61	778.43	250.18	0.00	24,239.89
334	28	02/08/34	1,028.61	786.21	242.40	0.00	23,453.68
335	28	03/08/34	1,028.61	794.07	234.54	0.00	22,659.61
336	28	04/08/34	1,028.61	802.01	226.60	0.00	21,857.60
337	29	05/08/34	1,028.61	810.03	218.58	0.00	21,047.57
338	29	06/08/34	1,028.61	818.13	210.48	0.00	20,229.44
339	29	07/08/34	1,028.61	826.32	202.29	0.00	19,403.12
340	29	08/08/34	1,028.61	834.58	194.03	0.00	18,568.54

PMT. #	YEAR	PMT. DATE	PAYMENT	PRINCIPAL	INTEREST	PMI	BALANCE
341	29	09/08/34	1,028.61	842.92	185.69	0.00	17,725.62
342	29	10/08/34	1,028.61	851.35	177.26	0.00	16,874.27
343	29	11/08/34	1,028.61	859.87	168.74	0.00	16,014.40
344	29	12/08/34	1,028.61	868.47	160.14	0.00	15,145.93
345	29	01/08/35	1,028.61	877.15	151.46	0.00	14,268.78
346	29	02/08/35	1,028.61	885.92	142.69	0.00	13,382.86
347	29	03/08/35	1,028.61	894.78	133.83	0.00	12,488.08
348	29	04/08/35	1,028.61	903.73	124.88	0.00	11,584.35
349	30	05/08/35	1,028.61	912.77	115.84	0.00	10,671.58
350	30	06/08/35	1,028.61	921.89	103.72	0.00	9,749.69
351	30	07/08/35	1,028.61	931.11	97.50	0.00	8,,818.58
352	30	08/08/35	1,028.61	940.42	88.19	0.00	7,878.16
353	30	09/08/35	1,028.61	949.83	78.78	0.00	6,928.33
354	30	10/08/35	1,028.61	959.33	69.28	0.00	5,969.00
355	30	11/08/35	1,028.61	968.92	59.69	0.00	5,000.08
356	30	12/08/35	1,028.61	978.61	50.00	0.00	4,021.47
357	30	01/08/36	1,028.61	988.40	40.21	0.00	3,033.07
358	30	02/08/36	1,028.61	998.28	30.33	0.00	2,034.79
359	30	03/08/36	1,028.61	1008.25	20.35	0.00	1,026.53
360	30	04/08/36	1,036.80	1026.53	10.27	0.00	0.00

FROM:

DAVID HANCOCK
ELECT APPRAISALS, INC.
PO BOX 7054
LAKELAND, FL 33807-7054

Telephone Number: 863-619-8000   Fax Number: 863-648-5917

INVOICE

INVOICE NUMBER
0604207
DATE
APRIL 25, 2006
4780 NE 4TH AVENUE
REFERENCE

TO:

ALL STATE MORTGAGE LOANS

Telephone Number: Fax Number:
Alternate Number: E-Mail:

Internal Order #:	0604207
Lender Case #:	
Client File #:	
Main File # on form:	0604207
Other File # on form:	0604207
Federal Tax ID:	59-3523089
Employer ID:	

DESCRIPTION

Lender: ALL STATE MORTGAGE LOANS		**Client:** ALL STATE MORTGAGE LOANS	
Purchaser/Borrower: GREG VASILENKO			
Property Address: 4780 NE 4TH AVENUE			
City: OCALA			
County: MARION	**State:** FL		**Zip:** 34479
Legal Description: SEE ADDITIONAL COMMENTS			

FEES	AMOUNT
FULL APPRAISAL	150.00
SUBTOTAL	150.00

PAYMENTS			AMOUNT
Check #: Date: 04/25/2006 Description: COD			150.00
Check #: Date: Description:			
Check #: Date: Description:			
		SUBTOTAL	150.00
		TOTAL DUE $	0.00

Please Return This Portion With Your Payment

FROM:

DAVID HANCOCK
ELECT APPRAISALS, INC.
PO BOX 7054
LAKELAND, FL 33807-7054

Telephone Number: Fax Number:
Alternate Number: E-Mail:

TO:

DAVID HANCOCK
ELECT APPRAISALS, INC.
PO BOX 7054
LAKELAND, FL 33807-7054

AMOUNT DUE:	$ _____
AMOUNT ENCLOSED:	$ _____
INVOICE NUMBER	
0604207	
DATE	
APRIL 25, 2006	
4780 NE 4TH AVENUE	
REFERENCE	
Internal Order #:	0604207
Lender Case #:	
Client File #:	
Main File # on form:	0604207
Other File # on form:	0604207
Federal Tax ID:	59-3523089
Employer ID:	

Form NIV1 — "WinTOTAL" appraisal software by a la mode, inc. — 1-800-ALAMODE

Table of Contents

APRIL 25, 2006

4780 NE 4TH AVENUE
SEE ADDITIONAL COMMENTS
OCALA, FL 34479

ALL STATE MORTGAGE LOANS

PRIVACY NOTICE

Pursuant to the Gramm-Leach-Bliley Act of 1999, effective July 1, 2001, Appraisers, along with all providers of personal financial services are now required by federal law to inform their clients of the policies of the firm with regard to the privacy of client nonpublic personal information. As professionals, we understand that your privacy is very important to you and are pleased to provide you with this information.

Types of Nonpublic Personal Information We Collect
IN THE COURSE OF PERFORMING APPRAISALS, WE MAY COLLECT WHAT IS KNOWN AS "NONPUBLIC PERSONAL INFORMATION" ABOUT YOU. THIS INFORMATION IS USED TO FACILITATE THE SERVICES THAT WE PROVIDE TO YOU AND MAY INCLUDE THE INFORMATION PROVIDED TO US BY YOU DIRECTLY OR RECEIVED BY US FROM OTHERS WITH YOUR AUTHORIZATION.

Parties to Whom We Disclose Information
WE DO NOT DISCLOSE ANY NONPUBLIC PERSONAL INFORMATION OBTAINED IN THE COURSE OF OUR ENGAGEMENT WITH OUR CLIENTS TO NONAFFILIATED THIRD PARTIES, EXCEPT AS NECESSARY OR AS REQUIRED BY LAW. BY WAY OF EXAMPLE, A NECESSARY DISCLOSURE WOULD BE TO OUR EMPLOYEES, AND IN CERTAIN SITUATIONS, TO UNRELATED THIRD PARTY CONSULTANTS WHO NEED TO KNOW THAT INFORMATION TO ASSIST US IN PROVIDING APPRAISAL SERVICES TO YOU. ALL OF OUR EMPLOYEES AND ANY THIRD PARTY CONSULTANTS WE EMPLOY ARE INFORMED THAT ANY INFORMATION THEY SEE AS PART OF AN APPRAISAL ASSIGNMENT IS TO BE MAINTAINED IN STRICT CONFIDENCE WITHIN THE FIRM.

A DISCLOSURE REQUIRED BY LAW WOULD BE A DISCLOSURE BY US THAT IS ORDERED BY A COURT OF COMPETENT JURISDICTION WITH REGARD TO A LEGAL ACTION TO WHICH YOU ARE A PARTY.

Confidentiality and Security
WE WILL RETAIN RECORDS RELATING TO PROFESSIONAL SERVICES THAT WE HAVE PROVIDED TO YOU FOR A REASONABLE TIME SO THAT WE ARE
BETTER ABLE TO ASSIST YOU WITH YOUR NEEDS. IN ORDER TO PROTECT YOUR NONPUBLIC PERSONAL INFORMATION FROM UNAUTHORIZED ACCESS BY THIRD PARTIES, WE MAINTAIN PHYSICAL, ELECTRONIC AND PROCEDURAL SAFEGUARDS THAT COMPLY WITH OUR PROFESSIONAL STANDARDS TO INSURE THE SECURITY AND INTEGRITY OF YOUR INFORMATION.

PLEASE FEEL FREE TO CALL US AN ANY TIME IF YOU HAVE ANY QUESTIONS ABOUT THE CONFIDENTIALITY OF THE INFORMATION THAT YOU PROVIDE TO US.

Uniform Residential Appraisal Report

0604207
File # 0604207

The purpose of this summary appraisal report is to provide the lender/client with an accurate, and adequately supported, opinion of the market value of the subject property.

SUBJECT

Property Address 4780 NE 4TH AVENUE	City State FL Zip Code 34479
Borrower GREG VASILENKO	Owner of Public Record GREG & DENISE VASILENKO County MARION
Legal Description SEE ADDITIONAL COMMENTS	
Assessor's Parcel # 15448-001-00	Tax Year 2005 R.E. Taxes $ 3,222.44
Neighborhood Name OCALA	Map Reference 36100 Census Tract 0013.01
Occupant Owner Tenant Vacant	Special Assessments $ 0.00 PUD HOA $ per year per month
Property Rights Appraised Fee Simple Leasehold Other (describe)	
Assignment Type Purchase Transaction Refinance Transaction Other (describe)	
Lender/Client ALL STATE MORTGAGE LOANS Address	

Is the subject property currently offered for sale or has it been offered for sale in the twelve months prior to the effective date of this appraisal?   Yes   No
Report data source(s) used, offering price(s), and date(s).

CONTRACT

I did did not analyze the contract for sale for the subject purchase transaction. Explain the results of the analysis of the contract for sale or why the analysis was not performed.   N/A

Contract Price $ 0   Date of Contract   Is the property seller the owner of public record? Yes No Data Source(s)
Is there any financial assistance (loan charges, sale concessions, gift or downpayment assistance, etc.) to be paid by any party on behalf of the borrower?   Yes   No
If Yes, report the total dollar amount and describe the items to be paid.

NEIGHBORHOOD

Note: Race and the racial composition of the neighborhood are not appraisal factors.

Neighborhood Characteristics				One-Unit Housing Trends			One-Unit Housing		Present Land Use %	
Location	Urban	Suburban	Rural	Property Values	Increasing	Stable Declining	PRICE	AGE	One-Unit	90 %
Built-Up	Over 75%	25-75%	Under 25%	Demand/Supply	Shortage	In Balance Over Supply	$ (000)	(yrs)	2-4 Unit	%
Growth	Rapid	Stable	Slow	Marketing Time	Under 3 mths	3-6 mths Over 6 mths	150 Low	NEW	Multi-Family	%
							600 High	40	Commercial	5 %
							475 Pred.	25	Other	5 %

Neighborhood Boundaries THE NEIGHBORHOOD BOUNDARIES ARE; TO THE NORTH, HWY 326, TO THE EAST, HWY 200A, TO THE SOUTH, HWY 40 & TO THE WEST, HWY 301/441.

Neighborhood Description

Market Conditions (including support for the above conclusions)

SITE

Dimensions Area Shape View	
Specific Zoning Classification A1 Zoning Description	
Zoning Compliance Legal Legal Nonconforming (Grandfathered Use) No Zoning Illegal (describe)	

Is the highest and best use of subject property as improved (or as proposed per plans and specifications) the present use?   Yes   No If No, describe

Utilities	Public	Other (describe)		Public	Other (describe)	Off-site Improvements – Type	Public	Private
Electricity			Water		WELL	Street DIRT		
Gas		NONE	Sanitary Sewer		SEPTIC	Alley NONE		

FEMA Special Flood Hazard Area Yes No FEMA Flood Zone C   FEMA Map # 1201600475B   FEMA Map Date 1/19/1983
Are the utilities and off-site improvements typical for the market area? Yes No If No, describe
Are there any adverse site conditions or external factors (easements, encroachments, environmental conditions, land uses, etc.)?   Yes   No If Yes, describe

IMPROVEMENTS

General Description		Foundation		Exterior Description	materials/condition	Interior	materials/condition
Units One	One with Accessory Unit	Concrete Slab	Crawl Space	Foundation Walls	CONC/PIER	Floors	WOOD/VIN/AVG
# of Stories ONE		Full Basement	Partial Basement	Exterior Walls	CBS /AVG	Walls	DRYWALL/AVG
Type Det. Att.	S-Det./End Unit	Basement Area	N/A sq.ft.	Roof Surface	F/G/S AVG	Trim/Finish	
Existing Proposed	Under Const.	Basement Finish	N/A %	Gutters & Downspouts	YES / AVG	Bath Floor	
Design (Style) RANCH		Outside Entry/Exit	Sump Pump	Window Type	A/S/H / AVG	Bath Wainscot	
Year Built 1977		Evidence of Infestation		Storm Sash/Insulated	NO	Car Storage None	
Effective Age (Yrs) 10-12 YRS		Dampness	Settlement	Screens	YES / AVG	Driveway # of Cars	2
Attic None		Heating FWA HWBB Radiant	Amenities		Woodstove(s) #	Driveway Surface CONCRETE	
Drop Stair Stairs		Other Fuel ELEC	Fireplace(s) # 1		Fence WOOD	Garage # of Cars 2 CAR	
Floor Scuttle		Cooling Central Air Conditioning	Patio/Deck PATIO		Porch ENTRY	Carport # of Cars	
Finished Heated		Individual Other	Pool POOL		Other	Att. Det. Built-in	

Appliances Refrigerator Range/Oven Dishwasher Disposal Microwave Washer/Dryer Other (describe)

Finished area above grade contains: 8 Rooms   4 Bedrooms   3 Bath(s)   3,973 Square Feet of Gross Living Area Above Grade

Additional features (special energy efficient items, etc.). THE SUBJECT IS A FOUR BEDROOM, THREE BATH HOME, WITH A COVERED ENTRY, AN OPEN PATIO WITH POOL, A SCREENED PORCH, FENCING AND A TWO CAR GARAGE.

Describe the condition of the property (including needed repairs, deterioration, renovations, remodeling, etc.). THE SUBJECT IS AN AVERAGE QUALITY SITE BUILT HOME IN AVERAGE CONDITION AND TYPICAL FOR THE AREA. NO FUNCTIONAL OR EXTERNAL INADEQUACIES WERE NOTED.

Are there any physical deficiencies or adverse conditions that affect the livability, soundness, or structural integrity of the property?   Yes   No If Yes, describe

Does the property generally conform to the neighborhood (functional utility, style, condition, use, construction, etc.)?   Yes   No If No, describe

Uniform Residential Appraisal Report

0604207
File # 0604207

There are N/A comparable properties currently offered for sale in the subject neighborhood ranging in price from $ N/A	to $ N/A	
There are 9 comparable sales in the subject neighborhood within the past twelve months ranging in sale price from $ 150,000	to $ 600,000	

FEATURE	SUBJECT	COMPARABLE SALE # 1		COMPARABLE SALE # 2		COMPARABLE SALE # 3	
Address	4780 NE 4TH AVENUE OCALA, FL 34479	1035 SE 11TH AVENUE OCALA, FL 34471		9220 SW 19 AVENUE ROAD OCALA, FL 34476		3395 SW 4TH AVE OCALA, FL 34475	
Proximity to Subject		4.02 miles S		7.07 miles SW		5.71 miles S	
Sale Price	$ 0	$	464,000	$	497,750	$	450,000
Sale Price/Gross Liv. Area	$ sq.ft.	$ 103.11 sq.ft.		$ 142.21 sq.ft.		$ 103.54 sq.ft.	
Data Source(s)							
Verification Source(s)		PUB REC/INSPECTION/MLS OR 4388 PG 1350		PUB REC/INSPECTION/MLS OR 4370 PG 0471		PUB REC/INSPECTION/MLS OR 4317 PG 1346	
VALUE ADJUSTMENTS	DESCRIPTION	DESCRIPTION	+(-) $ Adjustment	DESCRIPTION	+(-) $ Adjustment	DESCRIPTION	+(-) $ Adjustment
Sales or Financing Concessions		CONV TYPICAL		CONV TYPICAL		CONV TYPICAL	
Date of Sale/Time		03/24/2006		03/06/2006		01/20/2006	
Location	32-14-22	20-15-22		24-16-21		30-15-22	
Leasehold/Fee Simple	Fee Simple	FEE SIMPLE		FEE SIMPLE		FEE SIMPLE	
Site	A 2.22 ACRES	A .39 AC/INF	+30,000	A 4.66 AC/SUP	-30,000	A 3.02 AC/EQ	
View	STREET/HOME	STREET/HOME		STREET/HOME		STREET/HOME	
Design (Style)	RANCH	TWO STORY		TWO STORY		TWO STORY	
Quality of Construction	AVERAGE	AVERAGE		AVERAGE		AVERAGE	
Actual Age	29 YRS	32	+600	27	-400	30	+200
Condition	AVERAGE	AVERAGE		AVERAGE		AVERAGE	
Above Grade	Total Bdrms. Baths	Total Bdrms. Baths		Total Bdrms. Baths		Total Bdrms. Baths	
Room Count	8 4 3	9 5 4	-1,000	8 4 3		8 4 3	
Gross Living Area	3,973 sq.ft.	4,500 sq.ft.	-2,000	3,500 sq.ft.	+9,460	4,346 sq.ft.	-7,460
Basement & Finished Rooms Below Grade	SCR PORCH NONE	SCR PORCH NONE	-10,540	OPEN PATIO NONE	+2,000	OPEN PATIO NONE	+2,000
Functional Utility	AVERAGE	AVERAGE		AVERAGE		AVERAGE	
Heating/Cooling	FWA/CAC	FWA/CAC		FWA/CAC		FWA/CAC	
Energy Efficient Items	AVERAGE	AVERAGE		AVERAGE		AVERAGE	
Garage/Carport	2 CAR GAR	2 CAR GAR		2 CAR GAR		NONE	+6,000
Porch/Patio/Deck	ENTRY	ENTRY		ENTRY		ENTRY	
FENCE/OTHER	FENCE	FENCE/FP	-2,000	FENCE/FP	-2,000	FENCE/FP	-2,000
POOL/OTHER	POOL	POOL/WKSP	-1,000	POOL/BARN	-5,000	POOL/NONE	
Net Adjustment (Total)		+ - $	14,060	+ - $	25,940	+ - $	1,260
Adjusted Sale Price of Comparables		Net 3.0 % Gross 10.2 % $	478,060	Net 5.2 % Gross 9.8 % $	471,810	Net 0.3 % Gross 3.9 % $	448,740

I ☐ did ☑ did not research the sale or transfer history of the subject property and comparable sales. If not, explain

My research ☑ did ☐ did not reveal any prior sales or transfers of the subject property for the three years prior to the effective date of this appraisal.
Data Source(s)   PUB REC, MLS
My research ☑ did ☐ did not reveal any prior sales or transfers of the comparable sales for the year prior to the date of sale of the comparable sale.
Data Source(s)   PUB REC, MLS
Report the results of the research and analysis of the prior sale or transfer history of the subject property and comparable sales (report additional prior sales on page 3).

ITEM	SUBJECT	COMPARABLE SALE #1	COMPARABLE SALE #2	COMPARABLE SALE #3
Date of Prior Sale/Transfer	NO PRIOR SALES WITHIN	01/2004	NO PRIOR SALES WITHIN	01/2005
Price of Prior Sale/Transfer	36 MONTHS	$260,000	36 MONTHS	$371,000
Data Source(s)	APRIL 25, 2006	OR 3641 PG 0990	APRIL 25, 2006	OR 3940 PG 0376
Effective Date of Data Source(s)		APRIL 25, 2006		APRIL 25, 2006

Analysis of prior sale or transfer history of the subject property and comparable sales   THE SUBJECT HAS NO PRIOR SALES WITHIN THE LAST THREE YEARS OR LISTINGS WITHIN THE LAST TWELVE MONTHS OTHER THAN THOSE DISCLOSED IN THIS REPORT. THERE HAVE BEEN NO PRIOR SALES OF ALL THE COMPARABLE SALES UTILIZED IN THIS REPORT WITHIN THE PAST THREE YEARS OTHER THAN THOSE DISCLOSED IN THIS REPORT IN THE SALES COMPARISON GRID.

Summary of Sales Comparison Approach   ALL THREE SALES WERE CONSIDERED INSTRUCTIONAL IN THE FINAL ESTIMATE OF MARKET VALUE WITH EQUAL EMPHASIS PLACED ON ALL THREE COMPARABLE SALES.***IN APPRAISING PROPERTY IN THIS AREA OF MARION COUNTY IT IS SOMETIMES NECESSARY TO USE COMPARABLE SALES LOCATED MORE THAN ONE MILE FROM THE SUBJECT PROPERTY. THIS IS NOT CONSIDERED AN ADVERSE MARKETING FACTOR. ALL COMPARABLE SALES ARE LOCATED MORE THAN ONE MILE FROM THE SUBJECT. COMPARABLE SALE #2 IS LOCATED ON AN INFERIOR SITE AND RECEIVED AN APPROPRIATE UPWARD SITE ADJUSTMENT. COMPARABLE SALE #2 IS LOCATED ON A SUPERIOR SITE AND RECEIVED AN APPROPRIATE DOWNWARD SITE ADJUSTMENT.

Indicated Value by Sales Comparison Approach $ 469,000

Indicated Value by: Sales Comparison Approach $ 469,000   Cost Approach (if developed) $ 469,703   Income Approach (if developed) $

BOTH APPLICABLE APPROACHES TO VALUE FALL WITHIN A CLOSE VALUE RANGE AND ARE MUTUALLY SUPPORTIVE. NO VALUE EMPHASIS WAS PLACED ON THE COST APPROACH. GIVEN THE AVAILABLE SALES DATA, THE FIGURE INDICATED BY THE MARKET APPROACH IS USED AS THE FINAL ESTIMATED VALUE.

This appraisal is made ☑ "as is", ☐ subject to completion per plans and specifications on the basis of a hypothetical condition that the improvements have been completed, ☐ subject to the following repairs or alterations on the basis of a hypothetical condition that the repairs or alterations have been completed, or ☐ subject to the following required inspection based on the extraordinary assumption that the condition or deficiency does not require alteration or repair:

Based on a complete visual inspection of the interior and exterior areas of the subject property, defined scope of work, statement of assumptions and limiting conditions, and appraiser's certification, my (our) opinion of the market value, as defined, of the real property that is the subject of this report is $ 469,000 , as of   APRIL 25, 2006 , which is the date of inspection and the effective date of this appraisal.

PRIVATE MORTGAGE INVESTING

Uniform Residential Appraisal Report

0604207
File # 0604207

SUBJECT LEGAL DESCRIPTION:

SEC 32 TWP 14 RGE 22 W 289 FT OF S 371 FT OF NW 1/4 OF NE 1/4 OF NW 1/4 EX COM SW CC
255 FT TO POB TH E 34 FT TH N 204 FT TH SWLY 206.81 FT TO POB TOGETHER WITH AN EASE
700 FT OF E 50 FT OF NW 1/4 OF NW 1/4 AS RECORDED IN OR 1546-869

SITE COMMENTS:

THE SUBJECT SITE CONSISTS OF A FAIRLY TYPICAL SMALL ACREAGE TRACT THAT IS AVERAC
AND APPEAL. VIEWS IN ALL DIRECTIONS ARE EITHER OF SIMILAR RESIDENTIAL PROPERTIES
SURFACE DRAINAGE APPEARS ADEQUATE AS SITE IS ABOVE STREET GRADE. THERE ARE NC
EASEMENTS OR ENCROACHMENTS.

NE 4TH AVENUE IS AN ALL WEATHER DIRT AND GRAVEL STREET THAT IS PUBLICLY MAINTAIN
COMMON FOR THIS AREA AND ARE ACCEPTED IN THE MARKET PLACE BY PROSPECTIVE BUY

CITY SANITARY SEWER AND PUBLIC WATER ARE NOT AVAILABLE TO THE SUBJECT SITE. INDI
WELLS ARE COMMON FOR THIS AREA AND DO NOT HAVE AN ADVERSE AFFECT ON THE MARI
NEIGHBORHOOD.

SITE AND DIMENSION COMMENTS:

THE APPRAISER HAS NOT BEEN PROVIDED WITH A SURVEY. THE INFORMATION OBTAINED IS
OFFICE AND IS BELIEVED TO BE CORRECT.

CERTIFICATION # 23 - "INTENDED USER" CLARIFICATION:

THE INTENDED USER OF THIS APPRAISAL REPORT IS THE LENDER/CLIENT. THE INTENDED US
THAT IS THE SUBJECT OF THIS APPRAISAL FOR A MORTGAGE FINANCE TRANSACTION, SUBJE
PURPOSE OF THE APPRAISAL, REPORTING REQUIREMENTS OF THIS APPRAISAL FORM, AND I
ADDITIONAL INTENDED USERS ARE IDENTIFIED BY THE APPRAISER.

COST APPROACH TO VALUE (not required by Fannie Mae)

Provide adequate information for the lender/client to replicate the below cost figures and calculations.
Support for the opinion of site value (summary of comparable land sales or other methods for estimating site value) THE SUBJECT SITE VALUE IS BASED ON
VACANT LAND SALES WITHIN THE SUBJECT AREA.

ESTIMATED [ ] REPRODUCTION OR [X] REPLACEMENT COST NEW
Source of cost data LOCAL MARKET
Quality rating from cost service AVG   Effective date of cost data 04/25/2006
Comments on Cost Approach (gross living area calculations, depreciation, etc.)
PHYSICAL DEPRECIATION IS CALCULATED USING THE EFFECTIVE
AGE/LIFE METHOD.
NO SIGNIFICANT FUNCTIONAL OBSOLESCENCE WAS OBSERVED.
NO EXTERNAL DEPRECIATION WAS NOTED DURING MY
INSPECTION. COST FIGURES ARE DERIVED LOCALLY.

OPINION OF SITE VALUE			=$	120,000
DWELLING	3,973 Sq.Ft. @ $	95.00	=$	377,435
	N/A Sq.Ft. @ $		=$	
ENTRY, APPL, SCR PORCH, POOL			=$	15,000
Garage/Carport	513 Sq.Ft. @ $	25.00	=$	12,825
Total Estimate of Cost-New			=$	405,260
Less	Physical	Functional	External	
Depreciation	67,557			=$(67,557)
Depreciated Cost of Improvements			=$	337,703
"As-is" Value of Site Improvements			=$	12,000

Estimated Remaining Economic Life (HUD and VA only) 50 Years INDICATED VALUE BY COST APPROACH =$ 469,703

INCOME APPROACH TO VALUE (not required by Fannie Mae)

Estimated Monthly Market Rent $ ____ X Gross Rent Multiplier ____ = $ ____ Indicated Value by Income Approach ____
Summary of Income Approach (including support for market rent and GRM)

PROJECT INFORMATION FOR PUDs (if applicable)

Is the developer/builder in control of the Homeowners' Association (HOA)? [ ] Yes [ ] No Unit type(s) [ ] Detached [ ] Attached
Provide the following information for PUDs ONLY if the developer/builder is in control of the HOA and the subject property is an att
Legal Name of Project
Total number of phases ____ Total number of units ____ Total number of units sold ____
Total number of units rented ____ Total number of units for sale ____ Data source(s) ____
Was the project created by the conversion of existing building(s) into a PUD? [ ] Yes [ ] No If Yes, date of conversion.
Does the project contain any multi-dwelling units? [ ] Yes [ ] No Data Source
Are the units, common elements, and recreation facilities complete? [ ] Yes [ ] No If No, describe the status of completion.

Are the common elements leased to or by the Homeowners' Association? [ ] Yes [ ] No If Yes, describe the rental terms and options.

Describe common elements and recreational facilities.

Uniform Residential Appraisal Report

0604207
File # 0604207

This report form is designed to report an appraisal of a one-unit property or a one-unit property with an accessory unit; including a unit in a planned unit development (PUD). This report form is not designed to report an appraisal of a manufactured home or a unit in a condominium or cooperative project.

This appraisal report is subject to the following scope of work, intended use, intended user, definition of market value, statement of assumptions and limiting conditions, and certifications. Modifications, additions, or deletions to the intended use, intended user, definition of market value, or assumptions and limiting conditions are not permitted. The appraiser may expand the scope of work to include any additional research or analysis necessary based on the complexity of this appraisal assignment. Modifications or deletions to the certifications are also not permitted. However, additional certifications that do not constitute material alterations to this appraisal report, such as those required by law or those related to the appraiser's continuing education or membership in an appraisal organization, are permitted.

SCOPE OF WORK: The scope of work for this appraisal is defined by the complexity of this appraisal assignment and the reporting requirements of this appraisal report form, including the following definition of market value, statement of assumptions and limiting conditions, and certifications. The appraiser must, at a minimum: (1) perform a complete visual inspection of the interior and exterior areas of the subject property, (2) inspect the neighborhood, (3) inspect each of the comparable sales from at least the street, (4) research, verify, and analyze data from reliable public and/or private sources, and (5) report his or her analysis, opinions, and conclusions in this appraisal report.

INTENDED USE: The intended use of this appraisal report is for the lender/client to evaluate the property that is the subject of this appraisal for a mortgage finance transaction.

INTENDED USER: The intended user of this appraisal report is the lender/client.

DEFINITION OF MARKET VALUE: The most probable price which a property should bring in a competitive and open market under all conditions requisite to a fair sale, the buyer and seller, each acting prudently, knowledgeably and assuming the price is not affected by undue stimulus. Implicit in this definition is the consummation of a sale as of a specified date and the passing of title from seller to buyer under conditions whereby: (1) buyer and seller are typically motivated; (2) both parties are well informed or well advised, and each acting in what he or she considers his or her own best interest; (3) a reasonable time is allowed for exposure in the open market; (4) payment is made in terms of cash in U. S. dollars or in terms of financial arrangements comparable thereto; and (5) the price represents the normal consideration for the property sold unaffected by special or creative financing or sales concessions* granted by anyone associated with the sale.

*Adjustments to the comparables must be made for special or creative financing or sales concessions. No adjustments are necessary for those costs which are normally paid by sellers as a result of tradition or law in a market area; these costs are readily identifiable since the seller pays these costs in virtually all sales transactions. Special or creative financing adjustments can be made to the comparable property by comparisons to financing terms offered by a third party institutional lender that is not already involved in the property or transaction. Any adjustment should not be calculated on a mechanical dollar for dollar cost of the financing or concession but the dollar amount of any adjustment should approximate the market's reaction to the financing or concessions based on the appraiser's judgment.

STATEMENT OF ASSUMPTIONS AND LIMITING CONDITIONS: The appraiser's certification in this report is subject to the following assumptions and limiting conditions:

1. The appraiser will not be responsible for matters of a legal nature that affect either the property being appraised or the title to it, except for information that he or she became aware of during the research involved in performing this appraisal. The appraiser assumes that the title is good and marketable and will not render any opinions about the title.

2. The appraiser has provided a sketch in this appraisal report to show the approximate dimensions of the improvements. The sketch is included only to assist the reader in visualizing the property and understanding the appraiser's determination of its size.

3. The appraiser has examined the available flood maps that are provided by the Federal Emergency Management Agency (or other data sources) and has noted in this appraisal report whether any portion of the subject site is located in an identified Special Flood Hazard Area. Because the appraiser is not a surveyor, he or she makes no guarantees, express or implied, regarding this determination.

4. The appraiser will not give testimony or appear in court because he or she made an appraisal of the property in question, unless specific arrangements to do so have been made beforehand, or as otherwise required by law.

5. The appraiser has noted in this appraisal report any adverse conditions (such as needed repairs, deterioration, the presence of hazardous wastes, toxic substances, etc.) observed during the inspection of the subject property or that he or she became aware of during the research involved in performing the appraisal. Unless otherwise stated in this appraisal report, the appraiser has no knowledge of any hidden or unapparent physical deficiencies or adverse conditions of the property (such as, but not limited to, needed repairs, deterioration, the presence of hazardous wastes, toxic substances, adverse environmental conditions, etc.) that would make the property less valuable, and has assumed that there are no such conditions and makes no guarantees or warranties, express or implied. The appraiser will not be responsible for any such conditions that do exist or for any engineering or testing that might be required to discover whether such conditions exist. Because the appraiser is not an expert in the field of environmental hazards, this appraisal report must not be considered as an environmental assessment of the property.

6. The appraiser has based his or her appraisal report and valuation conclusion for an appraisal that is subject to satisfactory completion, repairs, or alterations on the assumption that the completion, repairs, or alterations of the subject property will be performed in a professional manner.

Uniform Residential Appraisal Report

0604207
File # 0604207

APPRAISER'S CERTIFICATION: The Appraiser certifies and agrees that:

1. I have, at a minimum, developed and reported this appraisal in accordance with the scope of work requirements stated in this appraisal report.

2. I performed a complete visual inspection of the interior and exterior areas of the subject property. I reported the condition of the improvements in factual, specific terms. I identified and reported the physical deficiencies that could affect the livability, soundness, or structural integrity of the property.

3. I performed this appraisal in accordance with the requirements of the Uniform Standards of Professional Appraisal Practice that were adopted and promulgated by the Appraisal Standards Board of The Appraisal Foundation and that were in place at the time this appraisal report was prepared.

4. I developed my opinion of the market value of the real property that is the subject of this report based on the sales comparison approach to value. I have adequate comparable market data to develop a reliable sales comparison approach for this appraisal assignment. I further certify that I considered the cost and income approaches to value but did not develop them, unless otherwise indicated in this report.

5. I researched, verified, analyzed, and reported on any current agreement for sale for the subject property, any offering for sale of the subject property in the twelve months prior to the effective date of this appraisal, and the prior sales of the subject property for a minimum of three years prior to the effective date of this appraisal, unless otherwise indicated in this report.

6. I researched, verified, analyzed, and reported on the prior sales of the comparable sales for a minimum of one year prior to the date of sale of the comparable sale, unless otherwise indicated in this report.

7. I selected and used comparable sales that are locationally, physically, and functionally the most similar to the subject property.

8. I have not used comparable sales that were the result of combining a land sale with the contract purchase price of a home that has been built or will be built on the land.

9. I have reported adjustments to the comparable sales that reflect the market's reaction to the differences between the subject property and the comparable sales.

10. I verified, from a disinterested source, all information in this report that was provided by parties who have a financial interest in the sale or financing of the subject property.

11. I have knowledge and experience in appraising this type of property in this market area.

12. I am aware of, and have access to, the necessary and appropriate public and private data sources, such as multiple listing services, tax assessment records, public land records and other such data sources for the area in which the property is located.

13. I obtained the information, estimates, and opinions furnished by other parties and expressed in this appraisal report from reliable sources that I believe to be true and correct.

14. I have taken into consideration the factors that have an impact on value with respect to the subject neighborhood, subject property, and the proximity of the subject property to adverse influences in the development of my opinion of market value. I have noted in this appraisal report any adverse conditions (such as, but not limited to, needed repairs, deterioration, the presence of hazardous wastes, toxic substances, adverse environmental conditions, etc.) observed during the inspection of the subject property or that I became aware of during the research involved in performing this appraisal. I have considered these adverse conditions in my analysis of the property value, and have reported on the effect of the conditions on the value and marketability of the subject property.

15. I have not knowingly withheld any significant information from this appraisal report and, to the best of my knowledge, all statements and information in this appraisal report are true and correct.

16. I stated in this appraisal report my own personal, unbiased, and professional analysis, opinions, and conclusions, which are subject only to the assumptions and limiting conditions in this appraisal report.

17. I have no present or prospective interest in the property that is the subject of this report, and I have no present or prospective personal interest or bias with respect to the participants in the transaction. I did not base, either partially or completely, my analysis and/or opinion of market value in this appraisal report on the race, color, religion, sex, age, marital status, handicap, familial status, or national origin of either the prospective owners or occupants of the subject property or of the present owners or occupants of the properties in the vicinity of the subject property or on any other basis prohibited by law.

18. My employment and/or compensation for performing this appraisal or any future or anticipated appraisals was not conditioned on any agreement or understanding, written or otherwise, that I would report (or present analysis supporting) a predetermined specific value, a predetermined minimum value, a range or direction in value, a value that favors the cause of any party, or the attainment of a specific result or occurrence of a specific subsequent event (such as approval of a pending mortgage loan application).

19. I personally prepared all conclusions and opinions about the real estate that were set forth in this appraisal report. If I relied on significant real property appraisal assistance from any individual or individuals in the performance of this appraisal or the preparation of this appraisal report, I have named such individual(s) and disclosed the specific tasks performed in this appraisal report. I certify that any individual so named is qualified to perform the tasks. I have not authorized anyone to make a change to any item in this appraisal report; therefore, any change made to this appraisal is unauthorized and I will take no responsibility for it.

20. I identified the lender/client in this appraisal report who is the individual, organization, or agent for the organization that ordered and will receive this appraisal report.

Uniform Residential Appraisal Report

0604207
File # 0604207

21. The lender/client may disclose or distribute this appraisal report to: the borrower; another lender at the request of the borrower; the mortgagee or its successors and assigns; mortgage insurers; government sponsored enterprises; other secondary market participants; data collection or reporting services; professional appraisal organizations; any department, agency, or instrumentality of the United States; and any state, the District of Columbia, or other jurisdictions; without having to obtain the appraiser's or supervisory appraiser's (if applicable) consent. Such consent must be obtained before this appraisal report may be disclosed or distributed to any other party (including, but not limited to, the public through advertising, public relations, news, sales, or other media).

22. I am aware that any disclosure or distribution of this appraisal report by me or the lender/client may be subject to certain laws and regulations. Further, I am also subject to the provisions of the Uniform Standards of Professional Appraisal Practice that pertain to disclosure or distribution by me.

23. The borrower, another lender at the request of the borrower, the mortgagee or its successors and assigns, mortgage insurers, government sponsored enterprises, and other secondary market participants may rely on this appraisal report as part of any mortgage finance transaction that involves any one or more of these parties.

24. If this appraisal report was transmitted as an "electronic record" containing my "electronic signature," as those terms are defined in applicable federal and/or state laws (excluding audio and video recordings), or a facsimile transmission of this appraisal report containing a copy or representation of my signature, the appraisal report shall be as effective, enforceable and valid as if a paper version of this appraisal report were delivered containing my original hand written signature.

25. Any intentional or negligent misrepresentation(s) contained in this appraisal report may result in civil liability and/or criminal penalties including, but not limited to, fine or imprisonment or both under the provisions of Title 18, United States Code, Section 1001, et seq., or similar state laws.

SUPERVISORY APPRAISER'S CERTIFICATION: The Supervisory Appraiser certifies and agrees that:

1. I directly supervised the appraiser for this appraisal assignment, have read the appraisal report, and agree with the appraiser's analysis, opinions, statements, conclusions, and the appraiser's certification.

2. I accept full responsibility for the contents of this appraisal report including, but not limited to, the appraiser's analysis, opinions, statements, conclusions, and the appraiser's certification.

3. The appraiser identified in this appraisal report is either a sub-contractor or an employee of the supervisory appraiser (or the appraisal firm), is qualified to perform this appraisal, and is acceptable to perform this appraisal under the applicable state law.

4. This appraisal report complies with the Uniform Standards of Professional Appraisal Practice that were adopted and promulgated by the Appraisal Standards Board of The Appraisal Foundation and that were in place at the time this appraisal report was prepared.

5. If this appraisal report was transmitted as an "electronic record" containing my "electronic signature," as those terms are defined in applicable federal and/or state laws (excluding audio and video recordings), or a facsimile transmission of this appraisal report containing a copy or representation of my signature, the appraisal report shall be as effective, enforceable and valid as if a paper version of this appraisal report were delivered containing my original hand written signature.

APPRAISER

Signature
Name   DOLLY O'MALLEY
Company Name   ELECT APPRAISALS, INC.
Company Address   P. O. BOX 7054
LAKELAND, FL 33807-7054
Telephone Number   863 6198000
Email Address   ORDER@ELECTAPPRAISALS.COM
Date of Signature and Report
Effective Date of Appraisal
State Certification #
or State License #
or Other (describe)   State #
State FL
Expiration Date of Certification or License   11/30/2006

ADDRESS OF PROPERTY APPRAISED
4780 NE 4TH AVENUE
OCALA, FL 34479
APPRAISED VALUE OF SUBJECT PROPERTY $ 469,000
LENDER/CLIENT
Name
Company Name   ALL STATE MORTGAGE LOANS
Company Address

Email Address

SUPERVISORY APPRAISER (ONLY IF REQUIRED)

Signature
Name
Company Name
Company Address

Telephone Number   863 6198000
Email Address   ORDER@ELECTAPPRAISALS.COM
Date of Signature
State Certification #   #RD4582
or State License #   ST CERT RES REA
State FL
Expiration Date of Certification or License   11/30/2006

SUBJECT PROPERTY

   Did not inspect subject property
   Did inspect exterior of subject property from street
   Date of Inspection
   Did inspect interior and exterior of subject property
   Date of Inspection   APRIL 25, 2006

COMPARABLE SALES

   Did not inspect exterior of comparable sales from street
   Did inspect exterior of comparable sales from street
   Date of Inspection   APRIL 25, 2006

Building Sketch

Borrower	GREG VASILENKO				
Property Address	4780 NE 4TH AVENUE				
City	OCALA	County MARION		State FL	Zip Code 34479
Lender	ALL STATE MORTGAGE LOANS				

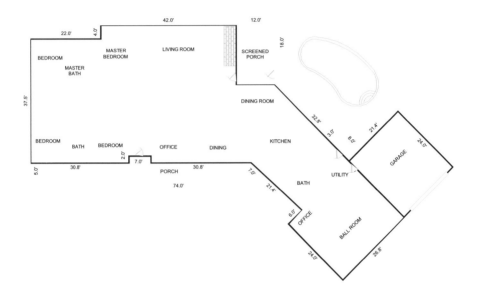

Sketch by Apex IV™

Comments:

AREA CALCULATIONS SUMMARY			
Code	Description	Size	Net Totals
GLA1	First Floor	3973.31	3973.31
P/P	Porch	368.79	
	Porch	216.00	
	Porch	24.00	608.79
GAR	Garage	513.60	513.60
	TOTAL LIVABLE (rounded)		3973

LIVING AREA BREAKDOWN		
Breakdown		Subtotals
First Floor		
0.5 x	0.0 x 0.0	0.00
	7.4 x 23.5	173.90
0.5 x	0.4 x 0.4	0.09
0.5 x	22.9 x 22.9	261.89
	0.6 x 22.9	14.04
0.5 x	14.4 x 30.3	218.08
	23.5 x 30.8	723.80
	18.0 x 26.2	471.60
	15.8 x 39.5	624.10
	22.0 x 35.5	781.00
	2.0 x 30.8	61.60
	24.0 x 26.8	643.20
12 Calculations Total (rounded)		3973

Subject Interior Photo Page

Borrower	GREG VASILENKO
Property Address	4780 NE 4TH AVENUE
City	OCALA County MARION State FL Zip Code 34479
Lender	ALL STATE MORTGAGE LOANS

SUBJECT FRONT

4780 NE 4TH AVENUE

Sales Price	N/A
Gross Living Area	3,973
Total Rooms	8
Total Bedrooms	4
Total Bathrooms	3
Location	32-14-22
VIEW	STREET/HOME
SITE	A 2.22 ACRES
QUALITY	AVERAGE
AGE	29 YRS

Subject Interior Photo Page

Borrower	GREG VASILENKO					
Property Address	4780 NE 4TH AVENUE					
City	OCALA	County MARION		State FL	Zip Code	34479
Lender	ALL STATE MORTGAGE LOANS					

Subject Interior

4780 NE 4TH AVENUE

Sales Price	N/A
Gross Living Area	3,973
Total Rooms	8
Total Bedrooms	4
Total Bathrooms	3
Location	32-14-22
View	STREET/HOME
Site	A 2.22 ACRES
Quality	AVERAGE
Age	29 YRS

Subject Interior

Subject Interior

COMPARABLE PHOTO PAGE

Borrower	GREG VASILENKO
Property Address	4780 NE 4TH AVENUE
City	OCALA
Lender	ALL STATE MORTGAGE LOANS

County MARION   State FL   Zip Code 34479

COMPARABLE 1
1035 SE 11TH AVENUE	
PROX. TO SUBJECT	4.02 miles S
SALE PRICE	464,000
GROSS LIVING AREA	4,500
TOTAL ROOMS	9
TOTAL BEDROOMS	5
TOTAL BATHROOMS	4
LOCATION	20-15-22
VIEW	STREET/HOME
SITE	A .39 AC/INF
QUALITY	AVERAGE
AGE	32

COMPARABLE 2
9220 SW 19 AVENUE ROAD	
PROX. TO SUBJECT	7.07 miles SW
SALE PRICE	497,750
GROSS LIVING AREA	3,500
TOTAL ROOMS	8
TOTAL BEDROOMS	4
TOTAL BATHROOMS	3
LOCATION	24-16-21
VIEW	STREET/HOME
SITE	A 4.66 AC/SUP
QUALITY	
AGE	27

COMPARABLE 3
3395 SW 4TH AVE	
PROX. TO SUBJECT	5.71 miles S
SALE PRICE	450,000
GROSS LIVING AREA	4,346
TOTAL ROOMS	8
TOTAL BEDROOMS	4
TOTAL BATHROOMS	3
LOCATION	30-15-22
VIEW	STREET/HOME
SITE	A 3.02 AC/EQ
QUALITY	AVERAGE
AGE	30

Location Map

Borrower	GREG VASILENKO	County MARION	State FL	Zip Code 34479
Property Address	4780 NE 4TH AVENUE			
City	OCALA			
Lender	ALL STATE MORTGAGE LOANS			

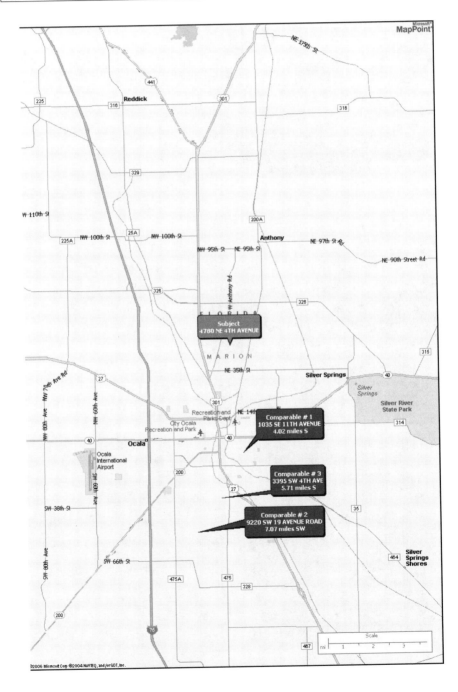

GLOSSARY

3/1, 5/1, 7/1 and 10/1 ARMs
Adjustable-rate mortgages that
have the interest adjusted at three-
five- seven- and ten-year periods.

7/23 and 5/25 Mortgages
Mortgages that have the interest
adjusted once, at seven years or
five years.

Abatement An allowance made
to a lease, or outside of a lease that
permits a period of free rent or
occupancy prior to the rent period.

Above building standard Options
available to a tenant (usually at
a premium cost) that are higher
quality than the standard options
available.

Absorption rate The rate at
which rental space is rented. Gross
absorption is total square feet rented
over a given period. Net absorption
is total square feet rented over a

given period, less space vacated
during the same period.

Abstract or title search A review of
all transactions and records related
to a property to determine if there
are any defects in the title of the
property that would prevent clear
transfer.

**Accelerated cost recovery system
or accelerated depreciation** A
method of depreciation that allows
a higher depreciation during the
first years of the ownership of a
property.

Acceleration When a lender
demands immediate repayment
of a mortgage due to a default on
the part of the borrower, or a loan
payment is accelerated because of a
due-on-sale clause in the mortgage.

Acceleration clause The clause in
a mortgage that allows the lender

to demand payment of the outstanding loan balance.

Acceptance When a seller accepts, in writing, the offer of a buyer.

Ad valorem Based on Latin according to value; it is a tax imposed on the value of a property, usually based on a government assessment.

Addendum Any additional change to a contract, after it has been signed, that all parties to the contract agree upon.

Additional principal payment Payments that can be made outside of the set periodic principal payment that will reduce the principal balance more quickly, thereby shortening the length of the loan.

Adjustable-rate mortgage (ARM) A mortgage with an interest rate that changes based on changes in some fixed, agreed-upon interest rate index, such as the prime rate.

Adjustable-rate mortgage (ARM) index The agreed-upon interest rate index used as the basis for an adjustable-rate mortgage.

Adjusted basis The base cost of a property plus capital improvements minus depreciation.

Adjusted funds from operations (AFFO) A measure of a Real Estate Investment Trust's performance using the Trust's

Funds From Operations (FFO) adjusted by recurring capital expenses necessary to maintain the properties in the Trust.

Adjustment date In adjustable-rate mortgages, the date upon which the rate is adjusted.

Adjustment interval or Adjustment period In adjustable-rate mortgages, the time between changes in the adjusted interest rate.

Administrative fee Management fee charged, either as a percentage of the assets managed, or a fixed fee per year.

Advances The servicer of a loan may cover a loan if a borrower fails to pay.

Advisor One who represents an investor in a transaction. Brokers, consultants, and investment bankers act as advisors. An advisor may be paid via a retainer or by a percentage of the value of a closed transaction.

Affordability analysis A study of a prospective buyer's capacity to afford a home. It takes into account income, price of home, funds available for deposit, type of mortgage to use, and potential closing costs.

Agency closing If a lender uses a title company or some other company to handle the closing on a property on its behalf.

Agency disclosure When an agent has the power to act for both buyers and sellers, most states require that the agent disclose who he is representing.

Aggregation risk When mortgages are pooled and then securitized for future sale, they are first warehoused together; there is a risk associated with this process.

Agreement of sale The document outlining the terms of a sale that represents that the buyer and the seller agree upon the sale and the terms.

Alienation clause A provision in some loans that requires the borrower to pay off the loan (in one lump sum, immediately due payment) if the underlying property is sold.

Alternative mortgage A type of mortgage that differs in terms from standard, fixed-rate, fixed-term mortgages.

Alternative or specialty investments Non-conventional types of property, such as long-term care facilities, mobile home parks, parking lots, forestry, or farm acreage, that may not be considered investment-grade real estate.

Amortization The paydown of a debt over time through regular payments; the cost of an item spread out over time, for tax or analysis purposes.

Amortization tables Pre-calculated tables that show how much a borrower's monthly payment will be on a mortgage.

Amortization term How long it will take to amortize a mortgage, stated in months: a 15-year mortgage has a 180-month amortization term.

Amortized Loan A loan that is completely paid off in installments.

Amortized Note A promissory note that is completely paid off in installments.

Anchor In shopping centers, the largest or most famous store or commercial property that brings the majority of customers to the shopping center.

Annual mortgagor statement A statement sent to borrowers annually that shows the amounts paid through the year and how it has been applied to principal, interest, and taxes.

Annual percentage rate (APR) An adjustment to a quoted loan rate that reflects actual costs, such as points, mortgage insurance, processing fees, etc.

Annuity A payment received at regular intervals in a fixed amount.

Application fee A charge made by lenders to cover the costs associated with the origination of a mortgage, such as appraisals, credit reports, etc. Some institutions do not have an application fee and charge each document independently.

Appraisal The estimate of a property value, usually by a professional appraiser, based on market replacement value and cash flow analysis.

Appraisal fee Fee charged for the appraisal of a real estate property.

Appraisal report The report filed by a professional appraiser giving the estimated value of a real estate property based on comparable properties and condition.

Appraised value An opinion by a professional (usually an appraisal professional) as to the value of a real estate property.

Appraiser A professional with knowledge of real estate markets and skilled in the practice of appraisal.

Appreciation The increase in value of an asset.

Appreciation return The periodic (usually quarterly) valuation applied to the appreciation of an asset.

Arbitrage Taking advantage of the price discrepancies of the good, product, or commodity in two different markets.

As-is condition The accepted condition of a property at the time a lease is contracted, regardless of faults or defects.

Assessed value The value assigned to a real estate property by taxing authorities for the calculation of the tax base.

Assessment The distribution of costs of improvements to a property via fees to the individual owners of the property. These fees are usually for public improvements such as sewer or curb installation or other district improvements.

Assessment The estimated value of a real estate property.

Asset management The management of property assets from appraising, acquisition, and financing; leasing and managing; accounting and reporting; including, ultimately, dissolution of property.

Asset management fee Fee charged for the management of a real estate asset.

Asset turnover Average total annual revenues from assets divided by total assets.

Assets Any item of value on a company's books, such as cash, real estate, and securities.

Assets under management Total value of real estate assets for which an asset manager has responsibility.

Assignee name Party or entity to whom an asset, including all of the obligations attached to it, has been transferred.

Assignment The transfer of an asset, including all of the obligations attached to it. Separate from a sublease where the total interest in the asset is not transferred.

Assignor Anyone who transfers his right to an interest in a real estate property.

Assumability The quality of a mortgage if it can be assumed by a buyer of a property from the seller of that property. Normally, the lender will conduct a credit review on the new borrower, and mortgages that are due at sale may not be assumed.

Assumable mortgage A mortgage that can be assumed by another party.

Assumption When a seller transfers the obligation of the mortgage of the underlying sales property to the buyer of the property, thereby assuring a pre-existing rate and conditions and saving closing costs.

Assumption clause The provision in a mortgage that allows a buyer to take over the pre-existing mortgage on the property from the seller.

Assumption fee In mortgage assumptions, the lenders may charge a fee to cover the costs of credit checks and recordings.

Attorn Agreement to recognize a new owner of a property and transfer of debt and obligation to him from the old owner.

Average common equity The total equity of a property over the last five quarters, divided by five.

Average downtime Average monthly time between expiration of one lease and beginning of another lease, as expected under current market conditions.

Average free rent Average monthly lease abatement allowed to tenants as an incentive, as expected under current market conditions.

Average occupancy Percentage of property occupied over the last 12 months, divided by 12.

Average total assets Assets of a company measured over the last five quarters and divided by five.

Back title letter The document an insurance company supplies to an attorney, in a real estate transaction, for examination regarding insurance on the title.

Back-end ratio A measure of a borrower's ability to pay a mortgage where the borrower's total outstanding debt is compared to monthly income.

Balance sheet A financial statement of the assets, liabilities, and net worth of an individual or entity.

Balloon payment The lump-sum payment due at the end of a balloon loan or mortgage.

Balloon, or bullet, loan or mortgage A type of loan, frequently used for mortgages, wherein interim payments are kept low because the bulk of the loan is payable at maturity, instead of being amortized over the life of the loan.

Balloon risk Risk that a balloon (lump sum) mortgage will not be paid at the end of the balloon period.

Bankrupt Unable to pay current debts and obligations.

Bankruptcy Federal proceedings that relieve a person or entity of their debts. After certain obligations are met, the net property is divided among the debtors, by the court, to fully satisfy all of the debts.

Base loan amount The amount upon which payments of a loan will be based; when closing costs and other fees are wrapped into the loan, it will increase the base loan amount.

Base principal balance Calculating the balance of a mortgage based only on payments and advances of principal, regardless of interest accrued or paid.

Base rent A fixed amount of rent set as a basis for future increases, which are usually made as percentage increases over the base.

Base year The expenses for the first year of a lease, which sets the basis for subsequent years.

Basis point One-one hundredth of one percent.

Before-tax income Income prior to deduction of any taxes.

Below-grade A part of a building that is constructed below the land

or "grade" level.

Beneficiary A person, usually a spouse or family member, who is designated by an employee to receive the benefit of his policies in case of death.

Beta A benchmark set to measure a stock's price relative to other similar stocks.

Bid An offer to buy.

Bill of sale A document that represents the transfer of ownership of personal property.

Binder A document issued by a title insurance company that details the property and outlines the guidelines under which title insurance will be issued.

Bi-weekly payment mortgage A mortgage that has a payment schedule of every two weeks instead of the standard month; it serves to shorten the term of the loan and is sometimes desirable by borrowers for budget purposes.

Blanket mortgage Any mortgage that covers more than one real estate property owned by the same borrower.

Blind pool A real estate investment vehicle that does not specify what properties will be invested in.

Book value Shareholders' equity less preferred stock.

Borrower In real estate, a person or entity who receives a mortgage loan and contracts to pay the loan in full under the agreed-upon conditions.

Break-even point When the owner of a real estate's income from that property is the same as his operating expenses and debt service.

Bridge loan A real estate loan for a shorter period than a standard mortgage, which allows a buyer time to look for long-term financing.

Broker An intermediary between parties in a financial transaction.

Brokerage The act of being an intermediary between parties in exchange for a fee; in real estate, there are real estate brokers and mortgage brokers.

Buildable acres The amount of acreage left for a building project after items such as open space, roads, rights of way, or non-buildable areas such as lakes and streams, etc., have been subtracted.

Building code Municipal law that dictates how structures will be built, which standards should be met, and what materials may be used.

Building standard plus allowance If a tenant intends to make his own improvements, the standard building costs are credited to him to use toward his own improvements.

Build-out Improvements in rental space requested by a tenant, allowing the tenant the base amount of improvements the landlord would have put in.

Build-to-suit Property offered for lease whereby the developer or landlord will build according to a tenant's specs.

Buydown mortgage If a lender or builder offers lower than market rates (and subsidizes the difference) for the early years of a mortgage loan; the rates will adjust to market rates after this period.

Buyer's remorse A feeling of trepidation (caused by the fear of taking on such a large responsibility) of a first-time homebuyer after signing a contract or closing on a home.

Call date Clause inserted in a lease or a mortgage allowing the lender to demand payment of a balance prior to maturity.

Call option A clause in a loan that allows the lender to demand repayment at any time over the life of the loan.

Capital appreciation Increase in the market value of a property or portfolio of properties due to capital improvements added.

Capital expenditures Expenses in capital improvements; that is, improvements of a long-term nature that will be depreciated over their life. This is in contrast to ordinary expenditures that are used in day-to-day operations and leave no residual value.

Capital gain Proceeds of the sale of an asset after deducting the book value.

Capital improvements Improvements to capital items on a company's balance sheet that serve to extend the life of the capital item.

Capital markets Markets where capital to invest in business is raised.

Capitalization All of the securities issued by a company, measured by their dollar value.

Capitalization A formula that calculates a property's value based on the net income of the property.

Capitalization rate Net operating income of a property divided by the value of the property. It is a measure of determining the value of a property.

Caps (interest rate) A limit placed on the interest rate for an adjustable-rate mortgage.

Caps (Payment) A limit placed on the monthly payment for an adjustable-rate mortgage.

Carryback financing A financing arrangement whereby the seller holds a note for a partial amount of the sales price.

Carrying charges Fundamental costs of running a property that are absorbed by the landlord or developer when the property is not leased.

Cash flow In real estate, the amount of cash a rental property generates; it is calculated by gross income less operating expenses and debt service. In general business, it is the amount of cash a company generates during a period, calculated by adding non-cash charges, such as depreciation to net income.

Cashier's check A check drawn by a bank, at a customer's request, that is drawn on the bank itself rather than the customer's account; it is immediately debited to the customers account and is immediately available to the payee.

Cash-on-cash yield The cash flow of a property as a percentage of average capital investment.

Cash-out refinance When a mortgage is refinanced at a new amount, so that the funds received from the new mortgage are greater than the amount due on the old mortgage, allowing the borrower to take cash out.

Certificate of Deposit Index (CODI) An index of six-month CD interest rates, used as a basis for some adjustable-rate mortgages.

Certificate of Discharge A written instrument executed by the mortgagee and given to the mortgagor when the debt secured by a mortgage is satisfied to show that the mortgage is released. Sometimes called a release of mortgage.

Certificate of eligibility A certificate issued by a local authority stating that a building meets code requirements and that the building inspections have been passed.

Certificate of occupancy (CO) A certificate issued by a local authority granting the right to occupy a building. It indicates that certain codes have been met and building inspections passed.

Certificate of Reasonable Value (CRV) Used by the Veterans Administration as an appraisal of a property's market value.

Certificate of veteran status A document received by veterans or reservists, with at least 90 days of active service, to validate their veteran status and make them eligible for lower-cost loans.

Chain of title A record that lists, in chronological order, the history of ownership of a real estate property.

Change frequency How frequently the interest rate and payments change in an adjustable-rate mortgage.

Chapter 11 The chapter of the federal bankruptcy code applicable to business reorganization.

Chapter 7 The chapter of the federal bankruptcy code applicable to business dissolution.

Circulation factor Footage of an office space required for circulation, which is not considered part of the net footage.

Class "A" A rating for real estate property indicating the highest rents because of high quality.

Class "B" A rating for real estate property indicating reasonable rents for reasonable quality.

Class "C" A rating for real estate property indicating low rents, but which are an attractive, cost-effective alternative to "A" and "B."

Clear title A real estate property title without any encumbrances, liens, or other defects.

Clear-span facility A building built with wide spaces between supports to allow clear, open spaces for such uses as warehouses or parking lots.

Closed-end fund A fund with a fixed number of shares, which is not obligated to issue new shares or redeem outstanding shares (open-end funds are).

Closing The procedure whereby title documents are signed by the buyer and seller of a property, and the loan is put in place via the property mortgage.

Closing costs All expenses relative to the exchange of the title on a real estate property, including title and appraisal fees, loan origination costs, etc., which are settled at the closing.

Closing statement The

document that outlines all of the funds that change hands at the closing between the financing institution, the buyer, the seller, and the real estate agents.

Cloud on title An encumbrance on real estate property that may or may not be valid and has to be investigated.

CMBS (Commercial Mortgage-Backed Securities) Commercial real estate loans are "securitized" and traded as financial instruments.

CMO (Collateralized Mortgage Obligation) A type of mortgage-backed security backed by a pool of mortgages.

Co-Borrowers One or more people who have signed the note and are equally responsible for repaying the loan.

COFI Index (Cost of Funds Index) An index frequently used as the basis for adjustable-rate mortgages; it is the weighted average of the interest rates paid in the 11th Federal Home Loan Bank District.

Co-investment Ownership by two or more groups of funds of a real estate investment; proportion of ownership is based on proportion of investment.

Co-investment program A program to manage a co-investment. It is used to allow smaller investors to pool their resources and invest in larger properties.

Collateral Goods or assets encumbered by a loan or a mortgage to secure payment.

Commercial mortgage A mortgage issued for the financing of a commercial real estate property.

Commercial mortgage broker A broker who specializes in financing commercial real estate property.

Commercial mortgage lender A mortgage lender who specializes in financing commercial real estate property.

Commingled fund An investment vehicle that allows groups of investors (benefit plans, pension funds) to combine capital in order to take advantage of larger investment opportunities, better professional management, and/or more diversification.

Commitment When a lender fixes the terms of a mortgage for a specific period, allowing a buyer to shop around for property without the interest rate going up in the interim period.

Commitment fee The fee charged by the lender to fix the terms of a mortgage for a specific period.

Common area In a lease situation, the area of a building that is used by all of the tenants, as compared to individual lease space used by each tenant; this usually includes lobbies, hallways, stairwells, parking lots, etc.

Common area maintenance
Cost of the maintenance of
the common area, charged as
additional rent to tenants.

Comparables The price of
properties similar to the one
being offered, as a way to
determine its value.

Compound interest Interest that
is paid on a principal balance as
well as on the accrued interest.

Concessions Reductions
given by a landlord, such
as abatements, allowances,
reimbursement of expenses, etc.,
to encourage a tenant to lease.

Condemnation The taking
of private property, without
the consent of the owner, by a
government for public use. See
also Eminent Domain.

Conditional commitment When
a lender promises to make a loan
only if certain conditions are met.

Conditional sale When a sales
contract is not final until certain
conditions are met.

Conduit A system between
mortgage lenders and the
organizations that purchase,
securitize, pool, and market
mortgage loans.

Conforming loan A loan that
qualifies under the conditions set
by Federal National Mortgage
Association or the Federal Home
Loan Mortgage Corporation.

Construction documents All of
the specifications and drawings,
usually drawn up by an architect
or engineer, detailing the
requirements of a construction
project.

Construction loan Loan to
finance the construction of a
property; it is converted to a
mortgage upon completion of
construction.

Construction management
Management of an entire
construction project, making sure
the construction is on time and
according to code.

**Construction-to-permanent
loan** A construction loan that
eventually converts to a long-
term traditional mortgage once
construction is completed.

Consultant In real estate;
companies or individuals that
provide services necessary to
real estate investment projects.
This may include analysis of
investment strategies, financial
management and analysis,
review of portfolio performance,
etc.

Consumer Price Index (CPI)
Measurement of changes in price
of a set "basket of goods" to
determine inflation. In real estate
management, it is used as a basis
for increases in adjusted basis
leases.

**Consumer reporting agency (or
bureau)** An agency that reports
on the credit worthiness of a
potential borrower. Banks and

other lenders use this information to determine whether a loan will be granted and at what rate. The largest agencies of this nature are Trans-Union, Equifax, and Experian.

Contiguous space Lease spaces that are next to each other and can therefore be combined and rented to a single tenant.

Contract documents The plans, specifications, materials list, and any other documents necessary to construct a building.

Contract rent The obligation of a lessee for the rent, expressed in total dollars.

Contract sale or deed A real estate contract that does not take effect, and under which title does not transfer, until after certain conditions have been met.

Conventional loan A standard, long-term loan made by a financial institution for the purchase of a home.

Conversion clause A provision in an adjustable-rate mortgage that the mortgage can be converted, at some future date, to a fixed-rate mortgage.

Convertible adjustable-rate mortgage An adjustable-rate mortgage that contains a provision that the mortgage can be converted, at some future date, to a fixed-rate mortgage.

Convertible debt In real estate, a mortgage that can be converted to full or partial ownership of the property by the lender within a certain time frame.

Convertible preferred stock Stock that is able to be converted into preferred shares under certain conditions, as specified by the issuer of the stock.

Conveyance The transfer of property title deed between parties. May also refer to transfer of other real estate interests.

Cooperative mortgage A mortgage loan on a cooperative residence.

Core properties Successful real estate assets that generate stable income, good appreciation, and high total returns. They are usually fully or near fully rented most of the time by desirable tenants with structured long-term leases.

Co-signer A party other than the borrower who also signs a promissory note and acts as a guarantor for the debt.

Cost-approach improvement value Replacement cost of an existing structure less any accrued depreciation.

Cost-of-sale percentage The total costs of selling an investment property, expressed as a percentage of the sales price. Includes commission, closing costs, and other fees.

Coupon The interest rate on a note or mortgage.

Courier fee A fee to cover the

delivery of the documents, related to the mortgage loan, that are transferred between lenders, escrow companies, and other parties during a real estate transaction. This is usually settled as one of the closing costs.

Covenant Stipulations written in deeds or other instruments of debt indicating uses of property or performance of obligations related to the property.

Credit enhancement Additional support to make a debt more credit worthy, such as guarantees, subordinations, or over-collateralization.

Credit history The detailed history of a prospective borrower's credit engagements and payments.

Credit life insurance An insurance policy that pays a mortgage off in the event of the borrower's death.

Credit rating A measure of a potential borrower's credit worthiness, based on his credit history, earnings, other outstanding debt, etc.

Credit report The report that contains the detailed history of a prospective borrower's credit engagements and payments.

Credit repository Companies that gather financial and credit information on consumers and store it for use for credit reporting.

Credit risk score or credit score

A mathematical measure of an individual's credit rating, formulated by assigning values to the information in a credit report. The most common scores are called Fair Isaac and FICO.

Cross-collateralization A pool of mortgages that, together, collateralize one debt.

Cross-defaulting A feature in a group of loans that allows the entire loan to be called if only one of the loans defaults.

Cumulative discount rate The rate at which a rent is discounted after all landlord lease concessions.

Current occupancy The percentage of a property that is leased, out of the total area of the property.

Current Value The value at the time of appraisal.

Current yield In commercial mortgage-backed securities, the coupon divided by the price equals the current yield.

Deal structure How a financing package is designed: it can be leveraged or unleveraged, traditional, participatory, convertible debt, or a joint venture.

Debt An amount owed by one person or entity to another.

Debt service The expense of meeting principal and interest payments on a debt.

Debt Service Coverage Ratio (DSCR) The operating income from a property divided by the cost of the debt service for the same period.

Debt-to-income ratio A borrower's monthly obligations for long-term debt divided by his gross monthly income.

Dedicate To convert private property to public use.

Deed A legal document that conveys the ownership title of a property.

Deed in lieu of foreclosure Transfer of the deed of a property to a lender to avoid foreclosure.

Deed of trust Like a mortgage, it registers that real estate is encumbered to secure payment of a debt.

Default Failure to meet the obligations of a contract or a loan.

Deferred interest When the monthly payment on a mortgage does not cover the full interest payment on the note, and unpaid interest is added to the principal balance.

Deferred maintenance account An account, funded by the borrower, that holds funds for future maintenance of a property.

Deficiency judgment A judgment that requires a borrower to pay the balance of a debt if the property used to secure the debt does not cover it.

Defined-benefit plan A pension or retirement plan that pays a benefit that is defined by a pre-arranged amount, either a fixed monthly amount or a fixed percentage of salary.

Defined-contribution plan A pension or retirement plan that pays a benefit that is defined by the contributions paid into it over time, plus any earnings those contributions have accrued.

Delinquency Failure to make payments on time, which usually leads to foreclosure of a property.

Delinquent mortgage A mortgage where the borrower is behind on his payments. If he does not or cannot resume payments and catch up, he will be in default, and the foreclosing procedure may begin.

Demand Clause A clause in the note that states the note is payable on demand of the holder.

Demising wall A fixed wall that defines the separation between tenant spaces or between tenant space and the common area in a building.

Department of Veterans Affairs (VA) An agency of the U.S. Government that guarantees mortgage loans made to veterans.

Deposit Similar to earnest money, funds given by a potential buyer to a seller to hold an offer to purchase.

Depreciation A periodic allowance, made in accounting for assets, that assumes a loss in the value of the asset due to age, wear, and other factors.

Derivative securities Securities that are derived from other securities but are traded on their own. For Collateralized Mortgage-Backed Securities, the interest-only strip is the most common. (The interest is stripped from the security, and both are traded separately.)

Design/Build A company that does both the design and construction of a property.

Disclosure A required statement made by the seller regarding certain types of information on the property, such as the presence of lead paint or radon.

Discount point Upfront fees a lender may charge to keep an interest rate lower on a mortgage loan. One point is equal to one percent of the loan.

Discount rate The interest rate used to determine the present value of future payments.

Discretion The amount of authority a manager has for a client's account. An account that is "fully discretionary" means that the manager can make all decisions without gaining prior approval of the client.

Distraint To seize personal property in payment of a default in a loan.

Diversification Designing an investment portfolio so that risk is spread out over several types of investments, reducing both capital and interest rate risk.

Dividend Distribution of profit paid to stockholders. In the case of Real Estate Investment Trusts, 90 percent of their income must be paid as dividends.

Dividend yield The dividend of a security divided by the price of the security expresses its yield.

Dividend-ex date The date at which a stock purchaser is no longer eligible to receive that stock's dividend.

Document needs list A lender will require a list of documents from a buyer in order to process a loan application. Typically, these documents will include bank statements, pay stubs, etc.

Documentation preparation fee The fee that lenders, mortgage brokers, or other settlement agents may charge for the preparation of closing documents for a mortgage.

Dollar stop A maximum, agreed-upon amount each tenant is obligated to pay for operating expenses.

Down payment That part of the price of a real estate property that a buyer pays in cash and does not finance with a mortgage.

DOWNREIT A financing structure in which an REIT may purchase properties with units

323

of the REIT. A DOWNREIT is subordinate to the REIT, unlike an UPREIT.

Draw The series of payments made to a builder, contractor, or suppliers out of the proceeds of a construction loan.

Due diligence An investigation by any party to a real estate transaction to assure that the property is as portrayed, and all of the relevant documents are true, with no material information omitted.

Due on sale A feature in a mortgage agreement that makes the mortgage payable if the mortgaged property is sold prior to the maturity date of the mortgage.

Due-on-sale clause The clause in a mortgage that makes the mortgage payable if the mortgaged property is sold prior to the maturity of the mortgage.

Earnest money A deposit against the purchase of a property to indicate that the potential buyer has the intention to buy.

Earthquake insurance An insurance policy that provides coverage against earthquake damage to a home.

Easement A grant or agreement allowing other parties access to a property. Frequently easements are granted to utility companies, for instance, to install necessary towers.

Economic feasibility Whether or not it is feasible to construct a project, after analyzing costs, revenue, and potential return.

Economic rent The rental value, according to the market, of a property. Similar to "comparables" in the sale of a property.

Effective date A registration is effective and sales of a security can begin on the effective date.

Effective Gross Income (EGI) Income from a property (rent, other items) minus an established vacancy factor. Can also be calculated as rents collected, less expenses and debt service.

Effective rent The rent realized by a landlord after any concessions made to a tenant have been deducted.

Electronic authentication Method(s) used to assure that an electronically transmitted document is genuine and unchanged, and is from the expected sender.

Eminent domain A governmental entity's power to acquire private property for public use. The agency is required by law to provide just compensation.

Encroachment When a structure extends over the boundary line of a property, without the permission of the owner of the property.

Encumbrance A claim against or interest in real property that is owned by another party, which may affect the transferability of the property.

End loan When a construction loan is converted to permanent financing.

Entitlement Eligibility for a Veterans Administration home loan is called entitlement.

Entity A form of business organization.

Environmental impact statement Statements filed with local authorities and environmental agencies indicating what impact the project will have on the local environment.

Equal Credit Opportunity Act (ECOA) The Federal law that prohibits discrimination in lending based on an applicant's age, sex, marital status, race, religion, and national origin.

Equifax One of the three main credit reporting agencies.

Equity In real estate, the value of a property after mortgages, or any other claims against it, are deducted.

ERISA (Employee Retirement Income Security Act) The Employee Retirement Security Act of 1974, which legislates how certain pensions can be managed and invested.

Errors and omissions insurance In real estate, an insurance policy that insures against errors or omissions by a builder or architect.

Escalation clause A provision in a contract calling for an increase in price in the event of an increase in certain costs, or a purchase offer for a property that can be automatically raised if a higher bid comes in.

Escrow Funds deposited with a neutral third party to be delivered upon the completion of certain conditions; earnest money or other deposits are usually held by a real estate agent or an attorney; also funds held by a bank from mortgage payments to be paid for taxes.

Escrow account An account, separated from the rest of the funds of an escrow agent, established to hold escrow funds.

Escrow agent A neutral third party who holds escrow funds, either deposits for real estate transactions, or funds held from mortgage payments to meet real estate tax, mortgage insurance, or other payments.

Escrow agreement All of the conditions set forth regarding escrow funds or other property deposited in escrow, their management by the escrow agent, and their eventual disposition.

Escrow closing Once all of the conditions of a real estate transaction are met, and the title is fully transferred, all escrow is closed.

Escrow company A company that acts as a neutral agent to assure all conditions of a real estate agreement are met.

Escrow disbursements or escrow payments Funds disbursed from a real estate escrow account to pay taxes, mortgage insurance, or other property-related expenses.

Estate All of the assets and possessions of a person at the time of death; includes property, bank accounts, vehicles, furniture, works of art.

Estimated closing costs A good-faith calculation of all of the costs related to the sale of real estate property.

Estimated hazard insurance An estimate of the cost of hazard or homeowner's insurance, which covers certain types of damage to the home.

Estimated property taxes An estimate of how much in property taxes will be payable on a real estate property, given current state and county tax rates, and based on the property's assessed value.

Estoppel certificate A statement used to verify the current status of an existing lease to be relied upon by a prospective purchaser or lender.

Examination of title When a title company views the public records and other documents related to a real estate property to determine the chain of ownership.

Exclusive agency listing An agreement that a real estate broker will be paid a fee if a property is sold or leased during the period of the agreement.

Executed contract A contract that has been satisfied, in that all parties have met their obligations under the contract.

Exit strategy A plan developed by investors allowing for the option to disinvest a property or investment.

Experian One of the three main credit reporting agencies.

Face rental rate The rental rate, openly published by the landlord. This rate may be negotiated, depending on market conditions.

Facility space Relevant to hospitality properties, the space used for such facilities as a restaurant, shop, or gym that serves the guest but is not tied to room occupancy.

FAD (funds available for distribution) Funds received from operations less funds used for tenant improvements or other amenities, such as lease concessions.

FAD multiple A measure of performance of an REIT, it is the share price divided by the FAD.

Fair Credit Reporting Act The federal law that gives individuals the right to inspect their own credit files. The credit agency has the right to charge a fee for this service.

Fair Housing Act The federal law that prohibits discrimination in renting or selling a property based on an applicant's age, sex, marital status, race, religion, national origin.

Fair market value An appropriate sales price, at which a buyer would buy and a seller would sell, if there were no other extenuating circumstances and each party had full disclosure of the property.

Fannie Mae (FNMA) The Federal National Mortgage Association. This organization assists buyers and sellers in the mortgage market by establishing and administering a secondary market for loans originated by the FHA and the VA.

Farmer's Home Administration (FMHA) An agency of the U.S. government's Department of Agriculture providing credit to farmers and residents of rural areas.

Federal Home Loan Bank Board (FHLBB) Now known as the Office of Thrift Supervision, it is the government agency responsible for the regulation and supervision of federally chartered savings and loans institutions.

Federal Home Loan Mortgage Corporation (FHLMC or Freddie Mac) A quasi-government agency that buys conventional mortgages from FDIC-insured financial institutions and HUD-approved mortgage brokers.

Federal Housing Administration (FHA) A government agency that provides low-rate, low-down-payment mortgages to qualified buyers.

Federal National Mortgage Association (FNMA) see Fannie Mae

Fee simple interest Private ownership of real estate where the owner has the total right of control, use, and transfer of the property.

FFO (Funds From Operations) Net income plus depreciation and amortization, outside of gains or losses from debt restructuring or property sales. It is intended to reflect the performance of a company's real estate portfolio relative to it operating cash flow.

FFO multiple The share price of an REIT, divided by FFO.

FHA loan A mortgage that is insured by the Federal Housing Administration.

FHA mortgage insurance The insurance paid to maintain an FHA-insured loan.

Fiduciary A person or entity who has fiscal authority for a plan's assets; the management, distribution, or disposal thereof; or who gives investment advice regarding these assets. A fiduciary, or a fiduciary agent, includes trustees, board members, administrators, investment managers, and others in a responsible capacity. A fiduciary agent may be held personally liable for a breach of his duty.

Finance charge Interest or other charges paid by a borrower on a deferred payment or revolving line of credit.

Firm commitment A promise, made in writing by a lender to loan money to a borrower to purchase real estate property.

First mortgage The most senior mortgage on a property; this mortgage is paid off first in cases of default and has priority over second mortgages and any other encumbrances on a property.

First refusal right, or right of first refusal A clause in a lease that gives a tenant the first opportunity, before a property is marketed, to lease or buy additional space, at the same conditions as the originally leased space.

First-generation space Newly constructed or renovated space that has never been leased or occupied before.

First-loss position An investment position that carries the highest risk (and consequently the highest yield) on a property or asset in case of loss of value or foreclosure.

Fixed costs Costs that remain the same, regardless of use, occupancy, sales, or production of a property.

Fixed installment The fixed monthly payment due on a mortgage loan to pay the principal and interest.

Fixed rate Rate of interest that does not change or adjust over the life of the loan.

Fixed-rate mortgage A mortgage for which the interest rate stays the same for the life of the loan.

Fixed time Certain weeks in a year the owner of a timeshare can use the timeshare.

Flat fee An advisor or management fee for the management of a real estate portfolio, based on a fixed percentage of the value of the portfolio.

Flex space Building space that can be easily reconfigured to meet changing needs of the tenants, usually switching between office or showroom space to warehouse and distribution space.

Float In reference to stocks, the number of shares publicly traded.

Flood certification Insurance coverage that is required in certain areas that have been designated as flood areas.

Floor Area Ratio (FAR) Gross square footage of a building as a ratio of the entire square footage of the building lot.

For Sale By Owner (FSBO)

When an owner of a property attempts to sell his home directly to the public, without the assistance of a real estate broker.

Force majeure An event or series of events that cannot be controlled by party to an agreement that prevents him from meeting the terms of the agreement. A force majeure is typically a natural disaster such as a hurricane or flood, or a man-made disaster such as war.

Foreclosure The process by which a borrower in default under a mortgage loses his interest in the mortgaged property; usually, the property is then subject to forced sale so the proceeds can be used to satisfy the mortgage debt.

Four quadrants of the real estate capital markets

Private equity - Direct real estate investments acquired privately.

Public equity - REITs and other publicly traded real estate operating companies.

Private debt - Whole loan mortgages.

Public debt - Commercial mortgage-backed securities and other securitized forms of whole-loan mortgage interests.

Forward commitments Contractual commitment to offer financing, as long as required stated conditions are met. In real estate, a lender makes a forward commitment to fund a mortgage.

Front-end ratio A calculation made by lenders that looks at a borrower's potential monthly housing expense (principal, interest, taxes, and insurance) to his gross monthly income.

Full recourse Where the endorser or guarantor of a loan is fully responsible for the repayment of the loan in case of default.

Full-service rent A rental rate that includes operating expenses and real estate taxes; increases in those expenses are adjusted in subsequent years.

Fully amortized ARM An adjustable-rate mortgage structured so as to be able to amortize the balance over the amortization term at the interest accrual rate.

Fully diluted shares Number of shares of stock that would result if all convertible shares were converted to common shares.

Future proposed space Planned space in a commercial development that has not yet been constructed, or future, unconstructed phases of a multi-phase construction project.

General contractor The contractor who is responsible for the entire project; a general contractor will hire all of the subcontractors, such as carpentry, electrical, and plumbing contractors, and is responsible for the coordination between them.

General partner A member of a partnership who has the authority to obligate the partnership, and who shares in both the profits and losses of the partnership.

Gift Any funds a buyer receives from a relative or other source to assist in the purchase of a home. Lenders usually require a statement that these funds are a gift, not a loan that has to be repaid.

Government National Mortgage Association (GNMA or Ginnie Mae) Provides sources of funds for residential mortgages insured by the FHA or the VA.

Going-in capitalization rate A rate for capitalization which is calculated by dividing a property's assumed first year net income by the value of the property.

Good-faith estimate An estimate from a lender indicating the expected costs associated with obtaining a home loan.

Grace period The period of time after the due date that a borrower has to make a loan payment without being considered late and incurring a late fee.

Graduated lease A long-term lease where the rent changes based on future contingencies.

Graduated Payment Mortgage (GPM) A type of mortgage where the payments increase for a period of time and then level off.

Grant To give or transfer interest in a property by means of a deed or other instrument.

Grantee The person to whom this interest in property is conveyed.

Grantor The person who grants this interest in the property.

Gross building area The total of all of the areas of a property at floor levels including basements, mezzanines, and penthouses, but excluding setbacks and projections.

Gross income The total income before taxes and other salary deductions are made.

Gross investment in real estate (historic cost) Total investment in real estate comprised of purchase price, acquisition costs, and capital improvement, minus proceeds from sales.

Gross leasable area Total floor area of a property useable by a tenant and which generates rental income.

Gross lease The tenant pays a flat sum rent, and the landlord pays all of the tax, insurance, maintenance, and utility expenses.

Gross real estate asset value Total value of all positions in a real estate portfolio under management, including debt and equity positions, any joint ventures, and any mortgages or notes related to the real estate.

Gross real estate investment value Total value of all positions in a real estate portfolio under management, including debt and equity positions, any joint ventures, but excluding any mortgages or notes related to the real estate.

Gross returns Total returns from the operation of real estate.

Ground rent Rent paid for the use of land, usually on which to build a building. This type of lease is usually very long-term (99 years) and the lessor retains the land title.

Growing Equity Mortgage (GEM) A fixed-rate mortgage with payments that increase over time, with the additional funds applied to principal.

Guarantee mortgage A mortgage that is guaranteed by another party, in addition to the borrower.

Guarantor A person who makes a guaranty.

Guaranty Where a guarantor guarantees satisfaction of the debt of another party if the other party fails to satisfy that debt.

Hard cost The real construction cost of property or property improvements.

Hard Money (1) Cash loaned: contrasted with soft money, which means credit extended rather than cash. These expressions are often encountered in such a term as hard-money trust deed. (2) Some people use this term to mean a high-interest loan.

Hazard insurance An insurance policy for a home that insures against losses from hazards such as fire, windstorms, etc.

Highest and best use The use of a vacant land or improved property that is most sensible in terms of construction possibilities, financial feasibility, and highest value attainable.

High-rise A building that is higher than most surrounding buildings. In a large town, this may mean a building of over 25 stories, but in the suburbs, it may be only 7 stories to be considered a high-rise.

Holdbacks Part of a loan that is not disbursed until certain requirements are met.

Holding period Time an investor intends to own or hold a property from the purchase date to the eventual sale date.

Hold-over tenant A tenant who remains on a property after a lease has expired.

Home equity line A line of credit extended against the equity in a home.

Home equity loan A loan against the equity in a home; unlike an equity line of credit, this is a loan with a fixed amount with no additional draws allowed.

Home inspection A full examination of a home by a professional inspector to determine the condition of a home, usually prior to purchase.

Home inspector In most states, a licensed professional qualified to evaluate and judge the structural soundness and systems (plumbing, electric, HVAC) of a residence.

Home price The agreed-upon price of a home between the buyer and the seller. It is usually based on the appraised market value of the home.

Homeowners' Association (HOA) A group of owners that governs a subdivision, condominium or planned community; handles the legal issues; enforces the regulations; and collects fees from all owners to cover the costs of maintenance.

Homeowners' Association dues Dues paid to a homeowners' association to cover the maintenance and other communal expenses, typically on a monthly basis.

Homeowner's insurance Insurance covering the risk of home ownership, including damage insurance, liability insurance, and theft insurance.

Homestead An old term referring to a homeowner's primary residence.

Housing and Urban Development (the U.S. Department of) (HUD) A federal agency that oversees the FHA and other community and housing development programs.

Housing expenses-to-income ratio How much of a person's gross monthly income, expressed as a percentage, is spent on housing costs.

HUD-1 Uniform Settlement Statement A standardized settlement statement used at closings that outlines all the closing costs in a real estate transaction.

HVAC The heating, ventilation, and air-conditioning systems of a building.

Hybrid debt A mortgage that has some equity-like features in that cash flow and property appreciation revert to the mortgage holder at the sale of the property.

Implied cap rate The net operating income of an REIT divided by its equity capitalization and total debt.

Impounds Part of the monthly mortgage payment that is put into escrow to pay fees related to the home, such as insurance and property taxes.

Improvements Any enhancement to a property, including internal improvements or external improvements such as streets or sidewalks.

Incentive fee A management fee structure whereby the fee is determined by the performance of the real estate assets being managed.

Income capitalization value A determination of the value of a property by converting anticipated benefits into property value by capitalization of anticipated income or by discounting annual cash flow for the anticipated holding period.

Income property Real estate that is owned in order to derive a profit from it.

Income return Dollar return from the operations of a real estate property, expressed as a percentage.

Index A published interest rate that lenders use as a base to calculate the rate on adjustable-rate mortgages.

Indexed rate The indexed rate plus a margin to arrive at the interest rate charged. For example, if the prime rate is 4 percent and is used as the index, and the margin is 2 percent, the rate charged would be 6 percent.

Indirect costs Costs of development of a property not related to construction or improvement. Such costs include administrative expenses, architectural and engineering fees, debt service.

Individual account management Individually managed real estate investment accounts where the investment company acts as advisor and/or manager of the account.

Inflation An annual rate at which prices increase.

Inflation hedge An investment made to offset the effects of inflation since it increases at a greater rate than the inflation rate.

Initial interest rate The rate on a loan when it is first established. In an ARM, this rate changes over the life of the loan.

Initial Public Offering (IPO) When a private company initially offers its shares for sale on the public market.

Initial rate cap In some ARMs, a limit is fixed for the maximum the interest may increase over the initial interest rate.

Initial rate duration A period of time, for an adjustable-rate mortgage, during which the initial interest rate (which is frequently lower than market rates) will last.

Inspection fee Fee paid to a professional inspector to inspect a property.

Inspection report A report made by a professional inspector indicating the condition of a property.

Installment Regular, periodic payments made by a borrower to a lender.

Institutional-grade property

Real estate investments that are owned or financed by large institutional investors. They will typically be made up of core investments such as office, retail, and industrial space and will be supplemented by specialized real estate such as nursing homes, hotels, mixed-use properties, and others.

Insurance binder Temporary insurance policy while a permanent policy is obtained.

Insurance company separate account A real estate investment offered by a life insurance company. It allows funds which are governed by ERISA to avoid unrelated taxable income from certain types of investments.

Insured mortgage A mortgage that is insured or guaranteed by the FHA or private mortgage insurance.

Interest Money paid by one party for the use of another party's capital.

Interest accrual rate The rate at which interest accrues on a loan, or in the case of real estate, on a mortgage.

Interest-only loan A loan in which the borrower pays only the interest as it accrues on the loan, without any of the monthly payment going toward principal.

Interest paid over life of loan The total sum of interest paid by a borrower to a lender during the life of a loan.

Interest rate A fee, expressed as a percentage, charged for the use of a lender's money.

Interest rate buydown plan A scheme to assist buyers whereby the seller advances funds from the sale of the home to lower the interest rate on the mortgage to make the mortgage more affordable for the buyer.

Interest rate cap Maximum interest rate allowed on an adjustable-rate mortgage during an adjustment period.

Interest rate ceiling Maximum interest rate allowed on an adjustable-rate mortgage during the life of the loan.

Interest rate floor Minimum interest rate allowed on an adjustable-rate mortgage during the life of the loan.

Interest-only strip A derivative that trades only the interest and not the principal of a loan or security.

Interim financing Also known as bridge loans or swing loans, this type of financing covers a seller between the sale of one home and the purchase of another. Construction loans are also types of interim financing.

Internal Rate of Return (IRR) A type of analysis using discounted cash flow to determine the anticipated return on a real estate asset in a given holding period.

Inventory All of the real estate property in a certain market, regardless of whether it is available or useable.

Investment committee The body on a company's board that oversees the company's investments or the governing body overseeing pension investments.

Investment manager A company that manages real estate capital for others for a fee. It may have discretionary power and may manage this capital via separate account, co-investment accounts, or commingled funds.

Investment policy The formal policy of a company or an institution outlining the criteria by which investments may be made and assets managed. It usually sets goals, methods, and criteria, and outlines use of outside consultants, managers, and advisors.

Investment property Any real estate that generates income, from a rental home to an apartment building to a commercial complex.

Investment strategy The criteria used by management to structure a real estate investment portfolio by setting types, locations, sizes of properties, as well as ownership models and stages of the investment cycle.

Investment structures The various types of investment structures are: leveraged or unleveraged acquisitions, traditional debt, joint ventures, and triple net leases.

Investment-grade CMBS Mortgage-backed securities with a rating of BBB or better.

Investor In real estate, the money source for most lenders.

Investor status Taxable or tax-exempt. Qualified pension and retirement plans are tax-exempt; all others, including off-shore capital, are considered taxable.

Joint liability When two or more individuals have the responsibility to abide by the terms of a contract or debt.

Joint tenancy When a property is owned by two or more people in equal shares. Frequently used for husband and wife ownership of a property.

Joint venture An investment vehicle formed by two or more entities to buy, sell, and manage real estate assets.

Jumbo loan A loan that is larger than the limits set by the FNMA or the FHMLC.

Junior mortgage Mortgaged loan that is subordinate to the first mortgage.

Just compensation In eminent domain, compensation that is offered to the owner of a property being taken over for public use that is considered fair and just to both the owner and the public.

Landlord's warrant Warrant to sell a tenant's personal property to meet the obligations of a lease or some stipulation in the lease.

Late charge Penalty imposed by the lender when a borrower does not make a payment by the due date or within the grace period.

Late payment Payment received after the due date.

Lead manager An investment banking firm that is primarily responsible for the coordination of the new issue of a security.

Lease A written agreement between a property owner and a tenant giving the tenant rights of possession of the property and stipulating the payment to the landlord for that right for a specified period of time.

Lease agreement The formal document evidencing a lease arrangement between a tenant and a landlord.

Lease commencement date The date stipulated as the beginning of a lease period, whether or not a tenant takes possession.

Lease expiration exposure schedule A schedule that shows all the square footage of leases in a property that expire in the next five years, and whether or not they will be renewed.

Leasehold The interest in a property held by a tenant for a limited time; primarily used to describe the right to inhabit a property for the term of a lease; and at the end of the lease, these rights revert to the owner or landlord.

Leasehold interest The right to use a property for a certain, fixed period with no transfer of title.

Lease-purchase mortgage loan A mortgage that allows a tenant to put part of his rent payment toward mortgage payments on the property.

Legal blemish Faults in the clear title of a property, such as violations or a fraudulent title claim.

Legal description An official description of a property, using surveys, lot and block numbers, and any characteristics, and listing any easements or reservations.

Legal owner The person or entity that holds the title on a property.

Lender In real estate, a bank, savings institution or mortgage company that offers loans to buyers to buy homes.

Letter of credit An agreement by a bank or a commercial institution that a draft will be honored as long as certain conditions are complied with. In real estate, letters of credit frequently take the place of cash deposits to act as security for a lease.

Letter of intent A preliminary document outlining the terms of a contract to be drawn.

Leverage Using credit to

finance the cost of a real estate investment. It can be positive leverage when the interest rate is lower than the capitalization rate of the project, or it can be negative leverage when the rate of return on the project is reduced by the debt.

Liabilities A person's or entity's debts and financial obligations.

Liability insurance An insurance policy that protects a person or company against claims of negligence or inappropriate action resulting in bodily injury or property damage.

LIBOR (London InterBank Offered Rate) The interest rate at which banks offer to lend unsecured funds to other banks in the London money market. It is used as a benchmark for many other rates.

Lien A claim against a property. Mortgages and trust deeds are considered liens and must be paid off when the property is sold.

Lien waiver A waiver that may be required for a mechanic's lien in order for payments to be made out under a construction loan or for a general contractor to receive a draw against a construction contract.

Life cap Limits how much a loan's interest rate can change during the life of the mortgage; if the rate on an ARM is initially 4 percent and has a life cap of 6 points, the cap is 10 percent.

Lifecycle The stages of property development, usually pre-development, development, leases, operations, and redevelopment.

Lifetime payment cap In adjustable-rate mortgages, the amount payments can increase or decrease over the life of the mortgage can be limited.

Lifetime rate cap The maximum interest rate on a loan.

Like-kind property Instead of cash in payment for a property, a property may be exchanged for a like property. Arrangements such as this are governed by Section 1032 of the Internal Revenue Code.

Limited partnership A partnership made of some partners who manage the business and are responsible for debt and other partners who only contribute capital and do not manage the business or take responsibility for any amount over their capital contribution.

Liquid assets Assets that can be converted to cash quickly; cash, funds in savings and checking accounts, money-market accounts, and most CDs are considered liquid assets.

Liquidity How easily an asset can be converted to cash without losing any value.

Listing agreement An agreement between a real estate broker and the owner of a property whereby the owner agrees to compensate the broker if he sells the property at a certain price.

Loan Funds extended by a lender to a borrower with the intent that it will be paid back over time with interest.

Loan amount The amount the borrower promises to repay according to the loan contract.

Loan application The written act of requesting funds from a lender.

Loan application fee The fee charged by most lending institutions to start the process of a loan application.

Loan commitment The promise by a lender to make a loan for a specified amount and on specific terms.

Loan officer A representative at a lending institution empowered to act on behalf of that institution to lend funds within certain limits.

Loan origination fee Fees charged by lenders to cover the costs of arranging the loan.

Loan parameters The factors used to determine whether to provide a loan to the borrower.

Loan term The time within which a mortgage must be paid off; conventional mortgages have 15- or 30-year loan terms.

Loan-to-value ratio (LTV) The principal of a loan divided by the appraised value of the property.

Lock The act of guaranteeing that a quoted rate will be given on a loan for a certain length of time.

Lock-box structure Rent or debt-service payments are sent directly to a trustee by the tenant.

Lock-in The commitment by a lender that a quoted rate will be guaranteed for a certain length of time.

Lock-in period A lender's commitment to a borrower to guarantee (or "lock in") a specific interest rate for a limited amount of time.

Lockout An initial period in a loan during which it may not be prepaid.

Long-term lease In general, a lease with an expiry date of at least three years from signing.

Loss severity How much principal is lost when a loan is foreclosed.

Lot A parcel of land that makes up a part of a subdivision or a block. Boundaries of lots are recorded in official maps and plats.

Low-documentation loan A loan that has less than the usual requirements regarding verification of income and assets.

Low-rise A building that is lower than most surrounding buildings, usually only about 4 stories high.

Lump-sum contract A

construction contract at a fixed price, usually granted via a bidding process. The contractor is obligated to the contract price and must absorb any loss but can make more profit if he can bring the project in under cost.

Magic page Part of the offering prospectus of a new REIT, it describes how the REIT will meet its expectations for funds available for distribution.

Maintenance fee A monthly fee paid by the members of a homeowners' association for the maintenance of the common areas.

Maker The creator of a promissory note who promises to pay the note when due.

Margin A fixed percentage added to an index for adjustable-rate mortgages.

Mark to market Changing the value of an investment on the books of a company to reflect the current market value of the investment.

Market capitalization The current share price of a company multiplied by the number of shares outstanding. It is a way to measure the value of a company.

Market data approach An appraisal technique based on sales of comparable properties. Also called comparison approach.

Market rental rates The rent a property would receive in the open market, as measured by rental rates on comparable spaces.

Market study A projection of the future demand for a real estate project based on probable rent the square footage can absorb.

Market value The price a property would receive in a competitive and open market sale.

Marketable title A title that can be readily sold to a willing buyer because it has no encumbrances.

Master lease The main lease in a building or development in which subleases exist.

Master servicer An institution that collects funds from borrowers, advances funds to cover delinquencies, and in the event of default, takes a property through foreclosure, all on behalf of the trustee.

Maturity date When a loan matures and the principal balance on the loan becomes due and payable.

Mechanic's lien A claim filed by a contractor, laborer, or supplier against a property to assure payment for his work or supplies. Mechanics liens must be satisfied before construction funds can be distributed.

Meeting space Space made available for meetings, conferences, and banquets in a hotel.

Merged credit report A credit

report that uses the information from all three of the main credit reporting agencies (Equifax, Trans-Union and Experian).

Metes and bounds A method of describing land by distances and directions of the boundaries.

Mezzanine financing Financing that is in between equity and debt; senior debt has a higher claim to assets, and equity has a lower claim.

Mid-rise Depending on the location, a building that is medium in height above ground level. In a large city, it may be as high as 25 stories, but in the suburbs, it may be 4 to 8 stories.

Mixed-use Rental space in a building that may be for more than one use.

Modern Portfolio Theory (MPT) A way of quantifying risk and return on a portfolio. It was developed by Harry Markowitz and is now the basis for the principle of asset diversification. It concentrates on the total portfolio and the relation of assets to each other within the portfolio, rather than concentrating on the performance of individual assets.

Modification Any change in the terms of a loan agreement.

Modified Annual Percentage Rate (APR) An APR that is adjusted based on the length of time the borrower expects to hold the loan.

Monthly fixed installment That portion of a monthly mortgage payment applied toward the principal and interest.

Mortgage A debt instrument that conveys conditional ownership of a financed asset. A borrower provides the lender with a mortgage in exchange for the right to use the property being financed and agrees to meet the repayment terms.

Mortgage acceleration clause The clause in a mortgage that allows the lender to demand payment of the outstanding loan balance.

Mortgage banker A bank or other financial institution that originates mortgages for sale in a secondary market.

Mortgage broker An individual who acts as an intermediary in the mortgage brokerage process, bringing lenders and borrowers together for a fee.

Mortgage broker business A company that acts as an intermediary in the mortgage brokerage process, bringing lenders and borrowers together for a fee.

Mortgage constant The ratio of the mortgage payment to the total outstanding mortgage balance expressed as a decimal.

Mortgage insurance Insurance on some mortgages to protect lenders from default. Usually mortgages with smaller down payments (less than 20 percent) will require mortgage insurance.

Mortgage interest deduction An allowable deduction taken on a tax return for the interest payments on a real estate loan.

Mortgage Insurance Premium (MIP) The monthly payment for mortgage insurance.

Mortgage life insurance An insurance policy that pays off a mortgage in the case of the death of the borrower.

Mortgagee A bank or other financial institution that lends money to a borrower against a mortgage note.

Mortgagor A person or entity that borrows money from a bank or other financial institution against a mortgage note.

NAREIT (National Association of Real Estate Investment Trusts) A trade association representing the real estate investment trust industry.

NCREIF (National Council of Real Estate Investment Fiduciaries) An association representing the real estate investment community involved in research, seminars, and education; also produces a property index.

NCREIF Property Index (NPI) An index produced by the NCREIF that reports returns and appreciation of income property, based on data collected from members. It is divided

by the various types of income properties.

Negative amortization A debt structure that allows an investor to pay an interest rate that is below the contract loan rate, for an initial period.

Net asset value (NAV) The value of a real estate portfolio less leverage or joint venture interests.

Net asset value per share Assets divided by shares outstanding.

Net assets Assets less liabilities, valued at market.

Net cash flow On long-term mortgages, net income plus depreciation minus principal payments.

Net effective income An individual's gross income less federal income tax.

Net investment in real estate Gross investment less outstanding debt.

Net investment income Income (loss) on a portfolio after expenses but before gains and losses on investments.

Net operating income (NOI) Gross revenue less operating expenses and allowance for anticipated vacancies; it is used to indicate financial strength.

Net present value (NPV) Total present value of future cash flow plus present value of estimated proceeds from sale. A net present value greater than zero is thought to be a good investment.

Net purchase price Purchase price less debt financing.

Net real estate investment value The market value of real estate property less related debt.

Net returns Investor return less management fees.

Net sales proceeds Sales proceeds of an asset less commission, closing costs, and any marketing expenses.

Net square footage Space required for a given function.

Net worth A measure of the worth of a person or company; it is the difference between total assets and liabilities of the person or company.

No-cash-out refinance The opposite of a cash-out refinancing: the amount of the new mortgage is equal to the balance due on the old mortgage, with no additional cash to be taken out.

No-documentation loan When the amount of the new mortgage covers the remaining balance of the first loan plus closing costs and any liens, and yields no more than 1 percent of the new loan's principal in cash.

Nominal yield Yield an investor receives on an investment, before fees or inflation are taken into account.

Non-assumption clause Provision in a loan that will not allow the mortgage to be transferred to another borrower, without prior lender approval.

Non-compete clause A feature of a lease which disallows other businesses of the same kind as the lessee to lease in the same building. This limits the competition business will have in the immediate area.

Non-conforming loan A loan that is either too large or doesn't meet the qualifications to be purchased by Fannie Mae or Freddie Mac.

Non-discretionary funds Funds an investment manager may manage, but without full discretion over those funds; each transaction must have the approval of the investor.

Non-investment-grade CMBS Commercial Mortgage-Backed Securities which have a B or BBB rating, and therefore are not eligible for institutional investors. These securities have a higher yield than investment-grade securities.

Non-liquid asset An asset that is not easily turned into cash, such as real estate, personal goods, etc.

Non-performing loan A loan on which the principal and interest payments are not being made.

Non-recourse debt A loan that, if it defaults, will only yield the value of the underlying asset, regardless of the value of the loan.

Nonconforming Mortgage A mortgage that does not meet the purchase requirements of Fannie Mae and Freddie Mac.

Noninstitutional Lender A lender that is not an institution, such as retirement funds, endowed universities, and private individuals.

Nonjudicial Foreclosure A foreclosure by having property sold to satisfy the debt without going through court.

Nonrecurring closing costs Fees that will only be paid once, at the closing of a real estate property, such as appraisal fee, home inspection fees, title insurance, etc.

Notary Public A person empowered to administer oaths and to attest or certify documents to assure their authenticity.

Note A document signed by a borrower agreeing to repay a mortgage within a certain length of time at a specific interest rate.

Note rate The interest rate on a mortgage note.

Offer The price at which an individual is willing to sell a security or commodity.

Office of Thrift Supervision (OTS) Formally known as the Federal Home Loan Bank Board, it is the government agency responsible for the regulation and supervision of federally chartered savings and loans institutions.

One-year adjustable-rate mortgage An adjustable-rate mortgage with an interest rate that changes yearly, based on a certain index.

Open space Portion of a building complex dedicated to public use and enjoyment; many municipalities now require a certain percentage of open space in a complex development.

Open-end fund A fund that does not have a subscription expiration period; new capital is continually accepted, and new investments are continually made.

Operating cost escalation A clause in a lease that allows the lessor to increase the lease rent based on some measure of increases in costs, such as price indices, newly negotiated wage levels, or increased operating costs.

Operating expense The cost to operate a real estate property. These costs included maintenance and repairs, utilities, management fees, administrative costs, insurance, and taxes.

Opportunistic An investment or phase of an investment where it is underperforming but is expected to experience cash flow and value increases in the near future. These typically are highly leveraged and need to produce high yields.

Option When a buyer pays a fee for the right (but not the obligation) to purchase a real estate property within a set time frame.

Option arm loan A home loan that allows the borrower different payment options each month.

Original principal balance The principal of a loan at the outset, before any payments have been made against it.

Origination fee A fee charged by a lender to a borrower for arranging a real estate loan.

Originator A company specializing in creating and underwriting mortgage loans, both commercial and residential.

Out-parcel The individual site of each retail business in a shopping center.

Overallotment When an underwriter offers to sell more shares than he has agreed to buy from an issuer.

Owner financing When the seller of a property agrees to finance some or all of the purchase price of it.

Parking ratio Total rentable square footage of a building divided by its total number of available parking spaces.

Partial sales The sale of less than an entire real estate property, such as only a parcel of land or only one building in a multi-building complex.

Partial taking Under eminent domain, when a government or governmental authority takes over only part of a property.

Participating debt A debt where the lender holds participatory equity, yielding him increases in income and the value of the property, in addition to interest on the debt.

Partnership A voluntary association of two or more persons to carry on business for profit.

Party in interest Regarding ERISA, it refers to employers and unions, but not their affiliates or service providers of retirement plans, and includes fiduciaries only when they act directly on behalf of a plan sponsor.

Pass-through certificate Certificates representing an underlying pool of mortgages through which principal and interest payments are passed to the holders of the certificates.

Payee A person to whom a note states it is payable.

Payer A person who signs a note agreeing to pay it. Also called a maker.

Payment Change Date for adjustable-rate mortgages, the date on which the new monthly payment amount, based on the new interest rate, takes effect.

Payout ratio Earnings per share less extraordinary items paid as dividends to stock holders over the last 12 months, expressed as a percentage.

Pension liability The amount necessary to fund the vested portion of a pension fund.

Percentage rent A rent structure, commonly used in retail centers, whereby the rent is calculated as a percentage of the gross sales or revenue of the tenant.

Per-diem interest Interest charged or accrued on a daily basis.

Performance Changes in the account value of a fund, measured on a quarterly basis, which are attributable to investment income, appreciation, and gross return. The many different formulas used for performance make it difficult to compare one investment to another.

Performance bond A bond posted by a contractor to assure the performance of a contract. In the event of non-performance, the proceeds of the bond are used to complete the project.

Performance measurement The entire scope of measuring real estate performance; there are many different models and tools used to determine performance.

Performance-based fees Management or advisor fees that are determined by the performance of the assets being managed, frequently combined with acquisition or other management fees.

Periodic payment cap For adjustable-rate mortgages, a limit on the amount new monthly payments can increase during an adjustment period.

Periodic rate cap For adjustable-rate mortgages, a limit on how much the interest rate can increase or decrease during an adjustment period.

Permanent loan A property's long-term mortgage.

PITI (principal, interest, taxes, and insurance) A payment on a mortgage that includes the principal, interest, taxes, and insurance.

Plan assets The total sum of all of the assets of a pension plan.

Plan sponsor An entity that establishes a pension plan, administers it, and makes the contributions to it. The term is frequently used to denote the staff administering the plan or the trustees of the plan.

Plat The map of a specific area, indicating all of the relevant features such as boundaries, streets, and easements.

Pledged Account Mortgage (PAM) A mortgage tied to a savings account whereby the savings account and the interest it accrues is used to gradually pay down the mortgage.

Points (loan discount points) Upfront fees a lender may charge to keep an interest rate lower on a mortgage loan; 1 point is equal to 1 percent of the loan.

Portfolio management The process whereby an entity formulates and implements an investment strategy according to the investor's objectives, or, in real estate, the management of several properties owned by one investor.

Portfolio turnover The time between the initial funding of an investment in a portfolio and when it is sold, expressed as an average over time.

Power of attorney A document that gives one person the power to act on behalf of another.

Power of sale A clause in a mortgage that gives the mortgagee the right to sell the mortgaged property in case of default.

Pre-approval A confirmation that a lender is willing to lend a certain amount to a borrower to purchase real estate. The lender will do an analysis to determine the credit worthiness of the potential borrower in order to make this commitment.

Pre-approval letter A letter indicating confirmation that a lender is willing to lend a certain amount to a borrower to purchase real estate.

Preferred shares Stocks that have priority over common shares in the case of dissolution of a company, though they fall behind most other creditors of a firm.

Preleased When a rental space is leased prior to the start of construction of the of the building or prior to the issuance of a certificate of occupancy.

Preliminary title insurance report A report by a title insurance company showing the condition of title to a property, including liens, restrictions, and so forth.

Prepaid expenses or fees Expenses paid before they become due.

Prepaid interest Interest expense that is paid before it becomes due.

Prepayment Paying a loan, or portions of it, before it is due.

Prepayment clause A provision in a note or deed of trust allowing the borrower to pay off all or part of the principal before it is due, with or without a prepayment penalty.

Prepayment penalty A penalty for paying a loan, or portions of it, before it is due.

Prepayment rights The ability of a borrower to make partial or full payment of a loan, prior to its maturity date, without any penalties attached.

Prequalification When a lender determines a buyer's ability to support a mortgage and of what amount.

Price-to-earnings ratio Current share price divided by the earnings per share from operations, measured over the last four quarters.

Primary issuance The point at which debt is first sold by the issuer.

Primary mortgage market Lenders, such as banks and other financial institutions, that make mortgage loans directly to consumers. They may, in turn, sell these mortgages in the secondary market.

Prime space First-generation space that is offered for lease.

Prime tenant Sometimes called the anchor, it is the major tenant in a shopping center and draws customers to the shopping center.

Principal An amount borrowed which is not yet paid.

Principal balance The amount of a loan left from the original principal which is not yet paid.

Principal paid over life of loan Scheduled payments of principal that will pay down the face amount of the loan over the length of time the loan is open.

Principal payments Payments that return principal to a lender, as compared to payment of interest.

Principle of conformity The concept that a house appreciates more in value when it is similar to other houses in the immediate

area.

Private Mortgage Insurance (PMI) Mortgage insurance is required by a lender when a down payment is less than 20 percent; when a private company offers this insurance, it is called PMI.

Private placement A security sale that is made directly rather than publicly and is therefore exempt from SEC requirements.

Private REIT A Real Estate Investment Trust whose shares are placed privately rather than traded publicly.

Pro rata In leases, the share of operating expenses attributable to each tenant proportionate to the leased space.

Processing fee A fee charged by lenders for the work necessary to process a real estate loan.

Production acres Area of agricultural or timber operations devoted to the crop; it does not include storage, office, or other support areas.

Prohibited transaction In ERISA, certain transactions are prohibited between a pension plan and a "party of interest": transfer or use of assets, exchange of property, loans or credit, furnishing goods or services, or acquisition of the employers real property.

Property tax The tax paid on private property, based on the assessed value and the local tax rates. Real estate property taxes are frequently included in a monthly mortgage payment.

Prudent man rule A standard by which a fiduciary agent is expected to act with the care, prudence, and diligence that a prudent man would use in a like situation.

Punch list The detailed list by the owner of a space of incomplete or unsatisfactory items in a construction project that a contractor has to fix or complete.

Purchase-Money Mortgage (PMM) A mortgage used to partially pay for a property.

Qualified plan An employee benefit plan that has been designated by the IRS as tax-exempt because, among other requirements, it has been placed in trust for the benefit of the covered employees.

Qualifying ratio The ratio a lender will calculate to determine how much money a buyer is qualified to borrow.

Quitclaim deed A deed that passes title without any guarantee that title is valid.

Rate cap See "Caps (Interest Rate)."

Rate lock See "Lock."

Rate-improvement mortgage A mortgage that allows a borrower to a one-time interest rate reduction without a refinancing.

Rating A measure of the credit quality of a security or asset, represented by a grade assigned to it by a recognized rating agency.

Rating agencies Firms engaged in the business of rating the securities of companies as to their credit quality to help investors decide on investments. The top rating agencies are: Standard and Poor's, Moody's, and Fitch.

Raw land Land in its natural state, before any improvements.

Raw space Raw space in a building, before any improvements.

Real estate agent A person licensed to negotiate the purchase or sale of real estate on behalf of a consumer.

Real estate fundamentals The basic factors that determine real estate values: supply and demand, price levels, and economic performance of a region.

Real Estate Settlement Procedures Act (RESPA) A law designed to protect consumers that requires a lender to give a borrower advance notice of closing costs.

Real property Land and any improvements to the land, such as buildings, parking lots, etc.

Real rate of return A measure of an investor's return which takes inflation into account; real rate of return = (1 + nominal yield) divided by (1 + the inflation rate) minus 1.

Realtor® A trademark indicating that a real estate broker is a member of the National Association of Realtors.

Recapture In leases, a clause that gives the lessor a percentage of profits over and above a fixed rental amount, or a clause that allows the lessor to terminate a lease if minimum sales are not met.

Recission In general, the cancellation of a contract; in real estate, the right of a buyer to cancel a real estate contract within 3 days of signing it.

Recording fees Fees to record a home sale with the local authorities so it becomes part of the public record.

Recourse A lender's right, in the event of default, to seize the personal assets of any guarantor.

Red herring A preliminary prospectus for an IPO. So called because it must contain a statement, in red ink, that the offering is filed but not yet effective.

Refinance Obtain a new loan to replace an existing loan on a property.

Regional diversification The attempt to diversify a real estate portfolio by differing areas; different managers and consultants define this diversification in different ways, some by geographic criteria, some by economic criteria.

Registration statement Forms filed with the SEC for a proposed new securities offering or for the listing of existing securities on an exchange.

Regulation Z A code in the Truth in Lending Act requiring a borrower to be advised (in writing) of all costs associated with a loan.

Rehab Substantial renovations to a building project to make it viable.

Rehabilitation mortgage A mortgage to finance substantial renovations to a building.

REIT (Real estate investment trust) A form of real estate ownership in which investors combine to acquire property or finance existing property. An REIT does not pay corporate income tax, but instead distributes substantially all of its income to investors.

Release clause A provision in a blanket mortgage or trust deed allowing the owner of the properties to secure the release of properties upon certain terms, usually the payment of a certain sum of money.

Release of mortgage A written instrument releasing the lien of a mortgage on real property. See also certificate of discharge.

Remaining balance Amount of unpaid principal remaining on a mortgage.

Remaining term The amount of time remaining on a mortgage.

REMIC (Real estate mortgage investment conduit) REMICs hold a pool of mortgages in order to issue multiple classes of mortgage-backed securities. It was included in the 1986 Tax Reform Act as a remedy for a corporate double tax.

Renegotiable rate mortgage See "adjustable-rate mortgage (ARM)."

Renewal option Gives a tenant the right to extend a lease.

Renewal probability The average percentage of tenants expected to renew their lease; it is used to estimate leasing costs and costs of downtime.

Rent Funds paid for the use and occupancy of a rental property.

Rent commencement date The date when a tenant is obligated to start paying rent.

Rentable/usable ratio Total rentable area of a building divided by usable area. It is used to determine pro-rata shares of common costs or to determine square footage basis for a tenant's rent.

Rental concession Any incentive offered by a landlord to induce a tenant to lease. Rent abatement, improvements to property, reduced rents, and moving allowances are a few of these types of incentives.

Rental growth rate Rate at which market rental rates are expected to rise in a given period.

Rent-up period Period immediately after construction of a building when renters are solicited and occupancy is stabilizing.

REO (Real Estate Owned) Property owned by a bank due to loan defaults and subsequent foreclosures.

Replacement cost An appraisal method that estimates the cost to replace a building with a building of the same usage, materials, standards, and design.

Replacement reserves A reserve that is established by periodic funding to provide for replacement of building components to extend the building's economic life.

Request For Proposal (RFP) A formal request by an entity inviting investment managers to make proposals for managing investments by submitting their strategies, performance on other portfolios, fees, references, and other determining information. The board or senior management of the entity will then review all RFPs for consideration.

Reserve account Any account that a borrower is required to fund in order to protect the interests of a lender. They may include capital improvement accounts, deferred maintenance accounts, etc.

Resolution Trust Corp. (RTC) Established by Congress to manage savings institutions that failed and eventually to sell the assets to recover taxpayer losses from these government-insured institutions.

Retail investor A direct consumer investor in securities marketed directly by investment companies.

Retention rate The last 12 months of earnings that have been reinvested in a company, calculated by subtracting the 12-month payout rate from 100.

Return on assets After-tax income divided by average total assets over an annual period.

Return on equity Income available to stockholders divided by average equity over an annual period.

Return on investments Income after taxes divided by average long-term debt, long-term liabilities, and shareholder equity over an annual period.

Reverse Annuity Mortgage (RAM) A type of mortgage where the lender makes periodic payments to the homeowner using the equity in the home as collateral for and repayment of the mortgage.

Reverse mortgage A type of mortgage where the lender makes periodic payments to the homeowner using the equity in the home as collateral for and repayment of the mortgage.

Reversion capitalization rate The rate at which reversion value is capitalized.

Reversion value The lump sum payment an investor expects to receive when an investment is sold or terminated.

Revolving liability A line of credit that allows a consumer to borrow a varying amount to purchase goods and services.

RevPAR (Revenue per available room) Total revenue from rooms in a hospitality facility divided by the average number of rooms.

Right to rescission In real estate, the right of a buyer to cancel a real estate contract within 3 days of signing it.

Risk management The determination of insurable risk, and the subsequent evaluation and implementation of the various insurance options available.

Risk-adjusted rate of return A method of determining return on investment that adjusts for volatility; it is the expected rate of return minus the rate of return of Treasury bills (a secure risk) divided by the expected standard deviation of the return on the assets.

Road show A circuit made by the principals or executives of a company that is planning a public issue of its stocks; they meet with various underwriters and investment analysts prior to the registration statement to explain and stir interest in the issue.

Roll-over risk The risk a lessor has that a tenant will not renew his lease.

Sale-leaseback A lease structure in which an owner of a property sells that property to an investor and then leases it back from the investor and continues to occupy it.

Sales comparison value A method of determining the value of a property by comparing it to recent sales of similar properties.

Sales contract The contract signed by the buyer and seller of real estate that states the terms of a sale that they agree to.

Satisfaction of mortgage A contract signed by the buyer and seller detailing the terms of a property sale.

Secondary financing or mortgage A second loan against a mortgage on real property secured by a lien junior to an existing first mortgage loan.

Secondary mortgage market The market where mortgages are bought and sold to investors.

Secondary, or follow-on, offering An additional stock offering made by a public company that has already had an initial stock offering.

Second-generation or secondary space Rental space that was previously occupied and becomes available for lease. It can either be leased by the landlord or subleased by the tenant.

Securities and Exchange Commission (SEC) A federal agency responsible for supervising and overseeing the issuance and exchange of public securities.

Securitization In real estate, the process of converting mortgage loans into tradable forms, such as mortgage-backed securities.

Security Property that is pledged as collateral for a loan.

Security deposit The deposit a tenant makes with a landlord to guarantee performance of the lease. It is usually a cash deposit, but can also be in the form of a letter of credit or bond.

Seisen (seizen) Ownership and possession of real estate by a claim of freehold estate.

Self-administered or self-managed REIT A REIT whose employees also perform the management functions of the property the REIT owns.

Seller carry back See "Owner Financing."

Seller financing See "Owner Financing."

Senior classes A type of security with first priority to the assets securing a loan.

Separate account When an investment manager or advisor is retained by a pension plan sponsor to secure real estate exclusively for that sponsor, using their stated investment policy.

Servicer The organization acting on behalf of a trustee for security holders.

Servicing The act of keeping a real estate loan in good order by collecting payments, paying taxes and insurance, etc.

Setback The distance from curbs or property lines that a building must be built.

Settlement costs or fees See "Closing Costs."

Settlement statement A standardized statement used at closings that outlines all the closing costs in a real estate transaction.

Shared Appreciation Mortgage (SAM) A mortgage where the lender or some other investor receives a portion of the future appreciation of a real estate property in exchange for a lower interest rate.

Shared-equity transaction A type of purchase where two buyers purchase a real estate property, one owning his portion as resident, the other owning his portion as investor.

Shares outstanding A transaction in which two buyers purchase a property, one as a resident co-owner and the other as an investor co-owner.

Simple Interest Interest computed only on the principal, as compared to compound interest which is computed on the principal and accrued interest.

Site analysis A study to determine whether a parcel of land is suited for its intended use.

Site development All of the necessary improvements to a site before anything can be built on it.

Site plan The plan that shows the buildings and improvements to a real estate property relative to the entire parcel.

Slab Concrete, reinforced by steel, that forms the floor of a building.

Social investing A type of investing that supports certain social or political objectives. ERISA will only allow social investing when it is also economically justified and the proper real estate fundamentals are considered.

Soft cost Portion of an investment outside of the actual cost of the investment and its improvements; in some cases, these costs are tax-deductible.

Soft money Credit extended as opposed to cash (hard money).

Space plan A drawing that shows the interior of a tenant space, indicating walls, doors, room sizes, and even furniture placement in some cases.

Special assessment A charge to owner(s) to cover the cost of public improvements necessary for the property.

Special servicer A firm engaged in the business of working out defaulted or delinquent mortgages.

Specified investing When an investor or investors specify specific real estate properties that their capital should be invested in.

Speculative space A space in a new construction that has not yet been leased.

Stabilized net operating income Income less expenses on a projected basis, adjusted to reflect fully stabilized operations.

Stabilized occupancy Projected income less expenses that are subject to change but have been adjusted to reflect equivalent, stable property operations.

Standard payment calculation Calculation used to determine the required monthly payments of a mortgage to repay the principal and interest over the life of the mortgage.

Step rate mortgage A mortgage in which the interest rate increases for a period of time at the beginning, and then stabilizes.

Step-up lease (graded lease) A lease that allows for specified

increases in the rent at set intervals during the lease.

Stipulations The terms within a written contract.

Straight lease (flat lease) A lease that calls for a fixed periodic rental payment during the term of the lease.

Strip center A small shopping center made up of a row of stores, usually anchored by one larger store such as a supermarket.

Subcontractor A contractor, who is usually a specialist in some area, such as electrical, plumbing, etc., who works under the general contractor on a building project.

Sublessee A person or entity that has the rights of use and occupancy of a rental space under a lease that is the primary responsibility of another party.

Subordinate loan Regarding mortgages, a second or third loan that has less seniority than a first mortgage.

Subordinated classes Regarding CMBs, those classes of securities with the lowest claim against the underlying assets.

Subordination When one or more classes of securities have less of a claim on assets than others.

Subsequent rate adjustments The interest rate adjustments on adjustable-rate mortgages after the initial interest rate period.

Subsequent rate cap The interest rate cap on adjustable-rate mortgages after the initial interest rate period.

Super jumbo mortgage Very large mortgages. Some lenders consider loans over $650,000 as jumbo mortgages, some over $1,000,000.

Surety A person or entity that guarantees the debt obligation of another.

Surface rights Mineral rights enabling the possessor of the rights to mine through the surface.

Survey A measurement of a parcel of land showing its metes and bounds.

Sweat equity Equity in a home created by work or improvements made by the owner of the property.

Synthetic lease A transaction that is treated differently for accounting and tax purposes; as a lease for tax purposes, and as a loan for accounting purposes.

Taking Condemnation or any interference with the right to property, but not necessarily physical seizure of the property.

Tax base Assessed value of real property in a tax jurisdiction. It is multiplied by the tax rate to calculate the real estate tax.

Tax lien A lien on a property for non-payment of property taxes.

Tax roll The record of all land parcels within a county, with names of owners, assessed values, and tax amounts.

Tax service fee A fee charged for monitoring the tax payments on a property to make sure the property is protected against tax liens.

Teaser rate A very low rate that is offered to borrowers for a short while as an enticement for the loan.

Tenancy by the entirety A type of ownership where a husband and wife hold title to a whole property, with rights of survivorship.

Tenancy in common A type of ownership where two or more owners hold undivided interest in a property, with no rights of survivorship; the interest may not necessarily be equal.

Tenant (lessee) One who holds a lease and rents real estate from a landlord.

Tenant at will One who holds a lease and rents real estate from a landlord without any agreement as to duration of the lease, and with the right of either party to terminate the lease.

Tenant Improvement (TI) Improvement made to a leased property by the tenant.

Tenant Improvement (TI) allowance Funds given by an owner to a tenant to make improvements to the leased premises.

Tenant mix A mixture of different types of tenants; most institutional investors like to see a mix of types of tenants.

Term The life of a loan.

Third-party origination When a lender uses another party to perform some part of the process to prepare a loan for the secondary market, either origination, processing, underwriting, closing, funding, or packaging it.

Timeshare Ownership of the use of a vacation or resort property for a limited, specific period of time.

Time-weighted average annual rate of return Annual rate of return that yields the same return as would have been yielded if the actual rate was compounded for each year.

Title The just and full possession of real property.

Title company A company that ensures clear title to a property and issues insurance protecting that title.

Title exam When a title company views the public records and other documents related to a real estate property to determine the chain of ownership.

Title insurance An insurance policy that protects a buyer or a lender against disputes as to valid ownership of a property.

Title insurance binder A document issued by a title insurance company that details the property and outlines the guidelines under which title insurance will be issued.

Title report Document indicating the current state of the title, such as easements, covenants, liens, and any other defects. The title report does not describe the chain of title.

Title risk Impediments that may stand in the way of proper transfer of title to real property.

Title search Review of all records relevant to a property to make sure there is clear title and no defects exist that would prevent title transfer.

Total acres The land area, measured in acres, of a real estate investment.

Total assets All items of value on a company's books, such as cash, real estate, and securities.

Total commitment The full amount of a mortgage to be funded, providing all conditions are met.

Total expense ratio Financial obligations of a borrower, including housing expenses and other debt, expressed as a percentage of gross monthly income.

Total inventory The total area in square footage of property, vacant or occupied.

Total lender fees Fees paid to a lender to obtain a loan, separate from fees associated with the transfer of property.

Total loan amount The final loan amount on a real estate property, including any closing costs that are to be included.

Total monthly housing costs The sum of all the payments relative to a homeowner loan, including, but not limited to, principal, interest, taxes, insurance, and homeowner association fees.

Total of all payments Total cost of a real estate loan which includes the principal and all interest payments.

Total principal balance The total debt of a mortgage which includes any refinancing amounts, payments, and interest accrued.

Total retail area The floor space of a retail center less the common area. It is used as a measure of how much space is generating sales.

Total return The sum of income and appreciation as a return on investment.

Townhouse An attached home.

Trade fixtures Property that belongs to a business in a retail lease and is removed upon termination of the lease.

Trading down Buying a home that is smaller and less expensive than one's current home.

Trading up Buying a home that is larger and more expensive than one's current home.

Tranche Securities are usually divided into classes or tranches, according to level of seniority and type of risk; lower-rated tranches have higher yields.

Trans-Union Corporation One of the three main credit reporting agencies.

Transfer tax A fee by state or local government levied on a property when it changes hands.

Treasury index The index of U.S. Treasury notes or bills that may be used as an index for adjustable-rate mortgages.

Triple net lease A lease wherein the tenant pays all expenses relating to the property, including taxes, insurance, maintenance, and utilities, in addition to rent.

Trustee In real estate transactions involving CNBs, a trustee is responsible for reporting and collecting principal and interest, and distributing proceeds to bondholders.

Trustor A person who conveys property to a trustee. In a trust deed, the trustor is the borrower or debtor.

Truth in Lending Law Also known as Regulation Z, a legal code that requires a borrower to be advised (in writing) of all costs associated with the a loan.

Turn-key project A construction

project where a third party handles all of the details of building and improving, and turns a completely finished project over to an investor.

Two step mortgage A mortgage where the borrower receives a below-market interest rate for a certain number of years (usually 7 or 10), and then the rate is adjusted.

U.S. Department of Housing and Urban Development See "Housing and Urban Development (Department of)."

Under construction After construction has begun on a project, and before the certificate of occupancy has been issued.

Under contract After the acceptance of a buyer's offer to purchase a property, and before closing, during which time the seller may not entertain other offers. During this period, due diligence is performed, financing is obtained and the title search is conducted.

Underwriter A company that will guarantee the issue of the stocks and bonds of a publicly traded company.

Underwriters' knot The type of knot approved by building code, which can be used at the end of an electrical cord to prevent the wires from being pulled away from their connection at the electric terminal.

Underwriting The process by which a lender evaluates risk and decides whether to extend a loan to a borrower and at what conditions.

Underwriting fee The fee charged by an underwriter to evaluate risk and decide whether to extend a loan to a borrower and at what conditions.

Unencumbered A property that is owned free and clear, has no liens, or encumbrances.

Unimproved land Raw land in its natural state with no improvements or buildings on it.

Unrated classes The most subordinated classes of CMBS.

Unrecorded deed Transfer of ownership of real estate property without the deed being recorded in government records.

Unsecured Without security.

UPREIT (Umbrella partnership real estate investment trust) A financing structure in which an REIT's assets, for tax purposes, are owned by a holding company.

Usable square footage Area within the demising walls in a building useable by a tenant.

Use Specific purpose and intended use that a building or a parcel of real estate has been designed for.

Usury An illegally high rate of interest.

VA (Veterans Administration)

A branch of the U.S. government that assists veterans through no-down-payment loans.

VA loan A loan granted through the VA, which requires no down payment.

VA Mortgage Funding Fee A premium which is fixed as a percentage of a loan on a no-down-payment loan.

Vacancy factor The amount of lost revenue projected from vacancies in a rental property; it is expressed as a percentage of the rentable square footage.

Vacancy rate Amount of available rental space as a percentage of total rental space.

Vacant space Available rental space being marketed by a landlord.

Valuation Estimated worth or price. The act of valuing by appraisal.

Value-added An investment in an under-performing or under-managed asset that will demand a higher return.

Variable Rate Mortgage (VRM) A mortgage that has a rate of interest that will vary over the term of the loan. The same as an adjusted-rate mortgage.

Variable rate A rate that changes over the life of a loan, usually tied to a published index rate.

Variance Permission granted by a municipality allowing a property to ignore some part of the zoning requirements based on special needs or circumstances.

Vendee A buyer.

Vendor A seller.

Verification of Deposit (VOD) A document issued by a financial institution verifying the balance and status in a borrower's bank account.

Verification of Employment (VOE) A document issued by an employer verifying the employment and salary of a borrower.

Virtual storefront A business run online as opposed to a physical store.

Waiting period The time after the initial filing of a registration but before its effective date.

Warehouse fee A fee that represents the lender's cost of holding a mortgage loan before it is sold on the secondary market.

Weighted-average coupon An average of the interest rates on a pool of mortgages using the balance on each mortgage as the weighing factor.

Weighted-average equity A method of calculating investment income, appreciation, and return using net assets at the beginning of a period, and adjusting for contributions and distributions, on a weighted bases.

Weighted-average rental rates An average of the rental rates in two or more buildings in a given market using the size of the leased units as the weighing factor.

Working drawings The plans, used by the contractors and subcontractors for a building project, showing in great detail the manner in which it should be built.

Workout When a borrower negotiates to restructure a loan in order to avoid foreclosure.

Wraparound mortgage A mortgage where an existing loan is combined with a new loan with the interest rate between the two. Payments are made to the second lender, who remits to the first lender after deducting his repayment.

Write-down The accounting procedure used when the market value of a property is lower than the book value of the property.

Write-off An accounting procedure to charge the company's books for a loss if an asset is no longer collectible.

Yield A measure of return on an investment based on dividends or interest received.

Yield maintenance premium A penalty that a borrower pays to compensate an investor in the case of early redemption of principal.

Yield Rate Yield expressed as a percentage of the total investment. Also called rate of return.

Yield spread The difference in yields between a chosen benchmark yield, such as that of U.S. Treasury securities and a commercial mortgage.

Zoning When a municipal government divides the sections of the municipality into different usage zones and then applies separate regulations for the design, structure, and use of buildings in these zones.

Zoning ordinance The set of laws and regulations used by municipalities to control the use of land and buildings in each of the separate areas or zones of the municipalities.

CALCULATIONS

SIMPLE INTEREST

Simple interest is calculated based only on the original principal amount.

The formula for calculating simple interest is:

Interest = Principal x Rate x Time

Be sure to state the rate and the time in the same way. In other words, if you are charging 14 percent per year, then you also have to list your time in years.

Let's look at an example:

You lend $100,000 at 14 percent interest per year for 2 years. To find out how much interest you will earn, plug the numbers into the formula:

$100,000 x 14% x 2 = $28,000

Now let's look at the same $100,000 at 14 percent for 6 months. Remember, you will have to state the rate and time in the same terms, so 6 months will become 0.5 years:

$100,000 x 14% x 0.5 = $7,000

COMPOUND INTEREST

How can you figure out how much money you will have (FV) in (n) years if you invest (x) dollars at (i) percent interest rate?

Here is the formula:

$FV = x (1 + i)$ ^n.

In other words, the future value of your money equals the initial amount invested times one plus the interest rate raised to the number of time periods invested.

For example, if you put $1,000 into a bond at 8 percent interest for 30 years, then the amount of money you would receive would be $1,000 times 1.08 to the 30th power. Mathematically, it looks like this:

$FV = $1,000 * (1 + .08)$ ^30

Thus, your bond would yield $10,062.66 in 30 years.

CASH FLOW

Cash flow is all of the property's money coming in minus all of the money going back out. It is like thinking about your property in terms of a checkbook. All the inflows are like deposits, and all the outflows are like checks or debits.

Inflows include rental income and other income plus vacancy and credit allowance.

Outflows include insurance, taxes, repairs and maintenance, supplies, utilities, and other debits.

CASH FLOW	
Date:	
Prepared by:	
INCOME	
Gross Scheduled Rent Income	
Other Income	
TOTAL GROSS INCOME	
VACANCY & CREDIT ALLOWANCE	
GROSS OPERATING INCOME	
EXPENSES	
Insurance (Fire & Liability)	
Property Taxes	
Repairs & Maintenance	
Supplies & Miscellaneous	
Utilities	
Other	
TOTAL EXPENSES	
NET OPERATING INCOME	
Less Annual Debt Service, First Mortgage	
Less Annual Debt Service, Second Mortgage	
Less Capital Additions	
Plus Loan Proceeds	
Plus Interest Earned	
CASH FLOW BEFORE TAXES	
Less Income Tax Liability	
CASH FLOW AFTER TAXES	

LOAN-TO-VALUE RATIO

The loan-to-value ratio is the ratio between the financed amount and the property's value. It is expressed as a percentage.

Loan-to-Value Ratio = Loan Amount/
Property's Appraised Value

Let's look at an example:

You loan $65,000 on a piece of property with an appraised value of $100,000. In this case the LTV ratio is $65,000 divided by $100,000, or 65 percent.

SELF-DIRECTED IRA TRUSTEES

**Trust Administration
Services**
5950 La Place Court
Suite 160
Carlsbad, CA 92008
800-455-9472
www.trustlynk.com

PENSCO Trust Company
P.O. Box 26903
San Francisco, CA 94126
800-969-4472
www.pensco.com

Fiserv Trust Company
717 17th Street
Suite 1700
Denver, CO 80202
800-521-6974
www.fiserv.com

Entrust
555 12th Street
Suite 1250
Oakland, CA 94607
510-587-0950
800-392-9653
www.iraplus.com

Asset Exchange
Strategies, LLC
512-528-0801
866-683-5228
www.myrealestateira
.com

Advanced Retirement
Marketing Services
P.O. Box 33446
Indialantic, FL 32903
877-777-1040
www.flexira.com/ins.htm

Sterling Trust Company
P.O. Box 2526
Waco, TX 76702
254-751-1505
800-955-3434
www.sterling-trust.com

Equity Trust Co.
Mid-Ohio Securities
225 Burns Road
Elyria, OH 44035
440-323-5491
www.trustetc.com

North Fork Bank
Corporate Headquarters
275 Broadhollow Road
P.O. Box 8914
Melville, NY 11747
877-694-9111
www.northforkbank.com

STATE USURY LAWS

Alabama	8%	
Alaska	12%	
Arizona	10%	
Arkansas	10%	
California	10%	
Colorado	12%	
Delaware	9%	There is no limit on collateral loans larger than $5,000. Also the ceiling rate may be exceeded on loans secured by real estate only through written agreement.
D.C.	8%	
Florida	10%	15% for loans above $500,000.
Georgia	8%	Loans secured by realty may carry a rate of up to 9%.
Hawaii	12%	
Idaho	10%	
Illinois	9%	

Indiana	18%	None on collateral loans.
Iowa	9%	There is no ceiling rate on real estate investment trusts.
Kansas	10%	Consumer loans other than supervised loans carry a maximum rate of 12%. There is no ceiling on any other type of loan.
Kentucky	8.5%	There is no ceiling on loans over $25,000 that are not on a single-unit family residence.
Louisiana	8%	Loans secured by real estate carry a maximum rate of 10%.
Maine	16%	No maximum rate applies if the loan is for non-personal or business purposes and the contract is in writing and involves more than $2,000.
Maryland	8%	Residential mortgage loans may be at 10%.
Massachusetts	None	
Michigan	7%	No ceiling rate applies to realty secured loans.
Minnesota	8%	No ceiling rate is applied to loans in excess of $100,000.
Mississippi	10%	
Missouri	8%	
Montana	10%	
Nebraska	9%	
Nevada	12%	
New Hampshire	None	
New Jersey	8%	Loans secured by realty carry a maximum of 8.75%.
New Mexico	10%	

New York	8.5%	Demand notes of $5,000 or over with collateral security may carry a rate of up to 25%.
North Carolina	8%	Ceiling rates on loans are graduated according to the size and purpose of the loans. First mortgages on single-family dwellings may be contracted for in writing at any rate agreed upon by the parties.
North Dakota	9%	
Ohio	8%	Loans in excess of $100,000 may be at any rate.
Oklahoma	10%	Oklahoma's Uniform Consumer Credit Code allows 18% to supervised lenders and 10% to others lending to consumers. There is no ceiling rate on other types of loans.
Oregon	10%	Loans in excess of $50,000 may be made at any rate.
Pennsylvania	9.5%	The maximum rate does not apply to loans of more than $50,000, loans of $50,000, or less secured by a lien upon real property.
Rhode Island	21%	
South Carolina	8%	The maximum rate on loans from $50,000 to $100,000 is 10% and on loans between $100,000 and $500,000, 12%. Loans larger than $500,000 may be at any rate.
South Dakota	10%	
Tennessee	10%	
Texas	10%	Corporate loans above $5,000 have an 18% ceiling.

Utah	18%	Revolving loans and non-supervised consumer loans carry a maximum rate of 18%. Supervised loans carry a maximum rate of 18% on all unpaid balances, or a total of 36% on unpaid balances of $390 or less; 21% on unpaid balances over $390 and not over $1,300. All other loans may be made at any rate.
Vermont	8.5%	Loans to finance real estate improvements or second residence may be at any rate.
Virginia	8%	Any rate may apply to nonagricultural loans secured by a first mortgage or realty.
Washington	12%	
West Virginia	8%	
Wisconsin	12%	
Wyoming	10%	Revolving loans and consumer loans other than supervised loans may carry a maximum rate of 10%. Supervised loans may be at a rate of the greater of 18% on all unpaid balances of $300 or less, 21% on unpaid balances over $300 and not over $1,000, and 15% on unpaid balances over $1,000. All other loans may be at any rate.

This table presents a synopsis of the maze of laws concerning usury in effect in the various states and the District of Colombia. Due to the complex nature of this area of the law, the table may not be completely accurate with respect to certain specific technical provisions.

MORTGAGE PROCEDURES BY STATE

ALABAMA

Conveyance is by warranty deed.

Mortgages are the customary security instruments. Foreclosures are nonjudicial.

The foreclosure process takes a minimum of 21 days from the date of first publication.

After the sale, there is a 1-year redemption period.

ALASKA

Conveyance is by warranty deed.

Deeds of trust with private power of sale are the customary security instruments.

Foreclosures take 90–120 days.

ARIZONA

Conveyance is by warranty deed.

Whereas deeds of trust are the security instruments most often used, mortgages and "agreements for sale" are used approximately 20 percent of the time.

Foreclosure depends upon the security instrument. For deeds of trust, the foreclosure process takes about 91 days.

ARKANSAS

Conveyance is by warranty deed.

Mortgages are the customary security instruments.

Foreclosure requires judicial proceedings, but there are no minimum time limits for completion.

CALIFORNIA

Conveyance is by grant deed.

Deeds of trust with private power of sale are the security instruments.

Foreclosure requires a 3-month waiting period after the recording of the notice of default. After the waiting period, the notice of sale is published each week for 3 consecutive weeks.

The borrower may reinstate the loan at any time prior to 5 business days before the foreclosure sale.

COLORADO

Conveyance is by warranty deed.

Deeds of trust are the customary security instruments.

Public trustees must sell foreclosure properties within 45–60 days after the filing of a notice of election and demand for sale, but they will grant extensions up to 6 months following the date of the originally scheduled sale.

Subdivided properties may be redeemed within 75 days after sale; agricultural properties may be redeemed within 6 months after sale. The first junior lien holder has 10 additional days to redeem, and the second and other junior lien holders have an additional 5 days each.

The public trustee is normally the trustee shown on the deed of trust, a practice unique to Colorado.

Foreclosures may be handled judicially.

CONNECTICUT

Most often, conveyance is by warranty deed, but quitclaim deeds do appear.

Mortgages are the security instruments.

Judicial foreclosures are the rule, either by a suit in equity for strict foreclosure or by a court decree of sale.

Court-decreed sales preclude redemption, but strict foreclosures allow redemption for 3–6 months, depending upon the discretion of the court.

DELAWARE

Although quitclaim and general warranty deeds are sometimes used, most conveyances are by special warranty deeds.

Mortgages are the security instruments.

Foreclosures are judicial and require 90–120 days to complete.

DISTRICT OF COLUMBIA

Conveyances are by bargain-and-sale deeds.

Though mortgages are available, the deed of trust, containing private power of sale, is the security instrument of choice.

Foreclosures require at least 6 weeks and start with a 30-day notice of sale sent by certified mail.

FLORIDA

Conveyance is by warranty deed.

Mortgages are the customary security instruments.

Foreclosures are judicial and take about 3 months. They involve service by the sheriff, a judgment of foreclosure and sale, advertising, public sale, and finally issuance of a certificate of sale and certificate of title.

GEORGIA

Conveyance is by warranty deed.

Security deeds are the security instruments.

Foreclosures are nonjudicial and take little more than a month, because there's a power of attorney right in the security deed. Foreclosure advertising must appear for 4 consecutive weeks prior to the first Tuesday of the month; that's when foreclosure sales take place.

HAWAII

Conveyance of fee-simple property is by warranty deed; conveyance of leasehold property, which is common throughout the state, is by assignment of lease. Condominiums may be fee simple or leasehold.

Sales of some properties, whether fee simple or leasehold, are by agreement of sale.

Mortgages are the security instruments.

Hawaii uses judicial foreclosures rather than powers of sale for both mortgages and agreements of sale. These foreclosures take 6–12 months and sometimes longer, depending upon court schedules.

IDAHO

Conveyance is by warranty deed or corporate deed, though often there are contracts of sale involved.

Either mortgages or deeds of trust may be the security instruments. Deeds of trust, which include power of sale provisions, are restricted to properties in incorporated areas and properties elsewhere that don't exceed 20 acres.

After the notice of default has been recorded, deed-of-trust foreclosures take at least 120 days, and there's no redemption period. Judicial foreclosures for mortgages take about a year, depending upon court availability.

There's a 6–12 month redemption period, depending on the type of property involved.

ILLINOIS

Conveyance is by warranty deed. Recorded deeds must include a declaration of the sales price.

Mortgages are the customary security instruments.

Judicial foreclosure is mandatory and takes at least a year from the filing of the default notice to the expiration of the redemption period.

INDIANA

Conveyance is by warranty deed.

Mortgages are the customary security instruments.

Judicial foreclosures are required; execution of judgments varies from 3 months after filing of the complaint in cases involving mortgages drawn up since July 1, 1975, to 6 months for those drawn up between January 1, 1958, and July 1, 1975, to 12 months for those drawn up before that. Immediately following the execution sale, the highest bidder receives a sheriff's deed.

IOWA

Conveyance is usually by warranty deed.

Mortgages and deeds of trust are both authorized security instruments, but lenders prefer mortgages, because deeds of trust do not circumvent judicial foreclosure proceedings anyway.

Those proceedings take at least 4–6 months.

Since Iowa is the only state that does not authorize title insurance, Iowans who want it must go through a title company in another state.

KANSAS

Conveyance is by warranty deed.

Mortgages are the customary security instruments.

Judicial foreclosures, the only ones allowed, take about 6 months from filing to sale.

377

Redemption periods vary, the longest being 12 months.

KENTUCKY

Conveyance is by grant deed or by bargain-and-sale deed. Deeds must show the name of the preparer, the amount of the total transaction, and the recording reference by which the grantor obtained title.

Mortgages are the principal security instruments, because deeds of trust offer no power-of-sale advantages.

Judicial foreclosure proceeding.

LOUISIANA

Conveyance is by warranty deed or by act of sale.

Mortgages are the security instruments generally used in commercial transactions, while vendor's liens and seller's privileges are used in other purchase-money situations.

Foreclosures are swift (60 days) and sure (no right of redemption). Successful foreclosure sale bidders receive an adjudication from the sheriff.

MAINE

Conveyance is by warranty or quitclaim deed.

Mortgages are the security instruments.

Foreclosures may be initiated by any of the following: an act of law for possession; entering into possession and holding the premises by written consent of the mortgagor; entering peaceably, openly, and unopposed in the presence of two witnesses and taking possession; giving public notice in a newspaper for 3 successive weeks and recording copies of the notice in the Registry of Deeds, and then recording the mortgage within 30 days of the last publication; or by a bill in equity (special cases). In every case, the creditor must record a notice of foreclosure within 30 days. Judicial foreclosure proceedings are also available.

Redemption periods vary from 90–365 days depending on the method of foreclosure.

MARYLAND

Conveyance is by grant deed, and the deed must state the consideration involved.

Although mortgages are common in some areas, deeds of trust are more prevalent as security instruments.

MASSACHUSETTS

Conveyance is by warranty deed in the western part of the state and by quitclaim deed in the eastern part.

Mortgages with private power of sale are the customary security instruments.

Creditors forced to foreclose generally take advantage of the private power of sale, but they may foreclose through peaceable entry (entering unopposed in the presence of two witnesses and taking possession for 3 years) or through the rarely used judicial writ of entry. Frequently, cautious creditors will foreclose through both power of sale and peaceable entry.

MICHIGAN

Conveyance is by warranty deed, which must give the full consideration involved or be accompanied by an affidavit which does. Many transactions involve land contracts.

Mortgages are the security instruments.

Private foreclosure is permitted; it requires advertising for 4 consecutive weeks and a sale at least 28 days following the date of first publication.

The redemption period ranges from 1 to 12 months.

MINNESOTA

Conveyance is by warranty deed.

Although deeds of trust are authorized, mortgages are the customary security instruments.

The redemption period following a foreclosure is 6 months in most cases; it is 12 months if the property is larger than 10 acres or the amount claimed to be due is less than two-thirds of the original debt.

This is a strong abstract state. Typically, a buyer will accept an abstract and an attorney's opinion as evidence of title, even though the lender may require title insurance.

MISSISSIPPI

Conveyance is by warranty deed.

Deeds of trust are the customary security instruments.

Foreclosure involves a nonjudicial process which takes 21-45 days.

MISSOURI

Conveyance is by warranty deed.

Deeds of trust are the customary security instruments and allow private power of sale. The trustee must be named in the deed of trust and must be a Missouri resident.

Foreclosure involves publication of a sale notice for 21 days, during which time the debtor may redeem the property or file a notice of redemption. The foreclosure sale buyer receives a trustee's deed.

MONTANA

Conveyance is by warranty deed, corporate deed, or grant deed.

Mortgages, deeds of trust, and unrecorded contracts of sale are the security instruments.

Mortgages require judicial foreclosure, and there's a 6- to 12-month redemption period following sale.

Foreclosure on deeds of trust involves filing a notice of default and then holding a trustee sale 120 days later.

NEBRASKA

Conveyance is by warranty deed.

Mortgages and deeds of trust are the security instruments.

Mortgage foreclosures require judicial proceedings and take about 6 months from the date of the first notice when they're uncontested.

Deeds of trust do not require judicial proceedings and take about 90 days.

NEVADA

Conveyance is by grant deed, bargain-and-sale deed, or quitclaim deed.

Deeds of trust are the customary security instruments.

Foreclosure involves recording a notice of default and mailing a copy within 10 days. Following the mailing, there is a 35-day reinstatement period. After that, the beneficiary may accept partial payment or payment in full for a 3-month period. Then come advertising the property for sale for 3 consecutive weeks and finally the sale itself. All of this takes about $4\frac{1}{2}$ months.

NEW HAMPSHIRE

Conveyance is by warranty or quitclaim deed.

Mortgages are the customary security instruments.

Lenders may foreclose through judicial action or through whatever power of sale was written into the mortgage originally. Entry, either by legal action or by taking possession peaceably in the presence of two witnesses, is possible under certain legally stated conditions.

There is a 1-year right-of-redemption period.

NEW JERSEY

Conveyance is by bargain-and-sale deed with covenants against grantors' acts (equivalent to a special warranty deed).

Mortgages are the most common security instruments though deeds of trust are authorized.

Foreclosures require judicial action, which takes 6–9

months if they're uncontested.

NEW MEXICO

Conveyance is by warranty or quitclaim deed.

Deeds of trust and mortgages are the security instruments.

Foreclosures require judicial proceedings

There's a 9-month redemption period after judgment.

NEW YORK

Conveyance is by bargain-and-sale deed.

Mortgages are the security instruments in this lien-theory state.

Foreclosures require judicial action and take several months if uncontested or longer if contested.

NORTH CAROLINA

Conveyance is by warranty deed.

Deeds of trust with private power of sale are the customary security instruments.

Foreclosures are nonjudicial, with a 10-day redemption period following the sale. The entire process takes between 45 and 60 days.

NORTH DAKOTA

Conveyance is by warranty deed.

Mortgages are the security instruments.

Foreclosures require about 6 months, including the redemption period.

OHIO

Conveyance is by warranty deed. Dower rights require that all documents involving a married person must be executed by both spouses.

Mortgages are the security instruments.

Judicial foreclosures, the only kind allowed, require about 6–12 months.

OKLAHOMA

Conveyance is by warranty deed.

Mortgages are the usual security instruments.

Foreclosures may be by judicial action or by power of sale if properly allowed for in the security instrument.

OREGON

Conveyance is by warranty or bargain-and-sale deed, but land sales contracts are common.

Mortgage deeds and deeds of trust are the security

instruments.

Oregon attorneys usually act as trustees in nonjudicial trust-deed foreclosures. Such foreclosures take 5 months from the date of the sale notice; defaults may be cured as late as 5 days prior to sale.

Judicial foreclosures on either mortgages or trust deeds allow for a 1-year redemption period following sale.

PENNSYLVANIA

Conveyance is by special or general warranty deed.

Mortgages are the security instruments.

Foreclosures take 1–6 months from filing through judgment plus another 2 months or more from judgment through sale.

RHODE ISLAND

Conveyance is by warranty or quitclaim deed.

Mortgages are the usual security instruments.

Foreclosures follow the power-of-sale provisions contained in mortgage agreements and take about 45 days.

Power-of-sale foreclosures offer no redemption provisions, whereas any other foreclosure method carries a 3-year right of redemption.

SOUTH CAROLINA

Conveyance is by warranty deed.

Mortgages are most often the security instruments.

Foreclosures are judicial and take 3–5 months, depending on court schedules. Foreclosure sales take place on the first Monday of every month following publication of notice once a week for 3 consecutive weeks.

SOUTH DAKOTA

Conveyance is by warranty deed.

Mortgages are the usual security instruments.

Foreclosures may occur through judicial proceedings or through the power-of-sale provisions contained in certain mortgage agreements. Sheriff's sales follow publication of notice by 30 days.

The redemption period allowed after sale of parcels smaller than 40 acres and encumbered by mortgages containing power of sale is 180 days; in all other cases, it's a year.

TENNESSEE

Conveyance is by warranty or quitclaim deed.

Deeds of trust are the customary security instruments.

Foreclosures, which are handled according to trustee

sale provisions, are swift, that is, 22 days from the first publication of the notice until the public sale.

There is normally no right of redemption.

TEXAS

Conveyance is by warranty deed.

Deeds of trust are the most common security instruments.

Following the posting of foreclosure sales at the local courthouse for at least 21 days, the sales themselves take place at the courthouse on the first Tuesday of the month.

UTAH

Conveyance is by warranty deed.

Mortgages and deeds of trust with private power of sale are the security instruments.

Mortgage foreclosures require judicial proceedings, which take about a year; deed-of-trust foreclosures take advantage of private power-of-sale provisions and take about 4 months.

VERMONT

Conveyance is by warranty or quitclaim deed.

Mortgages are the customary security instruments, but

large commercial transactions often employ deeds of trust.

Mortgage foreclosures require judicial proceedings.

There is a redemption period of 1 year for mortgages dated prior to April 1, 1968, and 6 months for all others.

VIRGINIA

Conveyance is by bargain-and-sale deed.

Deeds of trust are the customary security instruments.

Foreclosure takes about 2 months.

WASHINGTON

Conveyance is by warranty deed.

Both deeds of trust with private power of sale and mortgages are used as security instruments.

Mortgages require judicial foreclosure. Deeds of trust require that a notice of default be sent first and 30 days later, a notice of sale. The notice of sale must be recorded, posted, and mailed at least 90 days before the sale, and the sale cannot take place any earlier than 190 days after the actual default.

WEST VIRGINIA

Conveyance is by warranty deed, bargain-and-sale

deed, or grant deed.

Deeds of trust are the customary security instruments.

Foreclosures are great for lenders; when uncontested, they take only a month.

WISCONSIN

Conveyance is by warranty deed, but installment land contracts are used extensively too.

Mortgages are the customary security instruments.

Within limits, the actual mortgage wording determines foreclosure requirements.

Redemption varies from 2 months for abandoned property to a full year in some cases. Lenders generally waive their right to a deficiency judgment in order to reduce the redemption period to 6 months.

WYOMING

Conveyance is by warranty deed.

Mortgages are the usual security instruments.

Foreclosures may follow judicial or power-of-sale proceedings. Residential foreclosures take around 120 days; agricultural foreclosures, around 13 months.

RESOURCES

Dictionary of Real Estate Lending Terms, Richard B. Partain, 1989.

Investing in High Yield Private Mortgage Notes and Trust Deeds, Don H. Konipol, 2003.

Making Money Trading Mortgages, Delbert M. Ashby, 2004.

Publication 590: Individual Retirement Arrangements, IRS, 2005.

Real Estate Investors Guide to Private Mortgage Financing, Don H. Konipol, 2003.

Real Estate Loan Brokerage: How to Become a Successful Mortgage Broker, Richard B. Partain, 1991.

The Mortgage Encyclopedia, Jack Guttentag, 2004.

The New IRAs and How to Make Them Work for You, Neil

Downing, 2002.

The Note Holder's Handbook, Avalon Finance, Inc., 2003.

Untapped Funds, Hidden Wealth, Allen Cowgill, 2005.

What Every Real Estate Investor Needs to Know About Cash Flow…And 36 Other Key Financial Measures, Frank Gallinelli, 2004.

INDEX

ABOUT THE AUTHOR

*T**eri Clark's* interest in the new and different has led to a successful online writing career collaborating on nearly 100 books as an editor, researcher, ghostwriter, and author. The North Carolina resident, along with her husband, homeschools their four children. She can be reached at ghostwriting@gmail.com.

ABOUT THE CO-AUTHOR

atthew Stewart Tabacchi, originally from Pittsburgh, Pennsylvania, holds an associate's degree from Pittsburgh Institute of Aeronautics and maintains several mortgage licenses. These include a Mortgage Broker license (MB), a Mortgage Broker Business license (MBB),  as well as three Mortgage Broker Business Branch licenses (MBBB). Mr. Tabacchi worked for companies such as Aabco Mortgage and Accredited Mortgage and now has an Allstate Mortgage firm that maintains a state lenders license and is based in Ocala, Florida. There are currently four Allstate mortgage offices serving central Florida. Mr. Tabacchi entered the mortgage business in 1992 and has mastered all the secrets of private mortgage lending. Today, the majority of the loans his firm underwrites are private investor-backed mortgages. Of the hundreds of private investors and thousands of private mortgage contracts Mr. Tabacchi's firm has managed and orchestrated over the years, no investor has ever lost a nickel. Allstate Mortgage is a full-service mortgage firm providing services to private investors and mortgage clients. They can provide full loan servicing for the private investor, enabling the process to be highly profitable and virtually effortless — with no risk. You can reach Matt at 352-351-0200 or 866-351-0200, and he will be happy to answer any questions you may have and help guide you into the highly profitable world of private mortgage investing.

ALLSTATE
Mortgage Loans
& Investments, Inc.

Matthew Tabacchi
ALLSTATE MORTGAGE
809 NE 25th Avenue
Ocala, FL 34470
Phone: 352-351-0200
Fax: 352-351-4557
Web: **www.allstateocala.com**
E-mail: matt@allstateocala.com

❏ **Yes.** I would like more information on mortgage loans and investing. Please contact me.

Name _____

Address _____

City _____ State _____ Zip _____

Phone _____

Mail to: Allstate Mortgage Loans & Investments, Inc.
           809 NE 25th Avenue
           Ocala, FL 34470

MORE GREAT TITLES FROM ATLANTIC PUBLISHING

THE PRE-FORECLOSURE REAL ESTATE HANDBOOK: INSIDER SECRETS TO LOCATING AND PURCHASING PRE-FORECLOSED PROPERTIES IN ANY MARKET

The Pre-Foreclosure Real Estate Handbook explains everything you need to know to locate and purchase real estate bargains from banks, public auctions, and other sources. Whether you are a first-time homeowner or an experienced property investor, *The Pre-Foreclosure Real Estate Handbook* is a tremendous guide for buying pre-foreclosed homes in any market. You will learn the simple formula (developed from real-life experience) that can build massive wealth through real estate foreclosures. This book is a resource for novices and pros alike; it will guide you through every step of the process including finding properties, negotiating, and closing on your first deal. Exhaustively researched, it will arm you with hundreds of innovative ideas that you can put to use right away. This book gives you the proven strategies, innovative ideas, and case studies from experts to help you get more with less time and effort.

288 Pages • Item # PFR-02 • $21.95

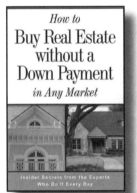

HOW TO BUY REAL ESTATE WITHOUT A DOWN PAYMENT IN ANY MARKET: INSIDER SECRETS FROM THE EXPERTS WHO DO IT EVERY DAY

This book explains everything you need to know to locate and purchase real estate with no down payment from individuals, banks, and other sources. Whether you are a first-time homeowner or an experienced property investor, this is a tremendous guide for buying real estate. You will learn the simple formula that can build wealth through real estate, with no money down. This proven formula works even if you have no real estate experience, bad or no credit, or very little money. This formula has been developed out of real-life experience. You will learn how to make smart real estate investments and use those investments to help you achieve financial success.

288 Pages • Item # BRN-02 • $21.95

FAST REAL ESTATE PROFITS IN ANY MARKET: THE ART OF FLIPPING PROPERTIES— INSIDER SECRETS FROM THE EXPERTS WHO DO IT EVERY DAY

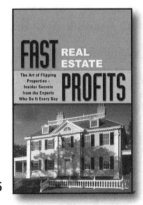

In real estate markets everywhere, real estate "flippers" have discovered that a small down payment, a little paint, some cleaning, and some time can net them tens (even hundreds) of thousands of dollars in profits, possibly tax-free. Finally there's a comprehensive, no-nonsense book that teaches you everything you need to build wealth through flipping properties quickly, legally, and ethically. You don't need great credit, a real estate license, or large sums of capital or experience to get started. There has never been a better time to invest in real estate.

288 Pages • Item # FRP-02 • $21.95

To order call 1-800-814-1132 or visit www.atlantic-pub.com